# THE CAMP DAVID SUMMIT – WHAT WENT WRONG?

TEL AVIV UNIVERSITY אוניברסיטת תל-אביב

The University Institute for Diplomacy and Regional Cooperation functions as an internal institute of the University and constitutes a part of the Gershon H. Gordon Faculty of Social Sciences. Its activities focus on two fields: in the field of diplomacy, the Institute deals with general theories of diplomacy, developments in world diplomacy, issues in the foreign relations of Middle Eastern countries, and the diplomatic conduct of Israel's foreign relations. In the field of regional cooperation the Institute deals with cases of regional cooperation in the world, regional cooperation in the Middle East, and cooperation between Israel and her neighbors – all in such areas as economics, infrastructure and environment. In its fields of specialization the Institute conducts research, publishes monographs, holds colloquia and international conferences, promotes doctoral dissertations and contributes to the Faculty's curriculum.

# THE CAMP DAVID SUMMIT – WHAT WENT WRONG?

Americans, Israelis, and Palestinians Analyze the
Failure of the Boldest Attempt Ever to Resolve the
Palestinian–Israeli Conflict

*Edited by*
Shimon Shamir and Bruce Maddy-Weitzman

A PROJECT OF

**The University Institute for Diplomacy and Regional Cooperation**
*Tel Aviv University*

**The Issam Sartawi**
**Center for Peace Studies**
*Al-Quds University*

**Konrad Adenauer Stiftung**
*Jerusalem*

## sussex
ACADEMIC
PRESS
*BRIGHTON • PORTLAND*

Copyright © Copyright Sussex Academic Press and The Tel Aviv University
Institute for Diplomacy and Regional Cooperation, 2005

The right of Shimon Shamir and Bruce Maddy-Weitzman to be identified as Editors of
this work has been asserted in accordance with the Copyright, Designs and
Patents Act 1988.

2 4 6 8 10 9 7 5 3 1

*First published 2005 in Great Britain by*
SUSSEX ACADEMIC PRESS
Box 2950
Brighton BN2 5SP

*and in the United States of America by*
SUSSEX ACADEMIC PRESS
920 NE 58th Ave        Suite 300
Portland, Oregon 97213-3786

*British Library Cataloguing in Publication Data*
A CIP catalogue record for this book is available from the British Library.

*Library of Congress Cataloging-in-Publication Data*
Shamir, Shimon.
    The Camp David summit – what went wrong? : Americans,
Israelis, and Palestinians analyze the failure of the boldest attempt
ever to resolve the Palestinian–Israeli conflict / edited by Shimon
Shamir and Bruce Maddy-Weitzman.
        p. cm.
    "Based on papers presented at an international conference".
    ISBN 1-84519-099-8 (h/c : alk. paper) — ISBN 1-84519-100-5
(p/b : alk. paper)
    1. Arab–Israeli conflict—1993–    —Peace—Congresses.
2. Palestinian Arabs—Politics and government—20th century
—Congresses.  3. Israel—Politics and government—1993–    —
Congresses.  I. Maddy-Weitzman, Bruce.  II. Title.
DS119.76.S546 2005
327.569405695'3—dc22

2005010173

Typeset & Designed by G&G Editorial, Brighton, East Sussex
Printed by The Cromwell Press, Trowbridge, Wiltshire
This book is printed on acid-free paper.

# Contents

# Contents

# Maps

Maps 1–3, courtesy of Samih al-Abed, Ministry of Planning, Palestinian Authority. Maps 4–8 courtesy of Israel Kimhi, The Jerusalem Institute for Israel Studies.

# Preface

This book is based on papers presented at an international conference, The Camp David Summit, 2000: What Went Wrong – Lessons for the Future, initiated by Tel Aviv University's Institute for Diplomacy and Regional Cooperation and held at the University in June 2003.

The Camp David summit was a formative event in the history of Israeli–Palestinian relations and possibly in the contemporary history of the Middle East as a whole. It constituted the most comprehensive effort ever to resolve the protracted conflict between Palestinians and Israelis, which is over a century old. Yet, not only did the summit end in failure, but it was immediately followed by the eruption of an unprecedented level of violence, still ongoing in early 2005. This tragic outcome generated an intense debate questioning the timing of the summit, the intentions of the parties, the adequacy of preparations, the efficacy of the negotiators, and the way the summit was concluded. In other words, the question still being asked today is, What Went Wrong?

Several books and articles have already been published by summit participants and observers, presenting individual interpretations of what took place. This book, however, is distinctive because it is the product of the only attempt made so far to bring together American, Israeli and Palestinian protagonists and juxtapose their diverse versions of the Camp David experience. Speakers at the Tel Aviv University conference were negotiators who had participated in that summit, as well as experts who had prepared the material for the negotiators, and academics who specialize in the methodology of peace negotiations.

It should be noted that the principal Palestinian Camp David negotiators who had been invited to the conference did not, in the end, attend; consequently they are not included in this volume. However, four distinguished Palestinians who had participated in various Palestinian–Israeli talks did take part in the conference, presenting insightful Palestinian perspectives on the Camp David summit. As their chapters demonstrate, some of these speakers offered diverse explanations for the absence of their compatriots, and all regretted that a great opportunity for authoritatively presenting the Palestinian delegation's version to the public was missed.

The reader should also bear in mind that several important developments on the Palestinian–Israeli scene took place after the delivery of the presentations in the conference, such as the construction of sections of the separation fence, the launching of Ariel Sharon's disengagement plan, the death of Yasser Arafat, and the election of Mahmud Abbas as his successor. However, these events necessitated only minor technical changes in the course of the revisions made by the authors and editors. The substance of the presentations remains as valid today as it was at the time of the conference.

The realization of this conference would not have been possible without the close cooperation between Tel Aviv University and Al-Quds University, and their respective presidents, Prof. Itamar Rabinovich and Prof. Sari Nusseibeh. On the operational level, the conference was the product of the dedicated work of the staff of Tel Aviv University's Institute for Diplomacy and Regional Cooperation, headed by myself, and the Issam Sartawi Center for Peace Studies, headed by Prof. Munther Dajani. We are also indebted to the third partner in this cooperative venture, the Konrad Adenauer Foundation, and to its representative in Israel, Dr. Johannes Gerster, who has provided invaluable support throughout the work on this project.

SHIMON SHAMIR

# JOHANNES GERSTER

# Greetings

## Violence Does Not Solve Problems

I BELIEVE THAT EVERY VICTIM IN THIS REGION is one victim too many, and that the majority of its people want to live in peace with one another. Here is a story from my experience in politics in Germany. In 1987, the President of the Soviet Union, Mikhail Gorbachev, visited Bonn. After a wonderful banquet, Gorbachev was chatting with Helmut Kohl and some friends in the Chancellor's office. Kohl looked out at the Rhine River and said, "Mr. President, the water of this river comes from Switzerland, meanders through France and Germany to the Netherlands, and flows to the North Sea. You can't stop the water. You can build walls, but you cannot change one fact: this water will flow to the North Sea. And I tell you, German unification will come, not today, not tomorrow, but perhaps sooner than you and I think."

That was in 1987. At that time, no one in the world thought that German unification would happen without war, in a peaceful manner. Three years later German unification was accomplished and voters in East Germany elected their first representatives to the *Bundestag*. I am completely sure that the unification achieved in Europe can be a model for the Middle East, that peaceful coexistence between Israelis and Palestinians will come. It has to come. The only question is the price we shall have to pay on the road there.

There is a wonderful Latin saying: *veritas facit pacem* ("truth produces peace"). That is the rationale of this conference – to examine sincerely the experience of Camp David, to search for the mistakes made and the reasons for its breakdown. The lessons from *What Went Wrong?* will surely assist future negotiations. This book will increase our knowledge of the past. With goodwill and correct perspective, there is hope for the future.

# BILL CLINTON

# Message from the President

*[handwritten Thai annotation]*

WARM GREETINGS TO ALL THOSE GATHERED IN TEL AVIV for "The Camp David Summit, 2000: What Went Wrong? Lessons for the Future." I am sorry I am unable to be with my good friends at Tel Aviv University and Al-Quds University, especially Professors Rabinovich and Nusseibeh, and I thank them for their initiative and cooperation in holding this important conference.

At this particularly challenging moment in history, I am heartened to know that Israelis, Palestinians, and Americans have joined together to consider the past, and in so doing, to identify and discuss the lessons of Camp David. These lessons do offer hope for the future, for there will come a day when both sides return to political negotiations – negotiations informed by what you accomplish at this gathering. Camp David was a stage in the process, not an endpoint. While we did not succeed in securing a final peace agreement, those discussions demonstrated that there was, and there remains, room to forge common ground.

I look forward to receiving a full report on what I know will be three days of thoughtful, groundbreaking discussion. I send my best wishes to you all for a productive and memorable meeting.

*[handwritten annotation: progress]*

# Opening Presentations

# SHIMON SHAMIR

# The Enigma of Camp David

THROUGHOUT HISTORY, PRINCIPAL LEADERS OF ADVERSARY STATES have occasionally met face-to-face with the aim of settling their disputes. Emperors, kings, princes, presidents and prime ministers convened meetings, either bilateral or multilateral, seeking to conclude peace between them and establish some kind of regional or global order. Since the beginning of the nineteenth century, these meetings have gone by such names as conventions, congresses or conferences, and since the 1950s, when they evolved as a quite common type of diplomacy, they have been dubbed "summit meetings."

The results of summit meetings have varied. Some summits produced agreements which became stabilizing factors in the relevant international relationships. Others appeared to be successful, but the consequences of the arrangements they had agreed on turned out to be disastrous. There were also summits that collapsed entirely, thereby exacerbating the situation and generating frustration and despair. The summit meeting convened at Camp David in July 2000 by President Bill Clinton, with Prime Minister Ehud Barak and Chairman Yasser Arafat, belongs to this third category.

The Camp David summit was a defining event in the history of Palestinian–Israeli relations and perhaps in that of the Middle East as a whole. It was the first attempt ever to reach a comprehensive solution to the hundred year-old conflict between the Jewish and Arab communities in the Holy Land. Yet, the summit did not yield any Israeli–Palestinian agreements. It was followed by the eruption of an unprecedented level of violence. Its failure intensified mutual suspicions and nourished bitterness and gloom. Moreover, it created new controversies. On top of all the existing

7

*Taking into consideration in*

ones, there is now the sharp disagreement over what really happened at Camp David.

Summit meetings are often followed by lively debates about the merits and drawbacks of each party's performance. Failed summits engender particularly sharp controversies, with each side blaming the other for the failure. It is rare, however, to find cases in which the parties not only blame each other for having held positions that were responsible for the failure, but cannot even agree as to what those positions were.

*include*

The debate over the failure of the Camp David summit encompasses a very wide range of questions. Some of these questions can be answered with a reasonable degree of certainty. Some are still being scrutinized by analysts and researchers in search of credible answers. And some, it seems, will never be answered definitely.

What follows is a "menu" of questions, arranged by category, concerning the theme of the conference – the search for "what went wrong."

➤ **Factors in the background of the summit**
➤ Were the faults of the Oslo process – in its essence or in its implementation – detrimental to the prospects of achieving an agreement at the summit? Did the continuation of settlement activity and Palestinian violence undermine the chances of success? Did the postponement of the last stage of the interim redeployment (in expectation of a comprehensive final status agreement) erode Barak's credibility? Was it eroded by his avoidance of transferring the three promised villages near Jerusalem?
➤ Was there an Israeli "Syria first" policy, and did it delay and undermine the process with the Palestinians?
➤ Did the Israeli unilateral withdrawal from Lebanon create a perception among the Palestinians that negotiations were not the best way to achieve their goals?
➤ How did the Palestinian threat to unilaterally proclaim a Palestinian state affect the prospects of the summit?
➤ Why did Arafat and Barak avoid preparing their respective publics for the need to make painful concessions, and how damaging was this?

➤ **Preparation**
➤ Were the Israelis and the Palestinians adequately prepared for the negotiations? Did they effectively employ experts to prepare dossiers on the various issues of the summit? Did they define their red lines and accurately evaluate their opponents' red lines in advance? Did they work out distinctions between "want" and "need"?

➤ Did they activate back-channel preparatory talks correctly in order to reduce the gap between the positions before the summit began? Why did the Stockholm talks yield so little? How damaging was Barak's simultaneous employment of two back-channel tracks uninformed about one another?

➤ Why did the two sides not benefit from the potentialities of track-II talks? Were the lessons of Track II understandings, such as those between Yossi Beilin and Abu Mazen, studied seriously?

### ➤ Intentions of the principals

➤ Did Barak go to Camp David with a sincere intention to reach an agreement, or did he go to "expose the true face of Arafat," as he explained *post hoc*?

➤ Was Arafat coerced to go to the summit, which he regarded as a trap, and was therefore determined to do no more than go through the motions without seeking an agreement?

### ➤ The time factor

➤ Was the timing of the summit right? Was it expedient to hold the summit when Clinton was on the verge of elections and Barak had a coalition that was falling apart?

➤ How did the time pressure work? Was Arafat the only one who was not affected by it and could walk away with impunity?

### ➤ Strategy

➤ Was it clear whether the purpose of the summit was to produce a broad or a detailed framework agreement?

➤ Should the negotiation have begun with the easier issues, with the more difficult ones, or with all of them simultaneously? Should there have been different teams assigned to the different issues?

➤ Was a strategy of tradeoffs systematically applied? Was it really necessary to lay down that "nothing is concluded until everything is concluded," or was it possible to substantiate agreements reached on particular issues?

➤ Was Barak's tactic of employing an "oriental bazaar" method in the bargaining over territorial dimensions counterproductive? Did it convince Arafat that by waiting the offer would improve?

### ➤ The conduct of the negotiations

➤ Were the negotiations conducted according to an orderly agenda?

➤ Were the Palestinians merely reactive in the negotiations, or did they initiate counter-proposals? Did they submit a Palestinian map?

➤ What was the nature of the Israeli proposals? Did the fact that they were submitted only verbally and through the third party diminish their validity? Were they presented in a "take it or leave it" fashion?

➤ Did the two sides share a similar "negotiation culture"?

➤ Were there conflicts within the delegations that affected them negatively?

➤ Were there leaks to the media that damaged the negotiations or facilitated them?

### ➤ The chief negotiators

➤ Did Arafat have difficulties understanding the Americans, and perhaps the Israelis as well? Did he refrain from getting deeply involved in the negotiations?

➤ Could Arafat bring himself to sign a final status agreement, or was he committed to a vision of total victory? Did he understand the historic opportunity that the summit offered? Why did he reject, or "accept with reservations," the Clinton Parameters? Was his encouragement of the *intifada* an indication that he never believed in a negotiated settlement?

➤ Was Barak overconfident in his ability to achieve a final status agreement at the summit and persuade the Israeli public to support it? Did he really believe that a hundred year-old conflict could be solved in two weeks?

➤ To what extent were the two leaders constrained by their constituencies? What were the limits of the concessions they could make?

➤ Were they too suspicious to share their intentions with their teams, thus hampering their efficacy?

### ➤ "Chemistry"

➤ Did the fact that Barak and Arafat hardly met face-to-face impede progress in the negotiations?

➤ Did the two sides pay enough attention to the emotional and symbolic needs of the other side? Did the Israelis project an arrogance of power and the Palestinians a victim mentality? Was Barak sufficiently mindful of his counterpart's dignity and sensitivities?

➤ Do such factors have any importance in negotiations based on interests?

### ➤ The third party

➤ Was Clinton too close to Barak to be able to convince Arafat that he was a genuinely honest broker?

➤ Was the US mediation effective in terms of systematic preparation, comprehensive strategy, agenda control, active involvement in the negotiations, and farsighted planning of alternative courses? Were the Americans adequately familiar with the interpersonal dynamics within the two delegations?

➤ Did the Americans apply sufficient pressure on the two sides to further moderate their positions? Should they have presented their plan earlier in the negotiations?

➤ Was a third party necessary at all, or would a bilateral meeting have been preferable?

## ➤ The Arab dimension

➤ Was it a mistake not to try to systematically mobilize the support of key Arab states for the negotiations? What would their positions have been?

➤ Was the attempt to solicit Mubarak to put pressure on Arafat too feeble and too late? What was Egypt's real interest regarding the peace talks?

## ➤ The Israeli and Palestinian positions

➤ *Territory* – The percentage of territory offered by the Israelis for the Palestinian state began in the 60s, climbed to the 80s and ended in the 90s; how far did it actually go? Were the calculations of percentages manipulative? What precisely was the Israeli area offered as a "swap" for annexed Palestinian territories, quantitatively and qualitatively? How viable could the Palestinian state proposed by the Israelis become in terms of contiguity and sovereignty? To what extent did the security arrangements demanded by Israel restrict Palestinian independence? How many settlements were to be dismantled?

➤ To what extent were the Israelis attentive to the Palestinian argument that they had already made their historic compromise by conceding 78% of historic Palestine and accepting the 1967 line?

➤ *Jerusalem* – How useful was Barak's decision to put the partition of Jerusalem on the table as a "surprise offer," without previous mutual consultations? Had the plan's implications for daily life in the city seriously been considered? What exact status (sovereignty, functional autonomy) were the Palestinians offered in the Arab neighborhoods and in the Old City?

➤ Was Arafat's denial of any Jewish historical link to the Temple Mount, and his rejection of the "sovereignty of God" and other compromise solutions, a blunder that shattered Israeli trust? Could he have made any concessions regarding the Holy Basin without the approval of the Muslim world?

➤ *Refugees* – Why was this issue hardly discussed at Camp David? Was it deferred because it was deemed resolvable at the final stage, or because, on the contrary, it was considered so contentious and emotional that bringing it up would shatter the negotiations?

➤ Was there at any point a Palestinian consent to limit the number of refugees returning to Israel, and at what level?

➤ *End of the conflict* – Was it a mistake to raise this issue, thereby opening up all the historic dimensions of the dispute? Could the Palestinians accept a "finality of claims" formula instead?

➤ *General* – Were Barak's offers fair and unprecedentedly generous, as maintained by the Israelis, or were they still such that no Palestinian could accept them, as argued by the Palestinians?

➤ On which of these issues did the talks break down? Was it the issue of Jerusalem/Temple Mount? Was it the issue of the Right of Return, looming large in the background?

### ➤ Post-Camp David talks

➤ Was the Israeli delegation at the Taba talks authorized to continue serious negotiations, or were they sent solely on an exploratory mission, as subsequently claimed by Barak? If Barak had concluded at Camp David that Arafat was "not a partner," why did he allow any continuation of the talks?

➤ Did the talks at Taba produce a promising basis for a peace plan acceptable by both sides?

### ➤ In retrospect

➤ Was blaming Arafat for the failure, by Clinton and Barak, unfair and harmful, or was it an inevitable conclusion from his conduct?

➤ Was it a mistake to allow the summit to collapse without a fallback plan? Once it was evident that the final status talks had reached a dead end, should efforts have been diverted toward another interim agreement, another Declaration of Principles?

➤ Did the Camp David summit prove that the Palestinian–Israeli conflict is not ripe for solution, and hence should not have been convened in the first place?

These are the questions intensively debated by the participants in the Camp David summit. Some of their accounts have already been published and several more are in the pipeline. Their answers are so divergent from one another, that one wonders if they were present at the same summit meeting. But of course they were, and the diversity of narratives is just another manifestation of the Rashomon syndrome – of the dependence of testimonies on the eye of the beholder. It is another corroboration of the dictum, "There are no truths but only perspectives."

The inquiry into "What Went Wrong" is only one of the two themes that appear in the conference title; the other is "Lessons for the Future." If we wish to look at the bright side of the Camp David experience, we may say that in spite of its failure, the peace summit was not in vain, and if properly studied it can teach us many rewarding lessons. Richard Holbrooke aptly wrote in his introduction to Margaret Macmillan's book on the peace conference that failed to prevent another world war, *Paris 1919* (New York: Random House, 2001):

> In diplomacy, as in life itself, one often learns more from failures than from successes. Triumphs will seem, in retrospect, to be foreordained, a series of brilliant actions and decisions that may in fact have been lucky or inadvertent, whereas failures illuminate paths and pitfalls to be avoided – in the parlance of modern bureaucrats, lessons learned.

Indeed, if the Palestinian–Israeli peace process resumes, which inevitably it will, negotiators will be better informed about all the pitfalls and obstacles on the road, and hopefully will come up with a better result.

## ITAMAR RABINOVICH

# The Failure of Camp David: Four Different Narratives

IN THE COURSE OF REVISING MY BOOK *WAGING PEACE*, I added two chapters, one on the "Barak Period" and one on the "Sharon Period." Naturally, the main theme of the Barak chapter was the collapse of the peace process – the failure of the Camp David conference and the outbreak of the wave of violence known as the second *intifada*. In the course of writing the chapter, I read most of the Camp David literature which, surprisingly, is quite voluminous. In the relatively short period that separates us from those events, a large number of books, essays and other statements addressing the events of Camp David summit and the reasons for its failure have been published.

To mention a few: a book by Gilead Sher, who is here with us; a book by Yossi Beilin; two books about the Barak government by Israeli journalists – one of them critical, the other less so; pronouncements by President Clinton; pronouncements by Prime Minister Barak himself; a very powerful interview given by Shlomo Ben-Ami to Ari Shavit in *Ha'aretz*; a piece co-authored by Robert Malley, who is also with us, and Hussein Agha, published in the *New York Review of Books*; a diary written at Camp David by Akram Haniyeh, the editor of *al-Ayyam* and an advisor to Yasser Arafat, which was published almost immediately following the proceedings; an essay by Ron Pundik, who is also with us, published in the quarterly journal *Survival*; and a book and several essays and interviews by Menachem Klein, who is here as well.[1]

Having sifted through the literature, I came to the conclusion that it can be divided into four categories that constitute not just versions of what occurred, but full-fledged narratives. A narrative is, of course, much more than a version. A narrative reflects a whole mindset, something that is very strongly embedded in one's thinking.

What I want to do here is enumerate the four categories and briefly comment about each of them.

**(1)** The first narrative is the **orthodox one**, represented by the pronouncements made by President Clinton, Prime Minister Barak, Shlomo Ben-Ami and Dennis Ross. These are the most distinctive representations of what I call the Israeli/American orthodoxy. According to this narrative, Israel tendered a serious offer for the solution of the conflict, and was not merely going through the motions, as some later charged. According to this narrative, whereas the content of the Camp David negotiations might be controversial, the response to the Clinton Parameters is not: this proposal was put on the table, accepted by the Barak government and not accepted by the Palestinian Authority.

There are, of course, differences in the style and the assertiveness of the presentations by the various individuals of this school of thought. Although following the summit President Clinton did not make a public, lengthy, systematic statement of his views, he has spoken in various forums, not all of them public, has been quoted extensively, and it is now very clear how he sees what happened. Dennis Ross has made no secret of his interpretation of what went on at Camp David, and after the publication of Malley's sharp criticism, he responded in kind. But perhaps Shlomo Ben-Ami's statements have been thus far the most powerful exposition of this narrative and we, his former colleagues at Tel Aviv University, know how eloquent he can be. In his interview in *Ha'aretz*, he argued that Arafat did not merely reject the offers made to him, but in fact did not want to make any deal at all, and proved that actually he was incapable of doing so. Ben-Ami's conclusions are thus very pessimistic. So, this is the orthodox narrative, emanating from both the Israeli and American establishments.

**(2)** To every orthodoxy there is a **revisionist counterclaim**, and the first such rejoinder came from Robert Malley and Hussein Agha. Essentially, this revisionist narrative tries to deny most of the main points that make up the orthodox narrative. It claims that a genuine Israeli offer did not exist, and if it did, it was not serious. The Palestinians could not be expected to accept the compromise envisaged by the Israelis because, basically, the essential Palestinian concession had already been made in Oslo. That is where they gave up the claim to most of Palestine, and they could not make additional territorial concessions.

And there is also an Israeli revisionist version, perhaps most eloquently presented by Ron Pundik, which comes fairly close to the Malley–Agha view. Most of those Israelis who tend to be identified with the Oslo agreement, like Pundik, come close to the revisionist view. This is easy to understand, because in the backdrop another debate is going on focusing on Oslo: Was Oslo the right thing to do or was it all wrong? If you are closely identified with Oslo, and wish to show that the agreement with the Palestinians at Oslo was the right thing to do, you must reject the pessimistic conclusions of Shlomo Ben-Ami and place the blame elsewhere, and Ehud Barak is usually the target. In some cases, there are also personal and political rivalries in the background that play an important role in fashioning the Israeli variation of the revisionist narrative.

**(3)**   The third category is the **deterministic narrative**. It argues that nothing could have been expected from the negotiations, because the summit was bound to collapse anyway. Here again, one can identify two main strands. One of them comes from the community of academics, experts and former officials. It is most powerfully and eloquently expressed in Henry Kissinger's book, *Does America Need A Foreign Policy?* The book contains an interesting chapter on the failure of Camp David. Consistent with Kissinger's well-known approach to Arab–Israeli peacemaking since the 1970s, he argues that Camp David was bound to fail because, in essence, no attempt at achieving a final status agreement between the Israelis and the Palestinians, or between Israel and the Arab world in general, can succeed. The reason for this, according to Kissinger, is that the minimum Arab demands have never met the minimum Israeli demands. There is a gap there that cannot be breached, unless one wishes to compromise Israel's security and future. Therefore, there is no point in trying. If you try, you are bound to fail, and if you fail, you generate a crisis. Kissinger's conclusion is that the parties must try to achieve interim agreements using a phased approach, play for time, build confidence and never try to aim prematurely for a final status agreement. He does not make do with this general statement, but actually offers a very detailed and astute analysis of the collapse of the peace process in the year 2000.

That is the academic/expert deterministic view. There is also a similar view that comes from the Israeli security establishment, usually from the Intelligence Division of the Israeli Defense Forces (IDF). It is most eloquently expounded by General Amos Gilad – more cautiously when he was in active service, and more openly and forcefully afterwards. He and other senior officers and figures in the Israeli defense establishment argue that Camp David was bound to fail because Oslo had been all wrong. Arafat, they say, was never sincere. As long as he was on the receiving end he was willing to take what was offered, but when the moment of truth arrived in 2000, he revealed that he never meant to make genuine peace with Israel. This deterministic view is embedded in a particular Israeli school of thought about the nature of the conflict with the Palestinians, the Oslo Accords and Arab–Israeli relations as a whole.

**(4)**   The fourth narrative is **eclectic in nature**. It appears in books and statements describing the events of Camp David in a way that does not present a specific clear-cut thesis. One example of a narrative of this type is the book by Gilead Sher, *Within Touching Distance*. Sher, who was a negotiator and subsequently Bureau Chief of Prime Minister Barak, does not seek to be overly critical. He presents an informative, detailed description of how the talks evolved and how they collapsed, but in his narrative there is no finger-pointing or over-arching themes. Another example of this category is Yossi Beilin's book, *A Guide to a Wounded Dove*. The book is dedicated to Ehud Barak "in admiration," but the text stands in contradiction to the dedication. Moreover, what in the book was only alluded to, burst out subsequently in an open controversy with Barak. Nonetheless, the book itself is marked by Beilin's reluctance to assertively blame Barak in print. Hence, I place him in the eclectic category.

These are, in my view, the four categories of narratives on the Camp David summit. I leave open the question which one is correct . . .

SARI NUSSEIBEH

# There Could Have Been Another Way

*[handwritten: notwithstanding / Nevertheless]*

I BELIEVE THAT ALL OF US WHO ARE COMMITTED TO PEACE are in agreement that regardless of what went wrong at Camp David, things should not have been allowed to go wrong *afterwards*. Some have argued, from opposite sides of the national divide, that the subsequent eruption of violence was – to draw on a familiar dictum – nothing more than a continuation of negotiations by other means. They have said, moreover, that the devastation of the political landscape was an intended and therefore unavoidable product of the failure to achieve a desired outcome to the negotiations. Thus Israel accused the Palestinian side of having set aflame the so-called *intifada*, while Palestinians accused Israel of trying to impose by force what the Palestinians did not and could not accept at Camp David.

To believe this interpretation to be true, of course, is to assume that it is totally naïve to contend that things should not have been allowed to subsequently go wrong. It is to assume that things could not but have gone wrong afterwards, since one side or the other, or even both, actually intended them to go this way, given their inability to achieve their respective objectives at Camp David.

However, given the way the political landscape has unfolded since the outbreak of violence in October 2000, it is hard not to believe that both sides simply miscalculated tragically, even assuming ill will on one side or the other. For now, Israel seems well on its way to imposing a more restricted solution, and the Palestinians seem well on their way to being subjected to something less than what was achievable at Camp David. This outcome cannot be a formula for a stable and lasting peace, and in any case could not have been the desired objective of either party at the time.

It is therefore more rational to assume that the devastation could have been avoided, whether on the assumption of the absence of ill will or, conversely, even on the basis of its existence, if the map had been read correctly and the potential miscalculations foreseen. Perhaps the miscalculations could even have been prevented in advance of Camp David itself.

Foreseeing the difficulty of bridging the gap on final status issues, some voices were heard at the time, my own among them, calling for a two-part agreement in preparation for Camp David: one on the issues over which there were no unbridgeable differences, and another on the list of the remaining issues. The Palestinian side could thus have declared its statehood in the image of its desired vision, while the Israeli side would simultaneously have recognized that state in a way that conformed to its own vision. There could also have been an agreement by the two sides to pursue negotiations in due course in order to bring the two visions closer to each other.

At the time, a unilateral declaration of Palestinian statehood was perceived as a belligerent stand, which it might well have been under a certain interpretation. But it may well have also been a means of escaping from what seemed, according to stated declarations at the time, an inevitable cul-de-sac. At Camp David, a workable agreement could have thus been reached which would have built upon previous peace efforts and laid solid foundations for a continuation of those efforts. We could have thus avoided years of human suffering.

In a sense, this idea of a provisional state and the Road Map are not very different in content, though they will be very different in terms of the overall political structure of the planned process. However, the creation of such a state under *present* circumstances could have the counterproductive effect of causing skepticism and mistrust among the Palestinian population, instead of being a positive psychological catalyst in the buildup of popular support for the peace process. That would very much be a function of having Ariel Sharon as the negotiating partner, rather than Ehud Barak, and of the Palestinian state being established within the confines of the enlarged prison walls on which the writing of the final borders is very clearly inscribed.

Anyway, that things went wrong both in Camp David and afterward is clear, and there are many reasons, hypothetical and real, why one can hold both sides responsible. However, viewed dispassionately, and in retrospect, one cannot help but recognize that while Camp David did not yield results on final status issues, it broke the ice on those issues and shook the foundations of long-held taboos. It is true that Palestinian expectations on Jerusalem, for example, were higher than what was offered by Barak, but given Israeli perspectives, Barak made an unexpected leap. One cannot help wondering whether, had the Palestinians made a similarly unexpected leap, say on the refugee issue, or on settlements or borders, it might not have been fruitful.

One cannot, in other words, help wondering whether a lack of initiative on the Palestinian side, more a function of negotiation culture in such situations than of hardened positions, contributed to the recoil and eventual frustration of the Israeli interlocutor. For I believe that it was abundantly clear that the Israeli interlocutor at Camp David wanted to close a deal. The Americans also wanted to close a deal. Only the Palestinians were skeptical from the outset, and therefore perhaps not tuned to the same mode.

But Palestinian skepticism, it must be stated, had its justified roots in the constantly churning wheels of settlement expansion, a process always running parallel to, but in the opposite direction from, any serious negotiation process. We know in any case, from the accounts of bilateral meetings held after Camp David, that the gaps were being narrowed and that whatever their remaining size, it would have been far better to construct a mechanism for managing these gaps than to allow a total breakdown, resulting in the human pain and suffering that followed.

Of course, it is always easier to be wise after the event, yet there are some observations I would like to make concerning that event. The first observation has to do with its nature. We know that different, often conflicting descriptions of the event compete for uniqueness or preferential status. However, given the many bilateral contact/negotiation lines that were all simultaneously or consecutively in play during that event, and the near absence of collective sessions, especially those in which the key interlocutors participated, one suspects that the subsequent conflicting descriptions of what really went on reflect different aspects of the reality of the event, rather than opposing versions of that reality.

We are all aware of how difficult it is to have two viewpoints converge in describing what we assume to be the same reality. So one can only imagine how much more difficult that process is when it comes to describing a multiplicity of contact lines operating simultaneously. In that sense, one can claim to know with far more confidence what occurred at Taba in January 2001, for example, than at Camp David.

My second observation has to do with third parties and the required nature of negotiations in this particular conflict. Very briefly, my sense is that each side has to "take the bull by the horns," and face its dilemma directly with a view to solving it, rather than depend on the ingenious efforts of third parties, however positively disposed they are to helping us. Frankly, Israel is not in need of a mediator to speak on behalf of Palestinian concerns, nor are the Palestinians in need of a mediator to speak on behalf of Israeli concerns. A resolution reached directly by the protagonists stands far more chance of lasting than one reached through third-party mediation.

These observations reinforce my own current belief in public engagement in the peace process, an element that was totally missing at Camp David. If the Oslo ship rocked us gently through the waters, closer and closer to the shoreline, Camp David shook the ship and awakened everyone in it to the reality of the rugged landscape of that shoreline. What we now need is the courage to disembark and reach that shore. This voyage does not concern only the captains of the ship; it concerns us all, ordinary Israelis and Palestinians, who seek a normal life of security and dignity. This is why the people must be brought into the process and why it should not be left only to erudite technicians and political leaders, however ingenious they may be.

This is also why I have proposed, jointly with Ami Ayalon, that the people be engaged in supporting the only workable principles for a resolution of this conflict, principles which – while allowing for further technical negotiations between the two sides – provide the way to address squarely all final status issues. It is the two peoples' destiny that is on the line, and this is their opportunity, perhaps the last one, to shape a workable, lasting two-state solution. If the people voice their preference, it is hard for leaders not to comply. Conversely, left only to leaders and third parties, the two peoples might never see the freedom and security they both so sorely need.

# MARTIN INDYK

# Camp David in the Context of US Mideast Peace Strategy

RECENTLY, I APPEARED ON A POLITICAL DISCUSSION SHOW in the US, "The Charlie Rose Show," with a well-known Arab journalist, Raghida Dergham. In praising President Bush for his decision, finally, to engage in Middle East summitry, she cast aspersions on President Clinton's Middle East diplomacy. Clinton, she insisted, had been all tactics and no strategy, whereas President Bush, she argued, has a strategy and is now implementing it. This particular bit of historical revisionism irritated me greatly, coming on the heels of over two years of criticism by the Bush Administration of President Clinton's use of summitry to try to resolve the Israeli–Palestinian conflict.

The charge that Clinton had lacked a strategy seemed, at least to me, one of his great defenders, wide of the mark, especially since it came at a moment when President Bush was himself engaging in the very same kind of summitry. So I decided, there and then, that the most useful thing I could do at this conference was to try to explain what President Clinton's strategy for Middle East peacemaking was, and compare it with the Bush strategy. The two summits, Camp David in July 2000 and Aqaba in June 2003, will be used to illuminate the two very different approaches to US Middle East peace strategy. I do this not only to set the record straight, but also to further understanding of the role the United States plays as the indispensable third-party mediator in efforts to resolve the Arab–Israeli conflict.

To that end, it is important to establish the context, at least from the American perspective. The first point I want to make is perhaps obvious, but cannot be stressed enough. When it comes to Middle East peacemaking, the US is not some neutral, even-handed mediator seeking a thankless Solomonic role in a seemingly hopeless dispute. As a superpower, the US pursues Middle East peace only when it suits its interests. To be sure, there is an element of naïve altruism in our policy, but that has never been more important than the sustained pursuit of American interests in a region vital to the US. In this regard, the US does have other alternatives to peace-making. We can preserve and promote our interests through deterrence, through containment, and as we have seen recently, through preemption. The Clinton Administration pursued peace because we believed it served our wider interests in the transformation of the Middle East.

When President Clinton entered office in January 1993, we were very conscious of the dire future facing the Middle East, of the battle that was unfolding between what we called the backlash states – who were actively seeking weapons of mass destruction, sponsoring terrorism and/or promoting Islamic militancy across the region – and the forces of modera-tion in Israel and the Arab world that were struggling to end their conflict. Concurrently, there was a bitter and bloody civil war being fought in Algeria between the regime and a violent Islamist opposition. Similarly, in Egypt, the Mubarak regime was facing a terrorist challenge from Islamic extrem-ists. In the Gulf, our vital interests in the security of the small, weak, oil-producing states of the Arabian Peninsula were being threatened by a wounded Saddam Hussein, bent on revenge, and a radical Ayatollah Khamene'i, bent on using terror to spread Iranian influence across the Middle East.

At the same time, Israel and all its Arab neighbors were embarked on a process of ending the Arab–Israeli conflict, which had begun a year earlier in Madrid. Moreover, the election in June 1992 of the Rabin government in Israel, a government with a mandate to make peace, had provided an oppor-tunity to the US not only to end the conflict but also, and more importantly from Washington's point of view, to use the peace process as the engine of transformation in the Middle East, as the driving force in a two-pronged strategy for defeating those who would threaten our interests. Even before Shimon Peres had articulated his vision of a "New Middle East," we saw the opportunity to pull this region across the threshold of the 21st century, by ending its primary conflict and overseeing the establishment of institutions that would transform this conflicted region into a more peaceful, more democratic and more prosperous domain, for the benefit of all its peoples and for the benefit of the US.

We were not naïve about this. In fact, we were deeply conscious of Middle East realities, and that is why we developed a two-branched strategy designed to contain the backlash states, particularly Iraq and Iran, while we made peace between Israel and its Arab neighbors. We labeled the first branch of this strategy "dual containment," and the second, "comprehen-sive peace." It was an integrated approach designed to generate a symbiotic dynamic between the two branches. To the extent that we could succeed in isolating and weakening the backlash states, we would reinforce the peace-makers. And to the extent that we could advance peace, we would strengthen the effort to contain the rogues.

Ironically, despite the fact that Camp David is what people remember best of that period of intense peacemaking activity, the centerpiece of Clinton's strategy for this transformation of the Middle East was not the effort to make peace between Israelis and Palestinians. Believe it or not, for a good part of the eight years of the Clinton administration, the Israeli–Palestinian negotiating track was a sideshow. In fact, the focus of our strategy was Syria. Damascus represented, in our view, the nexus between the two branches of our strategy. If we could succeed in bringing Syria into the circle of peace, Lebanon would quickly follow, we believed, and Israel would have peace with all the Arab states on its borders. The intractable and much more complicated Israeli–Palestinian conflict would be reduced, in our view, to its proper dimensions as a neighborhood dispute, and thereby made more easily resolvable. In the process, Iraq and Iran would be more thoroughly isolated and weakened, as other Arab countries joined the coalition for a new Middle East under the cover of a Syrian–Israeli peace agreement.

If we entered office with a clear sense of the strategic imperative of an Israel-Syrian rapprochement, we quickly reached the conclusion that it was also an achievable objective. When Yitzhak Rabin visited the White House in March 1993, President Clinton, meeting with him one-on-one, probed Rabin's willingness to withdraw fully from the Golan Heights and discovered that he had a partner for the deal. Not just one Israeli prime minister, as it turned out, but all four Israeli prime ministers during the Clinton era – Yitzhak Rabin, Shimon Peres, Binyamin Netanyahu and Ehud Barak – were willing to cede the Golan Heights to Syria for a peace deal. The challenge, therefore, was to bring the "Lion of Damascus," Hafez al-Asad, to the table to consummate the deal. That is why Secretary of State Warren Christopher made 21 visits to Damascus in the first four years of the Clinton administration, and that is why President Clinton held three summits with President Asad.

As it turned out, there were many problems with this strategy. To Washington, the Israeli–Palestinian conflict may have appeared to be a neighborhood dispute, but for Jerusalem it was an existential conflict. As much as each Israeli prime minister understood the strategic importance of a peace deal with Syria, the fact of the matter was that the conflict with the Palestinians always proved to be more pressing for Israeli governments. The Syrian problem could be contained but the Palestinian challenge could not. As a consequence, Rabin went off and made his deal with Yasser Arafat at the very moment that we in Washington thought we were brokering a breakthrough on the Syrian track. And with his policies of tunnel-opening and settlement-building, Netanyahu managed to drag us deep into the weeds of the Palestinian–Israeli dispute, compelling us to negotiate everything from the kinds of guns the Palestinian police would carry in Hebron to the names of the Hamas terrorists who would be arrested by the PA security forces.

Then there was the problem of our Syrian partner in this strategy. Hafez al-Asad enjoyed our attention, but he clearly did not like the idea of consummating a real peace with Israel. That proved to be just a bit too dangerous for a cautious Syrian Alawite who was frightened of losing his grip on Lebanon and his control of Syria's majority Sunni Muslim population. Nevertheless, after seven years of trying to conclude the deal with Syria, during which time three Israeli prime ministers offered Asad the Golan Heights, we thought that our moment had come with the election of Ehud Barak. Prime Minister Barak shared our strategic vision and was skeptical of the Oslo process. Thus, he quickly struck an understanding with President Clinton, at their Camp David summit in July of 1999, that they would together pursue a "Syria-first" strategy. That was the reason why Barak reached a quick agreement with Yasser Arafat at Sharm al-Sheikh in September 1999, which bought us six months of "breathing space" on the Palestinian track. The Palestinians thought the purpose was to negotiate a framework agreement for permanent status issues but, at least in my view, its purpose was to buy time on the Palestinian track in order to consummate the Syrian deal.

After a series of missteps, we also discovered in December 1999 that, unlike at any time during the previous seven years of diplomatic engagement, Hafez al-Asad was now apparently ready to do the deal. Aaron Miller, Rob Malley and I accompanied Madeleine Albright to Damascus on that visit, where I was struck by two important changes in Asad: (1) he was frail and suffering from dementia, evidenced by the fact that he kept confusing Barak and Clinton; and (2) for the first time in his life, he was in a hurry. Previously, he had insisted on Israel committing itself in advance of negotiations to full withdrawal to the June 4, 1967 lines. Now, in December 1999, he had only one condition for the negotiations, a condition he repeated three times in his conversation with the Secretary of State, "We have to finish them quickly."

It is an abiding reality of Middle East peacemaking that deals only are made when Arab leaders have a sense of urgency. That was true of Anwar Sadat when he made his historic visit to Jerusalem. It was true of Arafat when he decided to accept all of Rabin's conditions for the Oslo deal. It was true of King Hussein when he broke ranks with Arafat and Asad to conclude his peace treaty with Israel. And suddenly, just when we least expected it, that same sense of urgency was manifesting itself in Damascus, as the Syrian leader understood that he was coming to the end of his life. Since the topic of this conference is the Camp David summit, not the Clinton–Asad summit in Geneva that took place a few months earlier, I will not spend time analyzing what went wrong with our Syria-first strategy at that particular moment. Suffice it to say that Asad and Barak were like ships passing in the night.

When Asad was ready to make the deal in January at Shepherdstown, Barak was not, and when Barak was ready in late March to have Clinton present a detailed map of the line of full Israeli withdrawal to Asad in Geneva, it turned out to be too late for Asad. He now had a more pressing imperative before he died: to put his son Bashar in power. Making peace with Israel, in my assessment, would only have put that exercise at risk. At least that is what I believe he was thinking when he categorically said no to Barak's offer in Geneva, which caused the collapse of Clinton's Syria-first strategy, with dramatic consequences for our subsequent efforts to broker a deal on the Palestinian track, at Camp David and afterwards.

First of all, we lost the advantage that peace with Syria would have brought to those negotiations with Arafat. Had we made a deal in Geneva, Arafat would have been under pressure to take what he could before the rest of the Arab world normalized their relations with Israel. The failure of our Syria-first strategy reversed the pressures. Now, Clinton and Barak were in a hurry, and Arafat knew they had nowhere else to go for the deal that would seal Clinton's legacy and supposedly save Barak's prime ministership. Little wonder, then, that Arafat had to be dragged to Camp David and that, once there, he spent all his time looking for an exit strategy.

Secondly, Barak's willingness to withdraw to the June 4, 1967 lines on the Syrian front, with minor border adjustments around the Sea of Galilee, set a precedent for the Palestinian negotiators at Camp David. To be sure, they had also been insisting in their negotiations with Israelis on the June 4 lines, at least as the principle for negotiations on borders. But now, with the news going around that Prime Minister Barak was prepared to withdraw more or less to the June 4, 1967 lines on the Syrian front, it became an imperative that they had to insist upon. They would have to achieve the same deal.

Thirdly, and perhaps most importantly, when we look back at the unfolding events, the failure to get a Syrian–Israeli deal at Geneva led in short order to Israel's unilateral withdrawal from Lebanon. This granted Hizballah and the rogue states that supported it, Syria and Iran, a huge victory at a critical moment for the peace process. It demonstrated to the Palestinians the efficacy of force in producing Israeli withdrawal from Arab territory, and it seemed to have tipped the balance in Palestinian society away from those who argued that negotiations were the only way to secure Palestinian interests, toward those who had been training and equipping themselves to redeem Palestine in blood and fire. Had we achieved a Syrian–Israeli deal, all of these vectors would have been reversed. A comprehensive peace might well have been accomplished before Clinton left office. Instead, the all-important strategic context for the Camp David summit had deteriorated dramatically.

The rogues were in their heroic phase following their victory in Lebanon and the American failure to pry Syria away from them. Dual containment had already by that time been replaced by a more aggressive US policy toward Iraq and a more conciliatory policy toward Iran, but now the pressure was off of them and on us. Notwithstanding all the other mistakes, missteps and failures of leadership that doomed Camp David, these adverse developments in the strategic situation made it all but impossible to achieve a deal.

It is worth considering this salutary tale at a moment when the US has again plunged into attempting to effect Israeli–Palestinian reconciliation. Like Clinton, Bush wants to transform the Middle East. But he is driven by a sense of grave danger, rather than by a sense of great opportunity. After the September 11, 2001 terrorist attacks on the World Trade Center and the Pentagon, it became an American imperative to cut off the sources of terrorism in the Middle East by removing rogue regimes or pressing them to end their sponsorship of terrorism, and by what we call "drying up the swamp" that breeds more terrorists in friendly countries like Egypt and Saudi Arabia. Thus, instead of using Arab–Israeli peacemaking as the engine of transformation, Bush turned to war-making against Iraq. Containment was replaced by a policy of preemption, and the Palestinian cause was put on the back burner while the US toppled Saddam Hussein. However, with Saddam now gone, Bush has decided, ironically, to turn to the Palestinian issue, committing the prestige of his presidency and the time and energy of the White House to achieving a Palestinian state in short order.

It is interesting to note that there is no Syria-first option in this context. Syria, through a bout of incredible wooden-headedness, has managed to place itself firmly in the wrong camp, the one that sponsors terrorism. Bashar al-Asad has replaced his father and Arik Sharon, the old general, values the high ground of the Golan more than he values an uncertain peace with a newcomer in Damascus. So will Bush's strategy work any better than Clinton's? We can only hope and pray. But by putting all the emphasis on the Palestinian track and, as he says, "riding herd" on the parties, George Bush is taking a very weak Palestinian bull by the horns, one that lacks the capacity to confront the terrorists. In those circumstances, it will be very difficult for George Bush to succeed where Bill Clinton failed, and he will not have the assistance that would have come from the pressure exerted by fear of an agreement on the Syrian track.

However, while that part of the strategic context is missing at the moment, there are now other factors that are more important in shaping the strategic context. The US is again the dominant player in the region, with great influence. The rogue regimes are, as a result of our actions in Iraq, on the defensive. Israel is much strengthened, as the balance of power has tipped even further in its direction with the evaporation of the Iraqi army. There is an exhaustion factor operating on both sides, here in Israel and on the Palestinian side. As a result, there is a sense that the broad strategic context is now favorable for diplomatic progress.

That brings me to the last point. The US does quite well in using its immense power to shape the broad strategic context for peacemaking, to create, or at least help create the conditions in which those who would make peace can come to the fore, enter direct negotiations and try to resolve their bitter, complex conflict. We do not do so well when we get dragged down into the weeds, into the details.

However, the great irony of what happened at Camp David, and is repeating itself now, is that the Israelis and the Palestinians cannot seem to work out the details on their own. They seem to depend on the US to help them with the details. US Special Envoy John Wolf and his cohorts are engaged in a monitoring exercise. We have several diplomats here at the moment, working to try to put the details together. CIA teams, the president himself, his national security advisor and the secretary of state are all engaged in the process. The fact that the parties cannot get out of the rut without American involvement presents a conundrum. George Bush does much better in the broad, strategic context than in the details. Bill Clinton was a man of details. But either way, we have not been able to use our immense influence to produce a positive result, either at Camp David or thereafter. Therefore, the question remains: even though we have now shaped a better strategic context, will we be able to use our influence to resolve the myriad points of disagreement and achieve a solution to the conflict?

## Remarks during the Discussion

Let me offer a comment on the issue of time. I remember Prime Minister Barak asking me repeatedly throughout the first week of Camp David, "When is the last moment the president has to leave for the G-7 summit at Okinawa?" It was assumed, going into Camp David, that if we decide not to decide, it would mean that we would be at the terminating point of the summit. It was never imagined that Clinton would return from Okinawa to negotiate further. Thus, everyone perceived the existence of a very specific, eight-day time frame for Camp David. Prime Minister Barak wanted to understand exactly when the President had to leave. If you look at the detailed timing of Barak's proposal to divide the Old City (which was not an American idea, as Reuven Merhav tried to suggest), he timed it for the night before the morning when the President had to leave. That was very much, I believe, in keeping with the rules of the game of "chicken," with Barak trying to place Arafat in a situation in which he would have to make a decision without any further delay. The most important question one must ask, in analyzing both the Camp David 1978 summit (Egypt, Israel, US) and the Camp David 2000 summit, is this, "Who can afford to walk away?" In 1978, Anwar Sadat could not walk away without an agreement, while Menachem Begin could. Moreover, Jimmy Carter could not walk away without an agreement either, and he imposed an agreement on the weaker party, on Sadat, and basically promised him that he would subsequently get him a better deal on the West Bank. Of course, Carter did not get reelected and did not have the chance to fulfill that commitment. In my view, there was only one man who could walk away from each of these summits – Begin in 1978, and Arafat in 2000.

For both Barak and Clinton, time for achieving the deal that they each needed was running out. Clinton was in the last six months of his presidency, and needed the deal for his legacy, because without the deal his legacy is Monica Lewinsky. I do not say that as a joke, for it is a genuine tragedy. In Barak's case, he believed he had to conclude the deal during his first year in power. Indeed, he had already expended so much political capital in the process that his political future was hanging by a thread. He could survive politically only be concluding the deal. With Arafat, it was exactly the opposite. He could walk away without a deal and be a hero. Indeed, that is what happened. By saying no, he could gain more politically, both in the Palestinian and wider Arab spheres, than by saying yes. Thus, the question of who can walk away from a negotiation without a deal is perhaps a better predictor of results than all the other factors mentioned.

# Israeli Negotiators

# DANNY YATOM

# Background, Process and Failure

I WAS PRIVILEGED TO HAVE ACQUIRED A UNIQUE PERSPECTIVE on the peace process, thanks to the fact that I took part in all of the peace negotiations between Israel and its neighbors over the course of more than a decade. As the military secretary of the late Yitzhak Rabin, I participated in all of his meetings, overt and covert alike, with Arab leaders. The same was true when I worked under Shimon Peres and Ehud Barak. My perspective may not be entirely objective, but it certainly covers a long period of time, excluding only the three years when Binyamin Netanyahu was in office and I was head of the Mossad. During that period, to the best of my memory, there were hardly any communications between the Israelis and the Palestinians, except those leading to the Hebron agreement (January 1997) and the Wye Plantation Memorandum (October 1998).

Before I go on to discuss the summit, its goals and the causes of its failure, I will make a few comments about the backdrop to the summit, so as to better understand the goals that Israel defined during Barak's term.

There are five points that must be mentioned in this context. First, there was great frustration over the failure of the Geneva summit, a few months earlier, between President Clinton and Hafez al-Asad. We were pursuing two and one-half tracks at the time: the Palestinian track, the Syrian track, and the Lebanese annex to the Syrian track. Efforts were invested in both the Syrian and Palestinian tracks. Yet, whenever we made a move on the Syrian one, the Palestinians felt they were being manipulated, and whenever we made progress with the Palestinians – especially in Rabin's time – the Syrians felt that they were being trapped. Even though we reassured both sides that we had no intention of manipulating either of them, suspicion prevailed and cast a heavy shadow on our relationship with the Palestinians.

We were not the only ones trying to persuade the Palestinians that the talks with Syria were not meant to twist their arm. The Americans, who were persuaded by the many discussions that Barak had with Clinton that this was not the case, were trying to reason with them as well. But the Palestinians were apparently not convinced.

All this came to a head some four months before the Camp David summit when, on March 26, 2000, Presidents Clinton and Asad, after several hours of talks in Geneva, failed to break the deadlock on the Syrian–Israeli track. The Syrian track was then almost entirely blocked, and upon the death of Hafez al-Asad and the appointment of his son Bashar, it was terminally blocked and remains so until this very day.

A second point that must be mentioned here is the IDF's withdrawal from Lebanon. The pullout took place at the end of May 2000, and the Camp David summit began in mid-July. The IDF redeployed on the line demarcated by the UN after a number of modifications, mainly backward rather than forward, resulting from the fact that the UN surveyors often changed the border markings. Barak had made good on his campaign promise to pull the IDF out of Lebanon within one year of his election. Naturally, the withdrawal had both positive and negative effects on the sentiments of the Palestinians and the Syrians, and on their willingness to cooperate with Israel in pursuing the peace negotiations.

Third, the death of Hafez al-Asad shortly before the summit made a deep and lasting impression on the Middle East as a whole. In particular, it significantly lessened the chances for a renewal of Syrian–Israeli negotiations.

Fourth, during the year which preceded the Camp David summit, intensive efforts were made by the Palestinians and the Israelis through overt talks and, as later revealed, covert ones as well. Two different Israeli teams were involved in these efforts. One team, led by Oded Eran, dealt with general issues such as water. Another team, led by Shlomo Ben-Ami, who was Minister of Internal Security and at some point also served as foreign minister, met (sometimes secretly) with senior Palestinian officials, in attempts to bridge the differences between the two sides on four of the five issues to be dealt with in the permanent status agreement: refugees, borders, settlements and security arrangements. The Jerusalem issue was addressed only in passing, but later, of course, it came up at Camp David.

The purpose of Ben-Ami's efforts was to create an Israeli–Palestinian document laying out their understanding of the points of agreement and disagreement. Such a document, it was hoped, would enable the leaders from both sides to meet face to face and resolve the remaining disagreements through American mediation. President Clinton, President Mubarak, King Abdallah and, to an extent, Chairman Arafat, were convinced that this was the right way to deal with the conflict. They did not feel it wise to move directly to the details of the permanent status issues. They believed that it would be better to agree in advance only on the principles of the settlement of these issues, with the details to be fleshed out later on, as part of a permanent status agreement.

Although I can attest that the Israeli negotiating teams had considerable leeway, they came back empty-handed, without any achievement that might indicate that the Israeli and Palestinian positions had been brought any closer. The ritual that we would see at Camp David was already manifesting itself. The Israelis presented ideas, and at some point even maps that illustrated what was meant by the proposed sovereign, contiguous Palestinian state. The Palestinians, on their part, proposed nothing and avoided revealing their own positions. They failed even to make any good-will gestures that would have demonstrated that they had the ability and willingness to compromise. As a matter of fact, most of the reports submitted to Barak by Shlomo Ben-Ami and Gilead Sher looked like this: "We made the offer, and they asked what else we would be prepared to give." Barak and all of us concluded that these teams had done all they could and had reached a dead end.

Fifth, during the weeks preceding Camp David, there was a feeling amongst us that time was running out and that an opportunity might be missed. Underlying our concern was the fact that Arafat was being completely uncooperative, as opposed to Barak who had declared he would leave no stone unturned in order to achieve peace. Thanks to preparatory meetings, we already knew the Palestinian positions, which were generally fixed and inflexible, and they already knew our positions.

There were two options at that point. One was to advance in other creative directions, and the other was to go on treading water, knowing that time was working against us and against the process. Preliminary intelligence already showed that Arafat was thinking about unilaterally declaring the establishment of a Palestinian state, and we began planning our reaction. Barak raised the subject in numerous meetings with various leaders. He indicated that should the Palestinians make such a unilateral move, we would annex the major settlement blocs and the Jordan Valley. These moves, were they to occur, would mark the start of what threatened to be an escalation of tension. In any event, it was clear that if we could not negotiate effectively, the situation would deteriorate, leading eventually to chaos.

This may be a good opportunity to correct those who say that no preparations were made for the summit. In fact, extensive preparations had taken place. The Americans, including Aaron Miller, Dennis Ross, Madeleine Albright, Rob Malley and many others, came to the region and met with Arafat, Barak and other regional leaders, notably President Mubarak and King Abdallah. Leaders from other countries were also constantly updated and numerous telephone conversations were held between Clinton and Barak, and Clinton and Arafat, respectively. The Israeli side held the necessary preparatory discussions, some of which were quite thorough. Hence, anyone who says that no preparations were made, regarding either the technical or substantive aspects, simply was not there. And if he were, his memory must be playing tricks on them. It should be noted that it was hard to work with big teams preparing for negotiating such sensitive and problematic issues, because had there been any leaks regarding possible Israeli concessions, all hell would have broken loose. It was therefore vital to conduct the summit preparations with the utmost confidentiality.

Preparations on the Israeli side were therefore not the problem. The problem was the lack of preparedness on the Palestinian side. My impression was that they came to Camp David feeling that they had been coerced into it. This is the reason why the summit was unlikely to succeed.

Israeli and Palestinian societies have been intertwined for years, but both parties at Camp David wanted to separate from one another. As far as the Palestinians were concerned, the separation had to be absolute. They were unwilling to allow Jewish settlements to remain in their areas, a situation that could have paralleled the existence of Arab towns within the Green Line. In other words, they were not prepared to have Jewish residents, and certainly not to give them equal rights. Hence, it was absolutely clear at Camp David that we were headed for separation, not for anything else. At the same time, it was stated unequivocally that separation did not spell the end of economic cooperation. On the contrary, we were talking about free trade, or free trade zones, transcending the border line that was to be created. Above all, there were never talks about a Palestinian "entity," always about a Palestinian state. Those who present the end goal toward which we were working as anything less than a full-fledged sovereign state are mistaken.

Against this background, I would like to describe the goals of the actual summit, its progress and the causes of its failure. At the time of the summit, in July 2000, Clinton was still president, but presidential elections to choose his successor were to be held in November. Yet, Clinton was completely immersed in attempts to bridge the differences between the parties. He was thoroughly familiar not only with the general picture but also with its nuances, the ins and outs of the conflict. We wanted very much to substantiate America's serious commitment under Clinton and the willingness of his administration to play an active role in the peace process.

On our side, the first signs of cracks in Barak's coalition appeared prior to the summit. It was obvious that a wider coalition that would include the Likud and other parties would be less amenable to making the concessions that we believed could provide the basis for an agreement with the Palestinians.

Even the attempt prior to the summit to prepare an American paper, simply listing "I" and "P" positions, failed. Israeli and Palestinians delegations were sent to Washington in an attempt to create such a document, but in vain. These preparatory meetings clarified to both the Americans and the Israelis that a summit that would resolve the hundred year-old conflict was, at that point in time, not possible. The impression was that Arafat expected an agreement to be reached on all the difficult issues before the leaders would be invited to sign. This could not be realized and, given the endemic nature of the Israeli–Palestinian conflict, it cannot happen.

I believe that as opening positions, the offers that Israel made through the Americans were very forthcoming. Yet, Israel set down the following conditions:

(1)  No withdrawal to the borders of 1967;
(2)  Jerusalem would be united under Israeli sovereignty – this was only our opening position, and it changed during the summit, in an effort to be more flexible;
(3)  Most of the settlers would remain in settlement blocs under Israeli sovereignty;
(4)  Palestinian refugees would not be granted the Right of Return to places under Israeli sovereignty, under any circumstances, nor would Israel accept any ethical or legal responsibility for the fact that a refugee problem exists.

We told the Americans, who conveyed the message to the Palestinians, that our opening position afforded the Palestinians a good chance of getting much of what they wanted. Our opening position at Camp David gave the Palestinians a sovereign state on 85% of the territory of the West Bank and Gaza. During the summit, the figure went up to 95%. We demonstrated our readiness to make further concessions: a state with territorial contiguity within the West Bank (demilitarized), a safe passage between the Gaza Strip and the West Bank without any Israeli supervision or checkpoints, a free-trade agreement between Israel and Palestine, and permission to refugees to relocate to Palestine (but not to Israel). As for Jerusalem, it was obvious that a special arrangement would have to be reached, but we did not elaborate, and suggested that negotiations on the subject might have to be deferred because of the sensitivity of the issue.

From the Israeli perspective, our offer seemed a fair and decent one. Discussions that Ehud Barak held with many leaders from various countries indicated that others in the world saw it this way too. Our proposals were aimed at putting an end to the conflict and to mutual demands, or at least to put an end to claims on those issues on which agreement would be reached: settlements, borders, refugees, and so on.

These were to be our guidelines for the solution. We thought this approach would enable us to reach an understanding. We also thought it important that Arafat should hear about the package as a whole, since separate discussions of specific issues would draw attention away from the big picture and make it impossible to understand the advantages, links and trade-offs between the different elements of the package.

Obviously, then, our primary strategic goal was not "to expose Arafat's true face," as some have later charged. This was a consequence, and not the goal of the process. Our goal, defined by Ehud Barak, was to pursue any avenue that might lead us to peace by conducting, for the first time, substantive talks about the permanent status issues in an attempt to reach agreed solutions. This was to happen first as a framework agreement, in the context of binding guidelines that had to be decided by the leaders themselves. The framework agreement was to be followed by discussions aiming at detailed agreements, which were to end the conflict and all mutual claims, or, at least, end all claims regarding the matters on which agreement had been reached.

As I already stated, Israel continued to make concessions during the summit. Ehud Barak agreed, in effect, to give the Palestinians sovereignty over parts of Jerusalem. Although no final understandings were reached there, he agreed to consider this a basis for further negotiations, as the Americans suggested.

When the Americans presented their proposals, this was the first time I began to suspect that we would not succeed in concluding an agreement with Arafat. The Israeli delegation held a pointed seven-hour discussion with the participation of Barak, Ben-Ami, Amnon Lipkin-Shahak, Gilead Sher and others, as to whether we should accept the American plan. Eventually, most agreed with Barak's willingness to accept the American plan as a basis for further negotiations. Arafat, however, looked at the offer briefly before saying no to Clinton. Clinton tried to persuade him to reconsider, and eventually Arafat sent Sa'eb Erekat to Clinton to formally confirm his rejection.

The main points of dispute were the Right of Return and control of the Temple Mount. As for the Temple Mount, notwithstanding what has been said by both Mohammed and Munther Dajani, it is not accurate that the Palestinians understood from Israel that it was demanding exclusive sovereignty. We were prepared to make far-reaching concessions on the issue, to the point that we were considering such options as joint sovereignty, sovereignty of the permanent members of the Security Council or even sovereignty of Muslim countries. But the Palestinian delegation rejected all these proposals. They said to us in no uncertain terms, "Either full Palestinian sovereignty over the Temple Mount or nothing at all."

Israel had a part in the failure of the talks. Should it be attributed to misguided political perceptions and poor intelligence? I think not. The intelligence analyses we had at the preparatory meetings before the summit were completely consistent with the positions that the Palestinians eventually presented at the summit. These were evaluations of the Palestinian position on specific subjects such as refugees, the Right of Return and the Temple Mount. However, intelligence evaluations are not the basis for reaching an agreement. Intelligence analyses are a necessary tool for negotiations, but must not serve to rule out negotiations from the outset, or hinder attempts to convince the other side to move a little in our direction and narrow the gaps between us.

The following clarification must be made: we were not guilty of misunderstanding the depth of the concessions that were required of the Palestinians. What happened was a clash between conflicting national interests. We understood very well the Palestinian argument that they had already made all the possible concessions when they agreed to the borders of June 4, 1967. We understood this, but did not accept it. It was not a matter of misunderstanding, but of disagreement.

Some say that the negotiations failed because Israel's positions were too rigid or extreme. In answer to that, I want to mention that when our positions had been presented to the Americans before the summit, Dennis Ross said in one of these meetings that if these were our initial positions, we would have almost nothing left to negotiate with. Barak responded, "Yes, we are making offers that we believe are realistic. We are not going to Camp David to manipulate anyone." In other words, our opening positions did not offer 40% of the territory with the intention of adding another 40% during the talks. From the start we came with a realistic offer, generous and fair, but one that also left little room for negotiation.

Was there any danger that these proposals would serve, from then on, as the Palestinians' opening demands in any further negotiations? The answer, I believe, is no. If we ever reach a settlement with the Palestinians, it will probably be within the parameters that the Americans defined at Camp David. Granted, proposals that were already tendered cannot be erased or ignored, but it is obvious that there are very few further concessions that we can still make, because we have already offered almost everything that we possibly can. If the Palestinians fail to understand this, there will unfortunately be no agreement.

The failure of the Camp David summit and Ariel Sharon's visit to the Temple Mount were followed by the outbreak of the armed *intifada*, which continues to this day. In the beginning it was not an armed uprising and only involved stone throwing; only later did the Palestinians start using live weapons. Let me stress that it was not Sharon's visit to the Temple Mount on September 27 that caused the riots, but there is no doubt that it served as a catalyst. It is no coincidence that the riots started the day after his visit.

The riots did not take us by surprise because it was clear even before the summit that unless we did something to break the deadlock, the situation would deteriorate. I would like to reiterate that had Arafat unilaterally declared the establishment of a Palestinian state, we too would have taken unilateral steps, and the conflict would have escalated. We also knew that stalemate always leads to escalation. The IDF was preparing for a scenario of conflagration . The fact that the military was ready for the *intifada* was no miracle. It was the result of our evaluation that we should hope for the best but prepare for the worst.

To conclude, Arafat was wrong not to accept the American proposal and, in retrospect, most of the blame for the failure of the summit lies with him. Arafat was unable to rise to the responsibilities of a leader in the fullest sense of the word. He was not directly involved in the process and did his best to remain uninvolved. Throughout the summit, in fact, he was somewhat of an outsider.

The Americans did their job as best they could, although I believe that they did not apply enough pressure, mainly on Arafat. In one of his meetings with Clinton, Arafat said, "I do not know what the Israelis are talking about. The Temple Mount? The remains of the two temples? Where did they get that? There is no such thing. The Temple Mount is not sacred to the Jews; see the ruling of the Chief Rabbi, who said that Jews are not allowed on the Mount, proving that for the Jews the Mount is defiled, not holy." This was one of the only instances when Clinton lost his cool. He told Arafat that although he was not a Jew but a devout Christian, he could say that ever since he was a child he was taught that the remains of Judaism's holiest temple are on the Temple Mount.

The Americans could have put more pressure on Arafat in two areas: (a) they should have pressured him to accept their proposal as a basis for negotiations; and (b) they should have made him realize that the Palestinians also were required to make some concessions, and not only the Israelis. In addition, the Americans did not mobilize the Arab world to support Arafat. During the talks, Clinton made a feeble, unsuccessful attempt to do so in telephone conversations with Mubarak and King Abdallah. To the best of my knowledge, both snubbed Arafat.

We too were wrong not to have Ehud Barak invest all his efforts to conciliate Arafat. I argued with Barak on this point, emphasizing that no effort should be spared in trying to assuage Arafat's fears. I thought that Barak should meet with him and make him feel that he was respected. But that was not done, which was a mistake on our part.

The main lesson learned from the failure of the Camp David summit is that there is no alternative to continuing with negotiations, even "under fire." Preparations are needed. There is no way to get two parties to sit around the same table and resolve their differences when one of the preliminary conditions for sitting together cannot be secured without preparatory talks. To secure a cease-fire or cessation of terror, we must talk. Despite the disappointing outcome of the summit, I believe we cannot afford the luxury of sitting back and doing nothing. If we do that rather than be proactive, the situation will just deteriorate further.

## Remarks during the Discussion

I believe that the Syrian track did not interfere with the Palestinian one, and on this I differ with Aaron Miller. As Mr. Miller maintains, pursuing both tracks was Rabin's choice also. We did not think it right to follow one track or the other exclusively. It was clear to us that it was extremely important to try and advance on both tracks as much as possible and resolve our two main problems simultaneously.

## AMNON LIPKIN-SHAHAK

# The Roles of Barak, Arafat and Clinton

I WILL TRY TO SHARE WITH YOU MY IMPRESSIONS, recollections and understanding of the sequence of events at Camp David. We should look at the expectations that the protagonists in this drama had at the time. There were three key players: the Prime Minister of Israel Ehud Barak, the President of the Palestinian Authority Yasser Arafat, and the President of the United States Bill Clinton. All the others were almost just spectators, or at best, supporting actors. Each of the three main players came to Camp David with a different set of expectations. Overall, their familiarity with each other's character, needs and expectations was not sufficient to secure the success of the summit.

The election of **Ehud Barak** as prime minister marked a new phase in a not-so-new political process, in which all parties had already come a long way since 1993. Clinton was involved from the outset, and so was Arafat. Barak, in his previous roles, was involved as well. When Barak came to power in 1999, the political process had already suffered serious setbacks: the assassination of Yitzhak Rabin, which was an outcome of his role in the process, and the murderous Palestinian terrorist actions, which caused many Israelis to cast a vote of no-confidence in the process and confer the premiership on Binyamin Netanyahu. The victory of Ehud Barak, who was seen as Rabin's follower, renewed the hope for peace.

Barak's victory speech was the first source of disappointment for the Palestinians, as many of them later told me. They were sure they had played a supporting role in his election. After all, they had tried to spur Israeli Arabs to be actively involved in the election and tip the scales in Barak's favor. As you probably recall, this was an election in which votes were cast separately for Prime Minister and Knesset representatives. The Palestinians wanted

Barak to win because he represented for them hope. Instead of hearing a victory speech that addressed their needs and concerns, they heard Barak saying, "We will not give up Jerusalem; we will not give up the Jordan Valley; we will not allow refugees to return; and we will not go back to the borders of 1967." Although these statements reflected consensual Israeli principles and were probably well known to the Palestinians, to hear Barak emphasize them at his moment of victory was a major letdown which, in retrospect, from the Palestinian perspective, was only the first among many that followed. By the time of the Camp David talks, there had been various other letdowns, big and small, which served as roots of the failure of these negotiations.

The Sharm al-Sheikh meeting in September 1999, in which Israel and the US agreed to take a time-out on the Palestinian track and focus instead on the Syrian one, is worth mentioning in this context. Although nothing explicit was said to the Palestinians, they quickly understood this change and even accepted it. The Palestinians expressed surprise at the shift of Israel's focus to the Syrian track – so we heard from Aaron Miller after his meeting with Arafat – but the expression of this surprise was in fact only for the record, since the Palestinians were fully aware of what was happening. They did not object because in many respects the transition was convenient for them: they believed that no peace could be reached with Syria without an Israeli withdrawal to the borders of June 4, 1967, and that the Palestinian cause would only benefit from an agreement which accepted the principle of the June 4, 1967 lines. Furthermore, they felt that such an agreement would silence domestic opposition to an agreement with Israel, and that once an agreement between Israel and Syria were in place, it would be harder for Syria to continue to permit Hamas and other Palestinian factions sponsored by Damascus to oppose a similar Israeli–Palestinian arrangement. Nevertheless, Arafat made sure the world saw how offended he was, and told Miller he was being taken for granted.

Talks with the Palestinians nonetheless continued, and it was suggested to them that they set aside some of the interim agreements that had already been concluded and try instead to reach with Israel a framework agreement on permanent status. Indeed, this is what we sought to achieve at Camp David.

The failure of the talks with Syria at Shepherdstown and the futile meeting between Bill Clinton and Hafez al-Asad in Geneva brought the Israeli–Palestinian dispute back to center stage. But the Palestinian Authority displayed signs of nervousness and impatience even before the Geneva meeting. As a result, talks were held with the Palestinian Authority negotiators – mostly covert, and rightfully so – and an agreement was secured. One of the provisions of this agreement, to which the Americans were privy, was that three villages near Jerusalem would be handed over to the Palestinian Authority. A deadline for this handover was scheduled, but repeatedly postponed. The first deadline was postponed, with Arafat's agreement, when threats were made to dissolve the coalition government in Israel. The second deadline was canceled because it coincided with one of the Israeli memorial days. The third was postponed when it was suggested that the parties should wait for – and invest all efforts in – the final, comprehensive agreement. Meanwhile, word of the plan to allow the Palestinians to control the three towns was leaked to the press. The Knesset voted on it and approved the move, but threats that the coalition would be dissolved persisted.

Concurrently, secret negotiations commenced. At first, brief talks took place in Israel, with Abu Mazen (Mahmud Abbas) and Abu Ala (Ahmad al-Qureia) representing the Palestinians, and Shlomo Ben-Ami and myself representing the Israelis. During that period I learned that ours was not the only avenue being pursued: Gilead Sher and Sa'eb Erekat were also negotiating. In fact, Abu Mazen told us at one point about a meeting that had taken place with Gilead Sher, who brought with him a paper from the Prime Minister. I admit that this put us in a rather awkward position. Although we did not think too much of it, these surprising parallel talks were not helpful, as the Palestinians did not understand their meaning any better than we did. In any case, communications with Abu Mazen and Abu Ala, who seemed to be competing for the title of hard-liner, were futile and therefore discontinued. Our recommendation was to conduct talks with only one of them, not both. These talks led to the Stockholm channel, in which Ben-Ami and Sher took part.

The main force pushing to go to Camp David was Ehud Barak. He was truly and genuinely ready to reach a settlement, believing he had the solution for the conflict and the ability to implement it. He wanted to act quickly. Knowing that a settlement would be painful for the Israeli public to accept, Barak was convinced that the public would learn to live with it only if it were to be implemented swiftly. Opponents of the peace process were ready and eager to take action, and unless the move was swift, the cabinet would have to face protracted demonstrations and campaigns. Barak therefore convinced President Clinton that it was possible to secure an arrangement if the principals get involved. "Dayan's negotiating team [in 1977–78]," he argued, "was unable to accomplish in 12 months what Begin was able to get in 12 days." The Stockholm talks had made Barak aware of the differences between his positions and those of the Palestinians. He knew that Jerusalem had not been addressed there, but he had complete confidence in his ability to convince the Palestinians to reach an agreement on this issue as well and thus end the conflict. Despite the fact that he had a minority cabinet (following the Shas Party's withdrawal on the eve of the Camp David summit, on orders from Rabbi Ovadia Yosef), Barak embarked on his path with deep conviction and belief in his capabilities.

**Yasser Arafat**'s starting point at Camp David was, however, quite different. He was not ripe for an agreement, something that he fully admitted. He had been dragged into the summit under pressure from President Clinton. He was extremely suspicious and believed from the outset that the cooperation between Israel and Washington was much closer than that between the Palestinian Authority and Washington. Arafat behaved as though time was not of the essence. Granted, September 13 was the expiration deadline for the completion of the final status negotiations, but to him there was nothing sacred about this date or any other. Moreover, not only did he estimate that the differences between the parties were enormous, but he did not even want to try to bridge them. Bridging differences was not in Arafat's character. Neither in Oslo, nor in the May 1994 agreement on withdrawal from Gaza–Jericho, nor in any other stage of the negotiations, did Arafat bother to go into details and attempt to bridge differences. I think he found it comfortable to leave it to his officials to negotiate and make the necessary concessions, reserving for himself the authority to grant, or alternatively withhold, the final seal of approval.

Furthermore, the Camp David summit took place after Arafat had already seen that Syria had not suffered repercussions from President Asad's "no" to Clinton in Geneva. Hence, the American threat did not seem as ominous as before. In Arafat's mind, it was possible to defy Washington and penalties would not be meted out, at least not directly or immediately.

In addition, the summit took place after Israel had already declared its consent to withdraw to the borders of June 4, 1967 on other fronts. This point merits special attention. In the pullout from Lebanon, Israel worked hand-in-hand with the UN to demarcate every inch of the international border. Anyone traveling in the area today can easily see how hills were divided by the border simply because that was where the UN, with Israeli cooperation, placed the border stakes. Israel's consent to reinstate the exact line of the international border was given despite its substantial security-related investments on the Lebanese side of the border. Arafat and his people were surely aware of Israel's meticulousness in demarcating the international border. However, the Palestinian public did not perceive this as an Israeli virtue but rather as an indication of Israel's need to make concessions under pressure. In their eyes, Israel is always extremely reluctant to make concessions, and only agrees to do so under duress. In the case of Lebanon, the Palestinians felt that it was Hizballah's armed attacks that pushed Israel back to the international border.

Arafat, in my view, understood the weakness of Israel's political system.

He looked at Barak's narrow coalition, which on the eve of the Camp David summit had shrunk even further into a minority cabinet, and probably asked himself, "What if I were to say 'yes' and the Knesset rejects the agreement?" This never came to the test because Arafat had no intention of saying yes, but had he been forced into making a decision of this kind, this possibility surely would have influenced his thinking. Moreover, Arafat had always insisted that he needed time to mobilize Palestinian public opinion in support of the agreement and that this would be impossible without serious concessions on Israel's part. On the eve of the Camp David summit, he had only one demand of the Americans: that he should not be blamed if the talks fail. Although Washington accepted this demand, it clearly attests to his intentions.

Arafat's conduct of the negotiations was undoubtedly problematic, particularly *vis-à-vis* the Americans. He simply did not know how to deal with them.

President **Bill Clinton** was thoroughly familiar with all the players. He trusted Barak and appreciated his capabilities, and probably also wanted to believe that an agreement could be secured. In addition, timing was important to Clinton. July was much more convenient for him than August or September, because with elections coming up in November and the campaign expected to move into overdrive in September, it would be hard for the President to devote himself to steering a political process that was supposed to resolve an age-old dispute. It is also possible that the deadline for nominations for the Nobel Prize contributed to the way the timetable for the Israeli–Palestinian talks was defined.

No official talks took place on the first evening of the Camp David summit. In a private conversation, Arafat raised the matter of the Temple Mount, arguing that the real Temple Mount was not in Jerusalem but in Nablus. This is no joke; the bizarreness of this argument indicates how important Jerusalem was to Arafat. Bear in mind that before the Camp David summit no one had even mentioned Jerusalem, not in Stockholm or anywhere else. The matter was strictly taboo. Arafat was thus extremely concerned by Israel's claims to Jerusalem, and rightfully so.

Eventually, Barak presented the Israeli position on Jerusalem to the American delegation. In my mind, it was the most courageous concession made in the summit. For Barak, it represented a huge political risk, both in immediate terms and for his career as a whole. Apparently, he believed that this was his ace – the one card he could play that his opponent would have great difficulty rejecting. The Americans were impressed with the courage and generosity of the Israeli offer. After all, Barak's predecessors – Rabin, Peres, Netanyahu and even Barak himself prior to his election – had conditioned them to the mantra that Jerusalem would never be divided. Barak's proposal was an entirely new tune, surprising and far-reaching from any perspective. His offer had wide repercussions and invited various interpretations in Israel as well. No one remained indifferent.

Yet Arafat's response was most disappointing. He was asked to respond, but procrastinated. An attempt was made to mobilize the support of other Arab leaders, but instead they called Arafat on the phone and said to him, "You decide." It is my opinion that Arafat was simply incapable of making a decision on such fateful matters. This inability was clearly reflected in his public statements to the effect that making such a decision was tantamount to giving up his life, that if he made such concessions, he was as good as dead.

It was then that the real emotional rift occurred. Clinton departed for Okinawa, leaving the other delegates behind, awaiting Arafat's response. Shortly after that, we realized that in fact Arafat had no intention of offering any response. The Americans understood that as well. Acting to defuse the looming crisis in the talks, Secretary of State Madeleine Albright removed the item from the agenda. However, the future of the negotiations was unclear, as were the directions they would take.

President Clinton wasted no time upon his return from Okinawa, and took vigorous action to push the process ahead. At this stage Arafat had evidently already closed himself off, declining new and quite generous American proposals. As one of the previous speakers mentioned, the first map the Palestinians were offered included 85%–89% of the territory that Israel had conquered in the Six-Day War. At this point the Americans were offering land swaps to compensate for the missing percentage points. On the matter of refugees, President Clinton announced that he had secured another $8 billion from the participants of the economic summit in Okinawa, putting the total amount available for refugee rehabilitation, resettlement and compensation at around $40 billion. The President also stated he would initiate a process that would enable an unlimited number of Palestinians to move to the US during a given period of time. Granted, this was not a promise, but it was a far-reaching presidential statement, especially in American terms. The Americans also tried to find language that would be as soft as possible regarding the issue of control over the Temple Mount. No one disputed that the Palestinians would run the site, and Israel and the Americans were even ready to offer noncommittal language regarding sovereignty. But Arafat would not budge.

What can we conclude from this account? The opening positions of the Israelis and the Palestinians on all main issues – territory, refugees, Jerusalem – were far apart, and the leaders disagreed both on the substance of the problems and the timetable for their resolution. Given these differences, and given the fact that the leader of the Palestinian side was neither accustomed to nor incapable of working out the details of these issues, the summit's chances of success were slim to begin with. Arafat did not believe in the summit and did not want to reach an agreement there. He wanted to stretch the process out as long as he could, at best in order to warm up the Palestinian population to the prospect of concessions and a final settlement of the dispute. The Israeli leaders, on the other hand, wanted to accelerate the process and complete it with a signed agreement as soon as possible. They sought to secure a finished agreement that although including difficult and painful concessions, would finally put an end to the conflict, thus undercutting domestic opposition.

Arafat's difficulties with all the critical issues were clear. Everyone, possibly including Arafat, realized that no agreement could be reached unless the Palestinians gave up the Right of Return. Had he gone along with the American and Israeli offers at Camp David, he would have had to explain to his people that he, who throughout the years had repeatedly promised to return the refugees to the places they had left, was abandoning the Right of Return. Everyone also realized that some territorial concessions by the Palestinians would be required, since certain blocs of Jewish settlements would inevitably remain under Israeli control. This involved the abandonment of another unyielding "never" which Arafat would have had to account for. An additional common understanding was that the Western Wall and the Jewish Quarter of the Old City of Jerusalem would remain in Israeli hands, as would post-1967 Jerusalem neighborhoods such as Gilo and Neve Ya'akov. Accepting this would have compelled Arafat to explain to his people how it came about that he was giving up parts of pre-Six Day War Arab Jerusalem and its surroundings when he had repeatedly sworn that this would never happen. These reversals would not have been easy for the Palestinians to swallow, especially since they had not been prepared for them. Arafat believed that he did not have the backing of a public that was capable of endorsing such changes.

In addition, Arafat felt compelled to leave no room for critics to say that he had rushed into an agreement without putting up a real fight. In light of his longstanding radical posture and the firm stand he had demonstrated in front of the Arab and Islamic world, it would have been extremely hard for Arafat to resolve the three pivotal bones of contention in one fell swoop. This was too much for him to handle during the brief time period of the Camp David summit. What the Americans and Israelis expected from Arafat conflicted with his interests and disposition. It also was incongruent with the traditional way of negotiating in the Middle East. The circumstances seemed to be in his favor. Time was not of the essence: unlike Barak, he had no rapidly disintegrating coalition to worry about; unlike Clinton, he had no term of office that was coming to a close. It may very well be that Arafat believed that, since his interlocutors were under pressure, an unyielding stance on his part would result in a better offer than the one being tendered. Combining all these with the images of Israel's withdrawal from Lebanon and all the lessons from Israel's abortive talks with Syria, provides an explanation of the rationale underpinning Arafat's non-cooperation.

The Palestinian delegation gave off the clear feeling that some of its members did not agree with Arafat, preferring to advance the process rather than move toward the crisis that was clearly imminent by the summit's end. These Palestinian delegates conveyed the feeling that there was room to negotiate, and that Israel's positions, even if not acceptable as a basis for the final agreement, provided reasonable ground for further negotiations.

This was how the summit ended, with a bitter sense of failure. Israel had tendered proposals that were much bolder and more far-reaching than any that had been made in past meetings with the Palestinians, especially on the matter of Jerusalem. This failure, which reverberated not only in Israel but also throughout the region and the world, was primarily the responsibility of the Palestinians. Apparently, they did not comprehend how deeply disappointed the Israeli public was with their conduct at Camp David. This disappointment resulted in the election of Ariel Sharon as prime minister instead of Ehud Barak. This may have happened anyway; however the fact that the Palestinian Authority never tried to stop the armed *intifada*, even in the early stages when this could have easily been done, had a shattering impact on Israeli public opinion.

As for the lessons to be learned, I am afraid that in Israel no leadership ever learns from the experience of its predecessor. I do not know if the same will be true on the Palestinian side as well, in the post-Arafat era.

## Remarks during the Discussion

The human factor, that is inter-personal relationships, played a certain role at Camp David, but it was not a critical or determining factor. Good personal relationships can make a positive contribution, but in this case the lack of chemistry between the Israeli Prime Minister and the leader of the Palestinian Authority cannot be blamed for the failure of the summit. This factor may have aggravated the situation, but it certainly was not the prime cause of failure.

The role that the senior Palestinian officials played at the summit was significant. I believe it was not only Arafat who was forced into Camp David, but the entire Palestinian delegation. Their reluctance was evident. Over the course of the summit, some of the Palestinian participants began trying to achieve progress on some of the specific issues independently of the comprehensive framework agreement on permanent status. None of the Palestinian negotiators, at least those whose opinions I heard, ever thought that there was any chance of securing a complete agreement on all the issues.

The opinions of the Palestinian delegates did matter, even to Arafat. Despite repeated accusations that Arafat made all his decisions alone, he did in fact listen to his advisors and other officials. Nonetheless, it was he, and not they, who had the final say whether or not an agreement would be concluded or not. His decision to avoid an agreement at Camp David stemmed from his reading of the proposals that were on the table. When he asked himself whether the public in Gaza and Ramallah would lend their support to such proposals, I believe that his answer was no.

# YOSSI GINOSSAR

# Factors that Impeded the Negotiations

IN MOST CASES, I AM RATHER SKEPTICAL ABOUT HINDSIGHT, but in today's discussions I have already gained some important insights. First, let me note two comments made by former US Ambassador Martin Indyk, who played a senior role in the negotiations. His observation that the Camp David summit did not fail because of the dispute over the Palestinian Right of Return defies a campaign that has been underway since the collapse of the summit regarding the cause of this failure. If asked, most Israelis would now cite Right of Return as the primary reason. Another interesting point that I heard from Mr. Indyk is that he was not at all surprised when Yasser Arafat rejected the proposals made at Camp David, but *was* surprised when he turned down President Clinton's. This comment is very important. The proposals made at Camp David in July 2000 and those made by Clinton in December of that year are often treated *en bloc*. Commentators often do not distinguish between them. They overlook what Mr. Indyk has noted with a great deal of fairness, namely, that the offers made by President Clinton in December 2000, known as the Clinton Parameters, were in fact much more favorable to the Palestinians than those made at the Camp David talks.

A comment to Prof. Mohammed Dajani: Since I happened to be present when the issues pertaining to the Temple Mount were raised at Camp David, I know for a fact that it was not Prime Minister Barak who brought up the question of sovereignty; Yasser Arafat raised this issue. To the great surprise of the Israeli delegation, the entire Palestinian leadership failed to understand the significance of the Temple Mount to Jewish tradition and Israel's collective identity. As Amnon Lipkin-Shahak explained, it was this misunderstanding that was the main source of the disappointment and loss of trust on the part of the Israelis, and not the sovereignty issue as such.

I would also like to say how sorry I am that none of the principal Palestinians who played an active role in the negotiations are present here today. I listened respectfully to the explanations given by Mr. Dajani for their absence, but nevertheless would like to hope that just as the Israelis and Americans reflect here on their thoughts and actions, with critical thinking and intellectual integrity, the Palestinians will be doing the same on their side. It is important that they hold such discussions, draw lessons, and give voice to their thoughts. Today we Israelis have mostly been flogging ourselves, but we all know that we are just as good at accusing others. We do not want to point fingers at the Palestinians, and hope that they can do it for themselves where relevant.

My impressions from the Camp David summit may partly coincide with those of others at this conference, and partly diverge. Let me first make a general remark. For a long time now, I have believed that until Israelis humanize Palestinians as a society and as individuals, and thus also rationalize the Israeli–Palestinian conflict, the conflict will not be ripe for the conclusion of any peace agreement. This observation certainly held true at the time of the Camp David summit. Perhaps the violence of the *intifada* after Camp David has brought to the consciousness of the Israelis the reality and authenticity of the conflict. At the time of the Camp David summit, however, the Israeli–Palestinian conflict was seen by most Israelis as an amorphous phenomenon, not clearly defined.

Israel's political leadership also underwent an evolution in their thinking. The initial attitude toward the Palestinians, expressed by Golda Meir and others, was that there was no such thing as a Palestinian people, and hence there was no validity to their claims. Eventually, at Camp David, Israel's Prime Minister was prepared to give the Palestinians all of East Jerusalem, including parts of the Old City, in order to achieve the "end of conflict" with them. Our politicians underwent this metamorphosis mainly due to practical, pragmatic reasons, but neither the leadership at the time of the summit nor any previous Israeli government knew how to lead the Israeli public through the process. They failed to humanize Palestinian society in the eyes of the Israeli public and make Israelis see Palestinians as a normal human society. Moreover, they failed to make their constituencies realize that this is an authentic national conflict that involves real problems and genuine aspirations of flesh-and-blood people. This problem has been present throughout the protracted conflict with the Palestinians, and in my opinion it was one of the impediments that plagued the process leading up to Camp David and one of the pitfalls of the summit itself.

We must remember that the summit took place after both the Netanyahu and Barak cabinets had expressed, through statements or actions, their dissatisfaction with the Oslo process, and had tried, whether for ideological or practical reasons, to skip over it. The first thing that Barak's cabinet did was reschedule the redeployment time-table determined in the Wye River Memorandum, which in fact was nothing but a protocol for the implementation of a segment of Oslo II. The Palestinians failed to understand this fundamental difference between an agreement and a protocol. Moreover, as Mr. Lipkin-Shahak mentioned earlier, the Palestinians expected a revolution in the political process once Barak took office. They expected rapid progress and swift implementation of the stages defined in the Oslo Accords, leading up to a permanent status agreement.

However, in the two months that followed Barak's assumption of power, there were a number of clashes with the Palestinians on the question of the additional stages of the second further redeployment (FRD), which was to cover approximately 11% of the territory. Endless arguments over the maps and over which places would or would not be ceded compounded the debates regarding the implementation of the redeployment.

In this context, it is important to mention Israel's unilateral withdrawal from Lebanon. Several Palestinian leaders told their Israeli counterparts, and word later spread to all senior Israeli officials, that Israel's action led the Palestinian public to believe that violence was the only language Israel understands. While Hizballah got exactly what it wanted, the Palestinians had to bicker over the difference between 5.1%, 5.6% and 6.1% of the territory, even though they felt they were cooperating with Israel in matters of security, including clamping down on terrorists who were operating against Israel. Indeed, this was true at least until May 2000. This was a kind of cooperation that, as described by Palestinians, worked "in Israel's service and to the benefit of Israeli citizens."

I am, by the way, among those who firmly believe that the unilateral withdrawal from Lebanon played a role in the outbreak of the *intifada* in September 2000, or at least influenced the nature and intensity of the violence. I am referring to the influence that the pullout had on the Palestinian population, not necessarily the leaders. The Palestinian public, it should be remembered, watches every move the Israelis make.

Mention was made here of the Syrian track, which led the Palestinians to conclude unequivocally that in Israel's mind everyone takes priority over the Palestinians. Israel, they felt, was neglecting the peace process with them – which was precarious to begin with – and preferred to deal with those fronts that represented bigger threats to its security. Following the same logic, the Palestinians felt that Israel perceived the Lebanese/Hizballah front as more important, because it was more threatening than the Palestinian one. Palestinian officials said so explicitly to many Israeli representatives.

During January–February 2000, we were squabbling with the Palestinians over a handover of 6.1% of the territory, which the Palestinians contested for two reasons. The first reason was that Israel decided unilaterally which areas would be handed over to the Palestinians; the Palestinians objected to this, even though Israel was entitled to do so under the agreements. Israel allowed the Palestinians no say whatsoever – not even in the form of a recommendation or statement of opinion – as to the delineation of the areas that they would receive in the respective redeployments. The second reason was the Palestinian frustration regarding the Jerusalem-area villages. At the end of February, shortly before a Barak–Arafat meeting, I was working on a deal with the Palestinians. The terms were dictated by Barak and backed by the Americans. The deal comprised two main elements: (a) Palestinian covert involvement, through secret meetings between Palestinians and senior IDF officers, in choosing – out of a given list – the areas that would be handed over in the 6.1% redeployment; and (b) transfer of the three villages near Jerusalem – Abu Dis, Azariya and Issawiya – to Palestinian control. The first element of the deal was carried out in March, but the second element was not.

Another unconsummated portion of that deal involved the safe passage. I am not sure that anyone remembers that Oslo II had included the creation of a safe passage between the West Bank and the Gaza Strip that would allow the Palestinians to move relatively freely between the two areas. There were also other matters, such as the establishment of a committee on prisoner release. There were also references to the third FRD. Just one month earlier, at a meeting between the Israeli Prime Minister and foreign minister on one hand, and Arafat, Abu Ala and Abu Mazen on the other, the Palestinians had come to understand, almost by chance, that Barak was thinking about canceling the third FRD. Naturally, they were deeply disappointed.

Another important factor that must be mentioned is the anniversary of the founding of the State of Israel, which for the Palestinians is the day of *al-Nakba* ("the catastrophe"). In fact, it was on that day, May 15, 2000, that the first shot of *Intifadat al-Aqsa*, which eventually flared up in September, was fired. The incidents involved serious violence, including the participation of Palestinian security personnel and policemen who fired at Israeli troops. To be sure, such incidents had happened before, notably after the opening of the Hasmonean tunnel in Jerusalem in September 1996. But in retrospect, the *Nakba*-day violence foreshadowed the *intifada*'s eruption. One day earlier, the Knesset had approved the turnover of the three Jerusalem-area villages to the Palestinian Authority. Israel was hoping that the timing of the vote would send the Palestinians a calming message in advance of the May 15th anniversary, but this hope was shattered.

I would like to state unequivocally that the entire Palestinian leadership, including those leaders that some of us even today refer to as moderates or as potential partners, adamantly opposed the Camp David summit. To a man, they pressured Arafat to turn down the invitation. At Barak's request, I tried to convince the Palestinians to attend, and was shocked at their fierce opposition, coming not only from the most senior leaders but also from lower ranks. They were so much opposed that they fought over the question who would be allowed *not* to go. The Palestinians felt the summit was premature and would be an "ectopic pregnancy." It was not, in their view, part of the well-defined Oslo process. Hence, they maintained, the unimplemented interim agreements should first be observed. In general, they believed that there was much work to be done in bridging the differences on the various issues that constituted the Palestinian–Israeli conflict before the summit should convene. The differences over the three main issues – Jerusalem, refugees and territory – were very wide. (Of these three issues, Jerusalem – as other speakers have noted – was the only one that eventually was discussed at all at Camp David.) The Palestinians had felt that with such gaps on major issues, and in view of the fact that some of the interim agreements had not yet been implemented, the time was not yet ripe for a conference, certainly not a summit of the highest-ranking leaders. An idea was raised to hold a summit first without Arafat or Barak and invite them to join later, but the Palestinians rejected this option too. In sum, the Palestinians felt that this summit would be a big mistake and that the danger of failure overshadowed any benefit that it could possibly yield.

In addition to the question of "what went wrong" at Camp David, I think we should also be asking whether the summit benefited or injured the process with the Palestinians. This question merits discussion, not because there exist any clear-cut answers, but rather because it invites some serious thought.

As I mentioned, the Camp David summit was forced on the Palestinian leadership against its will. This is the primary explanation for the behavior of some of the most senior Palestinian delegates at Camp David. It deserves to be mentioned that Abu Mazen gave a long interview to *al-Hayat* (London), one year ago I believe, in which he described openly and in detail what the Palestinian leaders thought about the summit before it commenced. He more or less covered all the items I have mentioned, and concluded by saying that the Palestinians perceived the summit as a trap that Israel and the US were setting for them, a trap from which they had to escape.

Israel did not really know what the Palestinians would accept or reject. Some believed they would agree to a 20%–80% deal for the West Bank and Gaza (namely, the handover of 80% of the territory to the Palestinians). Others thought they would accept an arrangement of 10%–20%–70% (the 10% referred to territory in the Jordan Valley to be leased to Israel). I organized a meeting between Barak and Abu Mazen prior to the summit, because I thought it was important for the Israeli Prime Minister to hear the Palestinian positions not only through intermediaries like me but also directly from an authorized Palestinian personality. This meeting was covered in the media, and the only reason I am mentioning it here is to stress that Abu Mazen explained the Palestinian positions on all the issues and left no doubt as to the positions they would adopt at Camp David. This meeting once again showed how wide the gap really was on the three most important elements of the permanent status agreement: territory, Jerusalem, and the refugees.

Let me turn to the role that the Americans played at the summit. Despite the criticism that I have, in hindsight, of the American performance, I must repeat what I told Secretary of State Madeleine Albright in Paris in October 2000, when we were trying to find a way to deal with the *intifada*. I applauded the Clinton administration and the American delegation for the intellectual and emotional efforts that they invested in the peace process. Indeed, they undertook an incredible effort, which was expressed in many sleepless nights. This was already evident in Paris, when both the Israeli and Palestinian delegations were exhausted and the only ones still working were the Americans.

The literature on the 1978 Camp David summit with Sadat, Begin and Carter indicates that there was a point there when the US President realized that arranging direct meetings between the delegations and breaking down the conflict into specific controversial issues would lead nowhere. He then took matters into his own hands, spending the days with the future Chief Justice of Israel's Supreme Court, Aharon Barak, and Sadat's advisor, Osama al-Baz, and the nights with Foreign Minister Moshe Dayan and his Egyptian counterpart, Ibrahim Kamel. His involvement was so personal and intimate that the draft agreement – now posted on one of the walls at Camp David – is in his own handwriting.

By contrast, at the Arafat–Barak–Clinton Camp David summit, the American delegation was not really in charge. In fact, no one was in charge at all, and the summit took its own course. We had entertainment, we had golf carts, movies, bowling – we had it all. But there was no American leadership available. The question is not who the Americans should have pressured. The problem was that the presence of the American mediators was hardly felt. I am not saying that if it were Carter instead of Clinton the summit would have ended differently, but in the general picture, this element should also be noted.

The mutual distrust between Ehud Barak and Yasser Arafat, and Barak's unwillingness to meet with Arafat to discuss matters of substance, should also be mentioned. For the sake of fairness, I must say that in various arguments I had with him, Barak gave me detailed explanations for his reluctance to hold such a face-to-face meeting. Naturally I do not question his right to decide the method of dialogue. Barak believed that a direct meeting would lead to a documentation of his positions, and that Israel would then be forced to treat these positions as a starting point for any future negotiations, rather than as conditional positions. But many of the Israeli delegation, including myself (although I was not an official member of the delegation), felt differently. Interpersonal communications are, at times, mistakenly considered insignificant in political negotiations. In fact, personal touch and even intimacy play an important role and can produce results. We witnessed this in a number of cases of direct interaction between Israeli officials and Arafat, as well as with other senior Palestinian counterparts.

To my understanding, Barak's decision to avoid personal contact defies the very essence of the term "summit," which means that when necessary, or in times of crisis, the leaders themselves agree to sit together and resolve the most difficult issues, face-to-face.

It may come as a surprise to some of you that – as I see it – the leverage that any Israeli Prime Minister has over his Palestinian counterpart is much more effective than that wielded by the US President. Israeli prime ministers have traditionally believed that the President of the US wields much more power *vis-à-vis* the Palestinians than they do, but I believe that they have all been mistaken. I was convinced that Barak personally had much more influence over Arafat than Clinton had, and that whatever he said carried much more weight than any statement Clinton could make, but I was unable to persuade Barak of this. Unfortunately, Israel's prime ministers have consistently underestimated the power they have over the Palestinian leader and the potential of direct dealings.

As for the events of the summit itself, it is useful to recall the various crises that occurred and the way in which each delegation handled them. The ongoing crises highlighted the gap between the expectations of the two sides. There were moments when we in the Israeli delegation truly felt that we were making history, and then moments of crisis when we felt that historic opportunities were slipping away. The Palestinian delegation, on the other hand, did not feel at all that they were involved in history making, and the moments of crisis just made them anxious.

Finally, I would like to comment on the conclusion of the Camp David summit. It was said here today that the summit was just a milestone in a long peace process. That may be true, but this is not how the summit was portrayed at the time. The summit ended in acrimony, and the feeling was that this was the end. A noisy Israeli campaign, supported by the US, blamed the failure on the Palestinians and maintained that it was all over, that the other side had been put to the test and found wanting. Hence, there was no longer anyone to talk to and nothing to talk about – end of discussion. I think that diplomacy in general, and the Camp David case in particular, teaches that leaving the door open at the end of each stage is imperative for allowing the process to continue. Therefore, I agree that the Camp David summit must be seen as a milestone, rather than the finish line.

## Remarks during the Discussion

Martin Indyk asked about the Palestinians' stated conviction that when Israel and the US raised the possibility of a Jewish presence on the Temple Mount for prayers, what they actually wanted was to undermine the process. He asked me to elaborate on the Israeli moves on this issue and the Palestinian response to them, and the role that this issue played in the failure of the talks. Well, at the Prime Minister's request, preliminary inquiries had been made regarding the possibility of making some arrangements that would enable Jews to pray on the Temple Mount. These inquiries yielded no results. I also think they were insignificant, and I reject the interpretation we later heard that they had dramatically changed the Palestinians' attitude regarding the question of the Temple Mount. This was not how it happened, neither during the inquiries themselves nor afterwards, at the summit. It was a cautious attempt by the Prime Minister to look into yet another option that might be raised during the negotiations. That was the nature of the inquiry, and the Palestinian side treated it accordingly. Incidentally, the possibility of enabling Jews to pray on the Temple Mount had already been explored with Yasser Arafat in person, in the presence of his assistant. Anyone who attributes more to that episode than what I have just described is simply inventing things that were not there.

I would like to make one more comment about the personal factor in negotiations. I have already stated that I do not believe that this was the cause of the summit's failure, but I do believe that the human factor carries weight in any negotiations, including political ones. There are abundant examples from Israeli history in which individuals made a difference in negotiations, owing to their personality, skills and credibility, even when the most sensitive aspects of national defense were discussed. One prominent example is that of Efraim Halevy, who after the failed attempt to assassinate Khaled Mash'al in Jordan in September 1997, managed to save the situation thanks to his warm personal relations with the King. There are plenty examples from the Palestinian front as well where, for example, personal contacts made possible the release of persons held by Palestinians, but since I was involved in these efforts, I will not elaborate. In any event, there is no doubt that the human factor is relevant. Chemistry between the leaders is particularly significant and can contribute to the process, although I do not believe it is decisive on the question of whether an agreement can be secured or not.

I was asked about my call for humanizing the Palestinians in the eyes of Israelis despite frequent, long-standing calls on the Palestinian side for the annihilation of the State of Israel. Surely, the person who asked me this question does not believe that I would justify any call for Israel's destruction. All I said was that I believe that we Israelis are somewhat condescending toward the Arabs in general, and toward the Palestinians in particular. We respect the Palestinians a bit less than we do all other Arabs in the region. For example, we hold the Syrians in high regard. Compare the way the media and Israeli politicians talk about Hafez al-Asad with the way they treat the Palestinians leaders. There are many other similar examples. As a society, we must learn to treat Palestinians as human beings who have the same authenticity that we ascribe to ourselves. I believe that we are not yet ready to do so. Granted, Palestinian society also has quite a long way to go in this regard. It needs to learn to treat Judaism as a valid religion, Israeliness as a nationality and the State of Israel as the state of the Jewish people. No one disputes that. But that is not the point of this conference. I hope that there are Palestinians who will stand up and tell their fellow Palestinians exactly the same things we are telling ourselves here today. This is exactly what I have told Mohammed Dajani: I hope that on their side there are also meetings, discussions and attempts to draw conclusions and that people stand up and speak their mind openly, courageously and truthfully.

The question about the future and the prospects of the peace process merits a long seminar of its own. I do not have enough information today to evaluate the prospects of an agreement at this time. I hope and believe that eventually Palestinians and Jewish Israelis will live side by side in peace on this small parcel of land.

GILEAD SHER

# Lessons from the Camp David Experience

WHAT LESSONS, IF ANY, CAN BE DRAWN FROM THE FAILED SUMMIT at Camp David? In order to answer this question, one must first analyze the approaches of the two protagonists at Camp David and how these approaches affected what came afterward.

At Camp David, Israel sought to use the opportunity to reach a framework agreement on permanent status that would mean an end to the conflict and finality to all claims. The government of Ehud Barak focused on what was perceived as Israel's genuinely vital interest: the long-term existence of a Jewish democratic state within internationally recognized borders. It was a conscious decision in favor of a painful historic compromise, one that would respect the rights of the Palestinians, bring about an end to the occupation, and, as it was hoped, an end to the conflict – not necessarily love and friendship, but peaceful, stable coexistence. Camp David, which followed intensive preparatory negotiations in Sweden, was for Israel an extremely important benchmark in the process, rather than a final conclusion of it.

From the Israeli perspective, the Palestinians' approach to the summit was not uniform. Nonetheless, the common denominator was an approach that stemmed from a strong sense of grievance and a search for historic justice. It entailed exploiting political negotiations as a phase in the ongoing clash of cultures and peoples, as well as religions. We had no doubt that a portion of the Palestinian leadership, and particularly Yasser Arafat, regarded the achievement of an agreed political solution as just a temporary, tactical tool. It was not intended to bring about an end to the conflict, but to be used to enhance the Palestinian position in anticipation of the next phase in the struggle. In their view, time was on the side of the Palestinian cause.

There was thus a significant gap between the ways the two parties conceived the purpose of the Camp David summit. This conceptual gap affected the unfolding of events far more than any of the mistakes made by either of the parties, or the mistrust that characterized their relationship along the way.

Some individuals among the Palestinian negotiating team at Camp David did seek a compromise agreement, and manifested moderation. But their influence over Arafat was nil. The negotiators who faced us had no more than a virtual mandate. With a few of them, it would definitely have been possible to reach a reasonable agreement. But when the time came for a command decision, Arafat dismissed the achievements of his negotiators with a wave of his hand. Even before Palestinian violence erupted, Arafat did not consistently and clearly project a readiness to reach a true historic compromise with Zionism, based on the partition of the country into two independent political entities. And in the absence of any other directive from above, the ongoing hostility and wild incitement fell on fertile ground.

Arafat's tactic was to maintain the façade of participating in a political process. Behind this façade, however, his actual approach to the negotiations was totally passive. He was, as it turned out, waiting for the right moment and pretext to introduce an additional element into the arena: violence. He did not lift a finger to prevent the incitement to violence and the eventual outbreak of hostilities.

At Camp David, it was Yasser Arafat who critically failed. This is my personal view, of course, but I also believe that the bulk of Palestinian society also understands now that the tragedy that has befallen them has a name-tag on it. The Camp David talks could have paved the way toward ending the occupation. What the Palestinians called a conspiracy or a trap was in fact a genuine invitation to negotiate, to have a real give-and-take process, unlike their wish to automatically obtain the totality of their demands. From the end of September 2000 onward, the dominant Palestinian strategy was to exercise pressure on Israel through terrorism, to portray Palestinians in the eyes of the world as innocent victims, to evade any substantive political decision – yet at the same time to keep the appearance of willingness to continue the political process. Arafat's incompetence in managing Palestinian state-building was revealed in the form of widespread corruption, the use of terrorism and incitement as a political tool and consistent refusal to control his armed organizations.

So what now? How are we to move beyond the present situation of no trust, revengeful rage and tribal violence? When the dialogue does resume – as one must believe it will, notwithstanding the current grim reality – it is absolutely vital that we apply the appropriate lessons from the collapse of the Camp David summit. Here are some thoughts about lessons that should be learned:

**(1)** *The preparation of supportive public opinion.* The "historic compromise" underlying the agreement that was meant to be reached at Camp David was not well explained to the public. In Israel, explanations focused on what we were likely to be giving up, rather than the benefits of transforming the situation, namely, the "fruits of peace." It is obvious that serious attention and concerted effort must always be devoted to continuous, comprehensive public diplomacy – that is, explaining to the public the thinking behind the political process. But this did not happen in 2000, or at least not sufficiently. Added to this is the need to establish supportive international and Arab coalitions to sustain the peacemaking process.

**(2)** *Attention must be paid to the other sides' perceptions, not just their objective requirements.* On the issue of the Right of Return of the refugees, for example, it was image that held sway over substance. Here was an ethos that had been built up and nurtured over decades as one of the cornerstones of the Palestinian national struggle. The Palestinian negotiators considered it their duty to show, even if only verbally, that they were bringing an end to the tragedy of the refugees and that their dream of Return was about to be realized. As a result, for many of our Palestinian counterparts, the wording of this section in the draft agreement was perhaps more important than the practical mechanisms to be set up to help rehabilitate the refugees and mobilize the international community to aid them. I believed, and continue to do so, that some flexibility on our part over the wording would have satisfied such an emotional need and devotion to an image on the part of the Palestinians. They might have been quite content to have left it at that, and would not have demanded the actual Right of Return into Israel itself for all the refugees, which in my view is not part of their core interests and is, of course, inconceivable in Israeli eyes.

**(3)** *Careful thought must be given to the question of process management.* Sometimes this may be as important as the substance of negotiations. When parties move toward the resolution of such a historic conflict, the process must be kept very well structured. A strict framework with a rigid agenda is needed, from which the parties must not be allowed to deviate. This was definitely not the case at Camp David. To be sure, the facilitator hosting the summit got off to a good start. The summit began with an orderly procedure of presenting positions, defining interests and then giving each side its respective "assignments." However, there was no follow-up. The mechanism collapsed, and the businesslike, practical atmosphere that had marked the summit's beginning simply faded away. The process became unclear and disorganized. This pattern should not be allowed to repeat itself in future peace efforts.

**(4)** *Timing is crucial.* The Clinton proposals of December 2000 were based on the extensive negotiations that had taken place at Camp David; they summarized and fleshed out the level convergence of views reached up to that point. But they were ready as early as August 2000. Had Clinton presented his proposals at that time, capitalizing on the momentum generated by the summit, I believe the outcome might have been different. In the event, a very different momentum developed, a momentum of violence, and the historic opportunity was lost. Sadly enough, there was no realistic American contingency plan ready; no fallback or exit strategies were prepared for the eventuality that the summit would fail.

**(5)** *The permanent status issues are all interlinked.* In this conflict it is not possible to isolate any single issue from the others. The approach adopted by the Israeli negotiators was predicated on a readiness to discuss far-reaching ideas for solving all these issues, but nothing was considered agreed and binding "until everything was agreed." Thus any agreement on a single issue was not valid until all issues were resolved. For their part, the Palestinians regarded this approach as a conspiracy. Their suspicion that Israel was seeking a way to deceive them and the whole world, and perpetuate the occupation, prevailed over any reasonable explanations we offered them to the contrary.

I am quite confident that a permanent agreement will eventually be reached through negotiations. Until now, the conflict-resolution procedures employed were not able to cope with the myriad forces that influenced decision-making on both sides. Yet, the dialogue must continue, at all levels, between those elements in the respective societies who seek peace. The form of the final agreement will inevitably be a two-state solution, because a clear separation of the two peoples has been the underlying logic of the peace process ever since its inception in 1991. The two-state target to be reached at the end of the road requires several preparatory operational stages, some of which would dramatically change the current status quo. Initially, there must be a process of disengagement between the two peoples, followed by a cooling-down period and further transitional stages. Finally, the creation of a viable, demilitarized Palestinian state alongside Israel would conclude the process.

The challenge for Israel is to realize its vision and secure its future as a Jewish democratic state. This can be achieved only through a historic territorial compromise. The absence of a Palestinian partner after Camp David, one that possesses the capacity and willingness to take decisions, conclude agreements and implement them, should not be allowed to constitute an obstacle to Israel's long-term objectives. For the time being, Israel must disengage from the Palestinians, with or without an agreement.

The disputed issues will not change, nor will the solutions. When the time comes for the parties to end their terrible bloodshed, and when a responsible Palestinian leadership emerges, the two sides will find a way to agree on the formula of the permanent status. The agreement may emerge in phases: it may be preceded by Israeli-initiated unilateral separation, which will seek to ensure the democratic and Jewish character of the State of Israel. Eventually, the shape of the permanent status agreement will not be substantially different from what has been discussed before. Perhaps this is the ultimate, and ironic lesson from the collapse of the Camp David summit: that when such a time does come, we will be back to where we stood at Camp David, with the same solutions on the table. Let us hope that by then, both sides will have learned their lessons, for an agreement is indeed achievable.

## Remarks during the Discussion

I would like to refer to the controversy about the adequacy of preparations by the Israelis for the Camp David summit. We should distinguish between two things. There are preparations that are conducted within the parameters of the given policy. They consist of research, documentation, writing of papers, consultations, gathering of positions from relevant branches of government and the like. But in the course of the negotiations the principals may take decisions that go beyond the terms of reference that had guided the preparatory work. It is hardly possible to prepare for this sort of event. Therein lays the misperception of those who argue that Israel did not make the necessary preparations.

Prior to the summit, Israel conducted serious discussions on all the relevant issues, except Jerusalem. These discussions were held among all the appropriate bodies within and outside the cabinet. There were also preparatory discussions with the Palestinians, some of them in unofficial forums, where no minutes or records were kept, such as the Stockholm talks. There, we tried to put everything – again, except Jerusalem – on the table in preparation for the summit, and to formulate a joint paper. The result was a document of eight or nine pages, which marked considerable agreement on the contentious issues at hand, including the issue of the refugees. Having received reports on the talks from Abu Ala and Hassan Asfour, on the one hand, and from Shlomo Ben-Ami and myself, on the other, the Americans told us, "You have made a historic step toward permanent peace in the Middle East." Unfortunately, Abu Ala changed his mind and reneged on his acceptance of the documents – as had happened before with various agreements that were reached with Palestinian interlocutors.

Regrettably, the achievements attained in Sweden were not reported to Arafat with the same transparency of our presentation to the cabinet. Having realized this, and having understood that actually Arafat had no idea what to expect at Camp David, we decided to inform him of the developments ourselves. Shlomo Ben-Ami, Yossi Ginossar and I went to see him in Nablus, where we described to him and to others among the Palestinian leadership the agreements that had been reached in Sweden with the negotiators he had assigned. There was nothing more we could do as negotiators. We had done everything possible within the authority delegated to us, and were treading the fine line of exceeding that authority. Now was the time for the leaders to make the crucial decisions. They had to be summoned to a joint meeting where, with intensive bridging efforts to be made by the American president, they would hopefully achieve a historic compromise on behalf of their peoples. Unfortunately, Arafat did not see it this way. He did not approve of our talks in Sweden and dubbed this back-channel a "bad channel."

I was asked what our mandate was for those back-channel negotiations, and whether we had any real authority. One must understand that Israel's culture of negotiations and civil service norms of governance are entirely different from those of the Palestinians. We provide complete, comprehensive reports to our principals, and we receive instructions that we implement in accordance with the national policy. This cannot be said of the other side. We must learn to overcome such differences, and we have indeed tried to do so in various ways, but the existence of this obstacle should be recognized. Take, for example, the 1994 Cairo agreement and the problem that arose there in the last moment with the signing of the maps. Arafat simply would not sign, even though the ceremony, covered by all the international networks, was already underway. As dramatic as the incident may have been, it consisted of nothing more than last-minute blackmail, in line with Arafat's habitual tactics. These are facts that must to be taken into account in any retrospective analysis of what happened.

The "end of conflict" issue was one of the most central matters dealt with at Camp David. In Israeli–Palestinian negotiations, there is one important consideration that must be kept in mind: if we resolve first only the easier issues, then when we reach the difficult ones we are bound to face very rigid positions. At Camp David, we might have been able to reach an agreement on such issues as the security arrangements and territory, but that would have left us without our main leverage, the land. In my mind, the occupation of the Territories is not an asset but a burden – however, it constitutes an asset in negotiations. Giving up the territory in return for the resolution of some easier problems would have left us without our ace card for talks about the tougher core issues. It would have left us with no leverage for the next stage, in which Jerusalem and the Right of Return were to be discussed. The only trade-off for our primary asset, the Territories, would be a Palestinian withdrawal of the demand for the Right of Return. The core elements of the permanent settlement – refugees, Jerusalem, land and security – cannot be resolved in isolation. All these issues must be resolved together. The Palestinians wanted to leave the "end of conflict" issue to the end. Almost all the members of the Palestinian leadership that negotiated with us (except Arafat) said explicitly that they would keep us waiting for a decision on the "end of conflict" issue until the very last minute and only then they might agree. In other words, Palestinian procrastination, in this respect, was a negotiating tool.

The overall concept of the desired framework agreement on the permanent status was that it should provide a solution to certain problems that could be implemented immediately, along with a method to solve in the future those issues on which the parties could not fully agree at that point. This concept, however, called for all issues to be discussed *en bloc*. A framework agreement of this kind would thus comprise three elements: practical arrangements, general principles, and the road to be followed for resolving the open-ended permanent status issues when comprehensive negotiations could be renewed.

To those who ask why the first time that Israel's positions on the permanent status were put forth took place only at the Camp David summit, my answer is that, in fact, it was not the first time. The positions of the parties, the gaps between them, and the final decisions that could be made only by the leaders themselves – all these were no secrets. The sets of convergences, divergences and controversial core issues to be decided upon by the leaders were known to all parties well in advance of the summit. The leaders at Camp David were faced with the need to make difficult historic decisions – political and personal – that had national, religious, emotional and psychological ramifications. It is true that some of the delegates, mainly in the Israeli party, were given in advance a clear idea of the red lines of their government regarding the permanent status issues, but not all positions could be stated before the negotiations.

It is clear to me that the problem of the refugees is completely resolvable.

Prior to Camp David, all parties agreed on a mechanism dealing with refugees' claims. An international fund would be established, to which Israel would also contribute. The refugees would be rehabilitated in their present places of residence or in the Palestinian state once it is established or, alternatively, in countries outside the region, such as Canada, Australia and Norway, each of which have already stated they would accept tens of thousands of refugees. There would be no Right of Return to the State of Israel. Almost none of the Palestinian leaders – and I will take issue with anyone who says differently – truly believed that refugees would be allowed to return to Israeli territory. All the talk surrounding this issue was just empty propaganda and negotiating maneuvers. The fact is that the Right of Return was never the obstacle to reaching a permanent status agreement, neither at Camp David nor at any point thereafter.

# Palestinian Perspectives

# MUNTHER S. DAJANI

# Wrong Assumptions

I WOULD LIKE TO BEGIN BY APOLOGIZING for some of the scheduled Palestinian participants who will not, in the end, be attending. Some of them have legitimate reasons stemming from their involvement in the newly reactivated security track of the negotiations, but some of them just do not want to be here, and for that, there are no excuses. I blame them for not coming, and they bear the responsibility for their absence.

The immediate responses by both Palestinians and Israelis to the failure at Camp David were saddening and ironic as well. Arafat and Barak returned home with empty hands, having achieved no concrete results. Sadly, they were treated like heroes, an irony in my view, as it was their responsibility to do their utmost to try to come back with a signed agreement for the sake of both of their peoples.

I blame both Israelis and Palestinians for not doing enough at Camp David. At the inaugural session, the American host proposed meetings of experts to discuss water, the economy and similar issues at different levels of the summit. The Palestinians rejected the proposal, insisting on the need to focus first on the major issues of Jerusalem, refugees, land, borders and security. From my personal point of view, and I do not represent anyone but myself, this was a strategic and tragic mistake. Agreements could have and should have been reached on the more technical issues, as the Americans had suggested. That would have paved the way for addressing successfully the more difficult issues.

It was during Spring 2000 that the US began considering holding an Israeli–Palestinian–American summit to revive the Middle East peace process. The Palestinian response was that the prevailing conditions were not yet ripe for such a meeting. President Arafat was very frank with US

Secretary of State Madeleine Albright, telling her, "If a summit is held and fails, then this will weaken the hopes of the Palestinian people, and the possibility of achieving peace. Let us not weaken this hope." The Palestinians favored intensive preparatory negotiations with the Israelis to bridge the existing gaps on sensitive issues. However, this proposition was rejected, and the invitations to the summit were issued. The Palestinian leadership now felt they had no choice but to accept the invitation, even if they believed the summit to be ill-conceived and poorly prepared.

The Palestinians put their trust in US President Bill Clinton, since Palestinian–American relations had never been as good as they were during Clinton's eight years in office. President Arafat was invited to the White House at least twelve times during Clinton's tenure. He felt quite close to Clinton, believing him to be more objective in his views and a more unbiased mediator than previous US presidents. However, President Arafat utterly failed to comprehend the intricate ways in which the American system works. Moreover, since the Palestinians have a one-man system, they thought that there were similarities in the way the US democratic system operates. Hence, they tended to misjudge both Clinton's intentions and capabilities.

I believe that the Palestinian leadership still does not understand how the American system works. I shall always remember an incident in which one of the American television networks was covering a referendum organized by Egypt's President Sadat who, of course, always received 99.99% of the votes in such events. The network captured on film the cheating that took place, showing people sitting in a room fixing the referendum results. Public officials were recorded filling in blank ballots with "yes" votes. Hearing of the tape's existence, Sadat phoned US President Jimmy Carter, and asked him to intervene with that network and prevent it from broadcasting the footage. From Sadat's perspective, such action would be perfectly reasonable. To his astonishment, however, Carter replied that he could not do so.

By the same token, President Arafat felt that whenever there was something not to his liking, he could call President Clinton and fix it. However, as we know, in democratic systems things do not operate this way. The fact that President Arafat had visited the White House twelve times had not conferred upon him any special privileges to circumvent the American bureaucracy.

On the other hand, the Israelis, and the Americans as well, believed that the Palestinians were willing to pay a very high price to achieve their goal of a Palestinian state. They believed in "Palestinian ripeness," namely, that the Palestinian delegation, and with it the overall Palestinian environment, were ripe for an agreement that would give them less than their minimum national aspirations. In this regard, they miscalculated badly.

This became abundantly clear when the Palestinians were handed what we call a "monkey wrench" during the Camp David talks, namely, when it was proposed that Israel be granted sovereignty over the Temple Mount/*Haram al-Sharif*. Arafat was shocked, and everybody in the leadership agreed with him that the proposal was completely unacceptable (although some of the technocrats did not). For Arafat, the Temple Mount issue was not only a Palestinian matter, but also one that had Islamic and Arab dimensions. Had there been other Arab delegates present at the negotiations, such as the Saudis and the Egyptians, they could have assisted on that issue. But since President Arafat was there alone, without any Arab or Islamic support, I do not think he could have agreed with Israel on crucial issues such as Jerusalem, the Temple Mount or the refugees.

Subsequently, Arafat and others made fiery speeches regarding the *Haram al-Sharif*, declaring it had been *the* major point of disagreement at Camp David. In Palestinian society and throughout the Arab world, there was a wide consensus supporting the Palestinian position at Camp David. Nonetheless, I still feel that the parties could have agreed on some of the points and left the others for future talks, rather than aborting the negotiations entirely.

Coming back without an agreement was like shattering the last glimpse of hope, or, if you prefer, like snuffing out the flickering candle of hope at the end of the tunnel. This led to the situation that we are in today, as the *intifada* rages on.

Both delegations were to blame for not reaching some kind of agreement, at least an interim one, which was needed to prevent the termination of negotiations and the shattering of hopes for peace.

SAMIH AL-ABED

# The Israeli Proposals Were Not Serious

THANK YOU VERY MUCH FOR INVITING ME TO PARTICIPATE in this conference and giving me the opportunity to explain the Palestinian perspective on the Camp David and Taba negotiations. What I will present here are some facts and figures related to territory, because supposedly the essential part of the negotiations was to be based on the "land for peace" formula. I shall start this presentation with a small reminder regarding what we call the "shaping of Palestine" since the beginning of the conflict. **Maps 1-A** and **1-B** show British-Mandated Palestine and the UN Partition plan of 1947. **Map 1-C** shows the 22% of the area of original Palestine, namely the West Bank and Gaza, occupied in the June 1967 war and acknowledged in UN resolutions 242 and 338 as Palestinian. What happened to these territories in the aftermath of that war? Israel immediately began establishing settlements according to the Allon plan, in the Jordan valley and in the Jerusalem area. Then it began building what was called the "seven stars" along the western boundary of the West Bank. The reason I am referring to this is that it is important for understanding how the negotiations subsequently evolved.

After Oslo, at the beginning of 1994, there were a number of agreements, the first being the Cairo agreement of May 1994, through which we obtained part of Gaza and Jericho. In September 1995, we entered into another agreement, known as Oslo II. In this agreement we received about 2.8% of the West Bank, defined as Area A, and 23.7%, defined as Area B. The rest remained under the full control of Israel. The difference between Area A and Area B was that in Area B we did not have any control over military and security issues. According to the original Oslo Accords, final status negotiations were supposed to commence by May 1996, but nothing of the sort happened. The first scheduled further redeployment (FRD) took place following the October 1998 Wye River Memorandum. In that agreement, Area A was expanded to 9.8% and Area B was reduced to 18.6%. In the Sharm al-Sheikh agreement of September 1999, we received additional territory: Area A remained at 9.8%, Area B was expanded to become 24.6% and a small area of about 0.8% was designated as 'Green'/Nature Reserves. The second phase of the Sharm al-Sheikh agreement was determined on January 4, 2000, but never implemented. In that agreement, we were to receive additional land in Area A, now 11.7%, Area B remained almost the same, and the 'green' area was expanded to 2.9%. This is what we had been allocated prior to September 28, when the *intifada* broke out. Hence, the total area designated to be handed over to the Palestinian side by the Oslo process was: Area A – 11.7%, and Area B plus the 'green' area – 28.3%. The remainder of the territory was to be left for the final negotiation.

Now, I will show you what the Israeli territorial proposal at Camp David consisted of (**Map 2-A**). The white area was to be under Palestinian sovereignty; constituted only 81% of the 22%. The area of the Jordan valley was to be leased to Israel. The rest of the territory was supposedly to be annexed to Israel. Thus, what was offered to us at Camp David amounted, in effect, to three separate cantons: one in the northern part, one in the middle and one in the southern part. The areas that were to be annexed to Israel included 97 Palestinian towns and villages, inhabited by 370,000 Palestinians. That raises a question. If this was really Israel's demand, if Israel was willing to have 370,000 Palestinians annexed to Israel, then why all the hassle about taking back refugees?

The Palestinian side has been criticized for not accepting Israel's proposal at Camp David. We, for our part, thought that Israel's proposal was not a serious starting point for the negotiations. The whole idea of UN resolutions 242 and 338 is that they serve as the reference point for both parties, who will then sit down and deal with the issues that are of the greatest concern. If Israel has demands from the Palestinian side, then why not sit down and talk about them and see whether their demands really affect us, and in what ways? We can then mutually link each side's concerns, and arrive at a formula that protects our respective interests without harming our communities.

An additional complaint of ours was that the American and Israeli negotiators behaved like mathematicians, not statesmen. They were always speaking about percentages of land, without knowing exactly what the effect of their proposals would be on the population on the ground, and how they would impact on our mutual interests. Even land swapping became a mathematical equation. First they put forth a ratio of 9:1, then 3:1 and so on. The whole concept of focusing on percentages was not well thought out. When Palestinians saw how the Israeli proposal would disrupt the contiguity of the land under their control, they immediately rejected it. Why should this be called a good offer, when it was not, by any standard?

The very idea of "offering" us something was misleading, because the 22% of Palestine was not part of sovereign Israel, but part of the Palestinians' rights according to 242. If Israel had come and said, "perhaps, for strategic and future concerns, we need to modify the Green Line, but in a way that will cause minimal damage and will allow both of us to live with," that would have been an acceptable opening argument. We could have sat down and looked at those areas, examining Israel's interests there. If we could have accommodated the Israelis, and if there was no real harm to the Palestinians in terms of territorial contiguity, population, natural resources or other issues, then I cannot see any reason why we could not have reached an agreement.

However, in my opinion, Israel came to Camp David with a different approach, and I am speaking as one who was there. I did not participate in all the discussions that took place, but I was intimately involved in the territorial issue. In my view, the Americans were not ready at that time to manage the negotiations between the two sides. We felt that they were quite biased against us. We also felt that the Israelis were not seriously seeking to finalize an agreement at that particular time. By the way, none of the Israeli politicians, or the Americans, have ever mentioned that the Palestinians at Camp David put forth their own proposal, even though this proposal was discussed with both the Israeli and American teams, including President Clinton. Whether they liked it or not is a different matter, but there *was* a Palestinian counter-proposal that was put on the table, and it was discussed with the Israelis. Only a few people mentioned it. I believe that Gilead Sher included one line about it in his book, for the record.

In sum, the reason we said "no" to the Israeli proposal was because it would have been too difficult for any Palestinian to accept it. Moreover, if you look at the proposed borders of the State of Israel, you will find the proposal difficult to fathom.

Regarding the Jerusalem issue, the main problem for us is that in 1967 – as Reuven Merhav has rightly mentioned – Arab Jerusalem had been six square kilometers, and then the Israelis took over and started to expand in all directions. The first extension became an established fact and we had to live with it. However, this is not the proper shape of the city. When the new lines were drawn, nobody thought about it in practical terms, how the capital would look and how its future development would take place. The Israelis drew that particular boundary line because they wanted to include assets like the airport and exclude a maximum portion of the Palestinian population. Those were the criteria. Then, as Reuven Merhav has shown us, the Israelis started to draw other lines: another line around the city, and then a third line around the second line, introducing changes which we, the Palestinians, were expected to accept. This was absolutely unjust. Why should our people alone be expected to pay the price for solving problems of the city as the Israelis saw them?

If we are to seek a real solution that both peoples can live with, then we have to employ a different methodology, a different approach to the whole process of the negotiations. What was proposed at Camp David meant that those neighborhoods that are home to 280,000 Palestinians would be placed under a mixed regime. How would Jerusalem look according to the Israeli proposal? The inner Palestinian neighborhoods would be under Israeli sovereignty while the Palestinians would be granted administrative powers short of sovereignty. This means that we would be responsible for garbage removal, sewage, cleaning the streets, etc. Overall sovereignty over the Old City would go to Israel, with custodianship of the *Haram al-Sharif* to the Palestinians. The Israeli settlements around Jerusalem would be under Israeli sovereignty. We wondered what kind of a city this would be. At one time, the Israelis came to the Palestinians and said, "We want Jerusalem undivided." We said, "Fine, let's start talking about this option." But later on they changed their mind: now they wanted full separation. So we had to adapt ourselves and start discussing with the Israelis what this separation would entail.

Perhaps a future government will come and suggest a "half open and half closed" city. Perhaps only God can solve this problem. I do not know how *we* the Palestinians will solve it. The Israelis have not made up their mind about what they want in Jerusalem. Moreover, which Jerusalem are they talking about? Is it the six square kilometers of pre-1967 Arab Jerusalem, or the second or third rings mentioned by Reuven Merhav (see **Map 7**)? We want to know from Israel exactly what it wants Jerusalem to look like. We are willing to start discussions, we are willing to begin negotiating, but not on the basis of Israel's Camp David proposals, with which neither the Israelis nor the Palestinians can live. It seems to me that somebody had an interest in just having the groups meet at Camp David, and for that purpose all kinds of ideas had to be bandied about. At the end of the day someone had to be blamed for the failure, so the Palestinians were accused of failing to accept what was termed the best offer ever made to them.

Those are some of the reasons why we said "no" at Camp David. Many politicians neglect mentioning the subsequent December 2000 talks at Bolling Air Force Base, which were eventually overshadowed by the Clinton Parameters. In Bolling, the Israelis abandoned their demand for sovereignty over the Jordan Rift but insisted on leasing some of the area (**Map 2-B**). When we asked for how long, the answers ranged from 10 to15 years up to 999 years. The percentage of the area to be annexed still remained about

10%. What they tried to do with this proposal was to reduce the number of Palestinian towns and villages to be included in the areas to be annexed by Israel. However, the same concept of cantons without territorial contiguity was still there. When I asked how would our areas be linked, the answer from Shlomo Yanai was, "We can build you a bridge so you can cross from one area to the other." That shows how serious their "generous" offer really was. This is the way the state of Palestine was conceived by Israel, one that would be divided into different non-contiguous areas.

At Bolling, they looked at the issue of Jerusalem in a different way as well. A new notion appeared, called the "Holy Basin," which I think was not mentioned at Camp David. I cannot be sure about this, but if it was, it was only in passing. This time, in Bolling, the Holy Basin concept was discussed more seriously. In addition to the Temple Mount, the Israelis also wanted the Jewish and the Armenian Quarters. When we asked, "Why do you want the Armenian Quarter to belong to you?" the answer was, "Because of the accessibility it provides to the Jewish Quarter." We responded, "If that's the case, then there is no need for you to take the whole Armenian Quarter. A way can be found for the Israelis to reach the Jewish Quarter without having the whole Armenian Quarter under their sovereignty." This is an example of the type of questions for which we received no convincing answers from the Israeli side. Eventually, they were ready to give us overall sovereignty over Arab neighborhoods including those surrounding the Old City, as well as the Muslim and the Christian quarters of the Old City.

But looking at the map of Eastern Jerusalem, one can see the inherent problems according to the proposal that they had in mind (**Map 3**). They wanted to retain the settlements and the area contained in the master plan for Ma'ale Adumim. By the way, Ma'ale Adumim never was within the border of the city of Jerusalem. When Israeli negotiators talk about Jerusalem, it is never clear whether they are referring to the city of Jerusalem or the expanded Jerusalem area. Moreover, when they talk about the Jerusalem area, what are its boundaries? Nobody knows, it is an open question. It may extend in the north up to Ramallah, or south down to Bethlehem, or east toward Ma'ale Adumim, and even west toward Tel Aviv. According to the Israeli proposal, the areas left for the Palestinians were to be scattered about, unconnected. Obviously absent from their proposal was an overall integrated plan for the city as a whole. If Israel wants to find a solution to the issues posed by Jerusalem, then we can sit down and talk, define the issues and examine their various elements, including how a city can function and grow, and how it can also serve as a capital.

In Taba, it was different – revealing that what took place from Camp David till Taba was part of a process. However, the problem is that some Israelis deem Camp David to have been the end of the game. They see Camp

David as a simple message to the Palestinians, "This is our proposal, take it or leave it." Then they consider the collapse of the summit as the fault and mistake of the Palestinians because they did not accept the Israeli offer there. But if you look at the development of the process, you will see that the Israelis were gradually moving toward a better way of thinking, and a better way of finding solutions to the problem. On the January 27, a different map was tendered as part of the Taba discussions (**Map 2-C**).

You all know that at Taba it already was too late to conclude a deal, due to the imminent elections in Israel and the escalation of the *intifada*. Nevertheless, if we had another six months of serious negotiations and some fairness from the Americans, things could have been different. To be sure, we did not expect complete fairness from Washington, but we expected them at the end of the day to say, "Hey guys, listen, you must reach an agreement, the time has come, and we have this plan on the table. You have to make a decision within a certain period of time and we, on our part, will facilitate what is needed in order for you to reach an agreement." From the Israelis, we wanted more seriousness regarding the final status issues. People tend to say, "Let's put aside those hard issues." I believe that, on the contrary, these are the ones that should be discussed meticulously, and with greater seriousness. The whole concept of trying to agree on a framework, or principles for the negotiations, was not the right approach, because when you have a framework or broad principles that each side interprets differently, we are not closer to an agreement. Only if we start with the bottom-up approach, and discuss the issues more fully, with everything clearly laid out, can an agreement eventually be reached.

## Remarks during the Discussion

Regarding the question about the Christian areas of Jerusalem. The Israelis are always talking about a Jewish State. Ironically, within that Jewish State they want to have sovereignty over Muslims and Christians. This makes no sense. In addition, those areas had been under Arab control before 1967. Why should it be better for the Christians to be under Jewish sovereignty than under Muslim sovereignty? They have the right to choose. Israel cannot impose its sovereignty on them. Why not ask the Armenians and the other Christians what they prefer? We have views that are different from those of Michel Sabah, the Latin Patriarch of Jerusalem, and Hanna Atallah, the spokesman of the Greek Orthodox Patriarchate of Jerusalem.

Regarding the question of sovereignty. We insist on Palestinian sovereignty over the West Bank and Gaza areas, the 22% of original Palestine that we had before 1967, not over territories of Israel proper. The Israelis are always demanding sovereignty over areas they wish to have. If they have an interest in certain areas that they see as vital for the State of Israel, then they should be aware that there are also areas within Israel that are of vital interest for the Palestinians. These issues can be looked at, and perhaps territories can be exchanged. But you Israelis have always wanted to grab parts of the area that was ours before 1967, and you cast doubt on the legal status of that area. For your national ideology, maybe it is important to do so, but if you want such territories to remain in your hands, and if we are ready to exchange areas, then we should discuss it and reach agreement.

Regarding the Palestinian map. The Israelis and the Americans never mentioned it, but the Palestinian counter-proposal *was* expressed in a map. I have it and you can inquire about it. This map was presented before all the members of the Israeli team at Camp David – Gilead Sher, Shlomo Ben-Ami, Amnon Lipkin-Shahak, Shlomo Yanai and the rest. The American team headed by President Clinton, which included Sandy Berger, Madeline Albright, Dennis Ross, Aaron Miller and Rob Malley, also saw the map. Abu Ala, Hassan Asfour and I presented the map to Clinton and discussed it with him.

The Clinton Parameters were tendered a few months after Camp David. Yesterday, I asked the Americans whom I met in the hotel, "Why didn't the Americans put forward Clinton's proposal at Camp David as a starting point for the negotiations?" The answer was, "You were not ready for that." Once, when we were guests of Mr. Indyk, Dennis Ross had responded to the same question differently. He said, "I'm sorry, we should have done that but we were looking for a way to proceed with the bilateral negotiations."

I am convinced that I was correct when I said earlier that there was no American readiness to engage fully in the negotiations. Moreover, the Israeli team was not serious in their offer. At the same time, the Palestinians were not ready either to make the concessions that were requested of them at Camp David. So all three parties should place the blame on themselves, because none were ready to make a deal at that time. For the Americans and the Israelis to place the entire blame on the Palestinians is not fair. We admit that we made mistakes. There were differences within the teams that operated at Camp David – among the Palestinians as well as among the Israelis – which is probably another reason why the proper negotiating methods were not employed and why we did not reach an agreement. In sum, each of the three has to assume their share of responsibility for the failure, instead of blaming each other.

What might happen now will depend on the wisdom of the leaderships of both sides. I do not see any reason why the two sides cannot get together and start talking again about those questions, but unfortunately it seems that wisdom is currently in short supply among both the Israelis and the Palestinians. Politicians do not need to be intellectuals like university professors, but they must have the kind of wisdom that can guide them and their nations toward a better future.

# MOHAMMED S. DAJANI

# The "Blaming Game" is Wrong

LET ME BEGIN WITH A FEW PERSONAL COMMENTS. First, there are two types of scholars: those who claim they are objective and those who admit they are not. I belong to the second category. Second, we remember that there once were some visionary people who dreamt that a Jewish state would rise one day in Palestine; I belong to another group of dreamers who believe that a Palestinian state will rise one day next to the same Jewish state. Third, what follows will express my own personal views and opinions, which do not necessarily reflect the official Palestinian position.

I wish to explain why high-level Palestinians who were invited to this conference did not show up. Most of them would have liked to be here, believing the topic to be of crucial importance. They knew that it would be possible to learn a great deal from the deliberations of the conference and benefit from their lessons in the future. But unfortunately, the Israeli closure and checkpoints policy prevented them from attending. It is particularly difficult for Palestinians to obtain permits to come to Tel Aviv due to the present political tension. Unfortunately, even those who had permits to come could not join us due to security conditions.

In his inaugural address in 1961, John Fitzgerald Kennedy proclaimed, "Let us never negotiate out of fear, but let us never fear to negotiate." I believe that here lies the significance of the Camp David summit: we did not fear to negotiate. Whether or not such negotiations achieved their purpose is another issue. But any negotiations at least clarify the positions of adversaries and may help in bringing their views closer to each other.

To succeed, negotiators need the right approach, the right attitude, the right timing and the right environment. The negotiators at the Camp David summit did not meet these conditions; this may be one of the reasons why it did not fulfill the expectations. Unlike the leaders of the first Camp David summit, held in 1978 – Egyptian President Anwar Sadat, Israeli Prime Minister Menachem Begin and US President Jimmy Carter – who at the end of the summit were lauded for reaching an accommodation acceptable to all, the three leaders of the second Camp David summit, held in 2000, were criticized for not having reached any accommodation.

Initially, the Camp David framework generated a dynamic process of change. It created a hopeful setting for a creative peace process. Furthermore, it provided the protagonists with the security blanket of a powerful third party. The American continued involvement and full partnership was expected to lubricate the negotiating process, encouraging more flexibility, pragmatism and readiness for mutual accommodation.

The question is sometimes asked whether the US intervention was needed to convene the summit, and whether the US, which assumed the role of the third party, did not fail in its task to guide the two negotiating parties to a mutually acceptable accommodation.

Much criticism was directed at the US performance as a third party, but without US intervention and pressure on both parties, negotiations would not have taken place at all. Moreover, the US presence was required for preparing, managing and orchestrating the negotiation process, in order to increase the likelihood of achieving the desired outcome. Due to the intricacies of the situation, there were no direct negotiations between Barak and Arafat. In this unique kind of bargaining process it fell on the third party's shoulder to conduct most of the negotiations on behalf of the two sides. One important third-party role was to keep looking for "icebergs" from which the negotiations had to be steered away, and identify "minefields" which needed to be detonated – namely, those large, hidden, conflictual issues that may surface in the course of negotiations, causing them to collapse.

The role played by the US as a third party at the summit consisted of the following: it served as host, agenda-setter, peacemaker and conciliator, provider of fresh ideas, disseminator of fresh information and endorser of the negotiating parties. The Americans laid down the rules of the game. There was a strong presence at the summit of the US administration, with all its prestige and capabilities. The Americans were confident that the atmosphere generated by the rules of procedure and the constant pressure of their presence would produce the expected results.

As peacemaker, President Clinton exhorted the Palestinians and the Israelis alike, before as well as during the Camp David negotiations, to rise above their skepticism and show maturity, responsibility, realism and courage by making this great adventure of building peace in the region a success. He called upon both parties to seize the historic opportunity to establish peace between their peoples. At Camp David, President Clinton was forthcoming with fresh ideas and concepts to encourage the negotiation process. When the negotiations stalled, he offered comprehensive proposals, some of which afterwards became the basis for the Taba negotiations. The US was also the actor that, as the neutral third party, reported to the public on what happened at the summit.

However, there were some flaws in the role the Americans played as a third party. The Palestinians were critical of the US failure to act as an honest broker. I think that they should have been more realistic: they should have been aware that third parties, and the US as a superpower in particular, have their own agendas, interests and policies. Although Clinton attempted to be even-handed, he could not ignore the US policy of being Israel's close ally. The warm American–Israeli partnership alienated Arafat and made him feel that the cards were stacked against him.

In the London daily *Guardian*, David Clark described the role the third party played. He observed that Clinton needed a quick deal rather than a just deal, and chose to try to oblige Arafat to accept Israel's stand. Alain Gresh espoused similar views in *Le Monde Diplomatique*.

The Palestinians thus saw the third party as biased and heavy-handed. They felt that the Americans were pressuring them to make one concession after another, without pressuring the Israelis for reciprocal concessions. Having no state, army, political power or economic resources, the Palestinian negotiators nevertheless perceived themselves in the negotiations as an equal partner to the US, as a local power. The cultural–psychological barrier also contributed to the mutual alienation between the Americans and the Palestinians. The Palestinians' lack of good command of the language, acquaintance with the American culture, and understanding of the history of the Americans and the factors that shape their attitudes and decisions, created a rift that eventually pushed the Americans more firmly to the Israeli side. So did the Palestinians' rejectionist attitude toward American proposals, refraining from coming up with new counter-offers. They also lacked conflict resolution and negotiating skills.

Arab leaders were not present for consultation at Camp David, which made President Arafat feel isolated from the Arab world. The summit could have been enriched by an open channel of communication to King Abdallah of Jordan, Saudi Crown Prince Abdallah and President Mubarak of Egypt. Had there been such a channel, I imagine that Arafat's attitude during the negotiations would have been much more positive.

The Palestinians came to the summit not fully prepared, with a victim's mentality and with traumatic memories of the past. The Palestinian behavior on a number of occasions served to further widen the gap between the US and the Palestinians. For instance, the rejection by Abu Ala of a proposed Israeli map put on the table by Clinton, made the US President react angrily, "Okay, if you don't like the Israeli offer, make a counter-offer, show me your own map for us to compare." Another moment of this kind was when Yasser Abed Rabbo walked out on Dennis Ross, prompting Ross's reaction, "Who the hell are you to walk out on me? If you don't like the proposal, sit down and let's discuss the problem."

In responding to the points raised by other colleagues in this conference, let me point out that Palestinian Authority President Yasser Arafat initially was reluctant to go to the Camp David summit. When the Americans approached him with the idea, he was quite unwilling to accept it. His response was that the time was not yet ripe, that there should first be further intensive discussions to resolve the thorny issues. But the Americans insisted, and the Israelis wanted it, so he acceded. Perhaps when it ended without an agreement, his thought on the plane home might have been, "I hate to say it, but I told you so."

Basically, Arafat had a "don't take me for granted" attitude. Not hiding the fact that he had wanted to postpone the conference, Arafat went to Camp David with an attitude of, "Don't patronize me. I'm the odd number of the peace equation. I have been here before you and I will be here after you."

So, what went wrong in Camp David? First, we know that breakthroughs are sometimes achieved when a major concession is made, usually by the stronger party; in this case, the stronger party was unwilling to make any such major move. Second, neither party fully appreciated the value of those concessions that *were* offered by the other, and at times they were even unaware that such concessions had been made. Third, the outstanding issues were too numerous, too complex and too emotional to be woven together into a package deal in one, or even two summits.

Who is to blame for the missed peace opportunity? Each side blames the other. Israelis and Palestinians have two contradicting narratives to explain why the Camp David summit failed. The Israelis say, "We gave them a generous offer, which they refused; Arafat was inflexible and unreasonable." The Palestinians say, "Barak's 'generous' offer was neither an offer, nor generous. It made the emergence of a viable Palestinian state impossible. It did not address the Palestinians' unwavering and unqualified right to self-determination."

After Camp David, the myth of the "generous offer" gained much publicity. Much has already been said about it, yet it may be worthwhile to deal with it briefly again, just to assert Palestinian points of view, particularly on the lesser known aspects of this issue.

The myth was widespread indeed. *The Washington Post* wrote that "Israel offered extraordinary concessions" and *The Boston Globe* described them as "far-reaching concessions". *The Washington Post* even called them "unprecedented concessions." This myth also included the allegation that while the Israelis made offers, the Palestinians never made counter-offers.

Amnon Kapeliuk was one of the first writers to contradict this dominant narrative of the Camp David summit in his articles, "Camp David Dialogues" and "Conducting Catastrophe," in *Le Monde Diplomatique*. Deborah Sontag published a special report in *The New York Times* entitled "Quest for Middle East Peace: How and Why it Failed," in which she challenged the "simplistic narrative that has taken hold in Israel and to some extent in the US," that Arafat turned down Barak's generous offer and then "pushed the button and chose the path of violence." Her conclusion was that "many now agree that all the sides, and not just Arafat, were to blame." Robert Malley and Hussein Agha similarly challenged this myth in their article in the *New York Review of Books,* as did Charles Enderlin in his book *History of the Epoch of the Peace Process,* published in Paris.

The Israeli version, claiming that "Israel offered the Palestinians maximum concessions, which they rejected," speaks about the following arrangements: withdrawal from 96% of the West Bank; complete withdrawal from the Gaza Strip; establishment of a Palestinian state; creation of a Palestinian capital in East Jerusalem; some kind of sovereignty over the *Haram al-Sharif;* sovereignty over parts of Jerusalem's Old City; the dismantling of part of the settlements; the Right of Return for Palestinian refugees to the state of Palestine; and some territorial waters in the Dead Sea.

The Palestinian counter-version was that the Israeli offer at Camp David fell short of matching the Palestinian historic concession of recognizing the State of Israel within 78% of the territory of Mandatory Palestine. The Palestinians argue about each detail of the Israeli offer. They say that the Palestinians could not accept an arrangement that divided Palestinian territories into four cantons separated by Israeli areas and hindering Palestinian passage. On the territorial offer, they point out that the Israeli offer still fell short of the 22% of original Palestine, namely, the West Bank and Gaza, which is their minimal demand on the basis of a historic compromise. On Jerusalem, they point out that 63.5 square kilometers, which is 90% of the land annexed by Israel in East Jerusalem, belonged to 28 West Bank villages. The Israelis left out of their offer the huge belt of Jewish settlements, consisting of a wide buffer zone around the Palestinian territories. With regard to free movement, Israeli annexation of strategically important and highly valuable, vast areas of the West Bank, while retaining security control over other parts, would have made it impossible for the Palestinians to travel

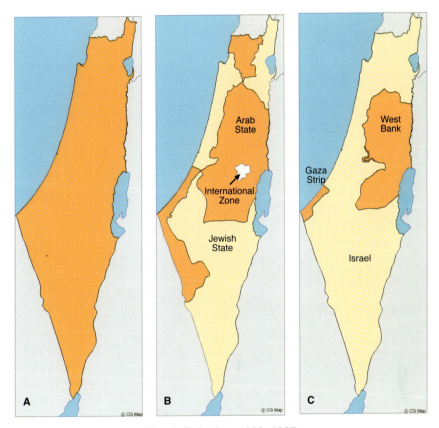

**Map 1** Palestine, 1923–1967
A: British Mandated Palestine
B: 1947 Partition Plan
C: 1949 Armistice Lines
Courtesy of Samih al-Abed, Ministry of Planning, Palestinian Authority

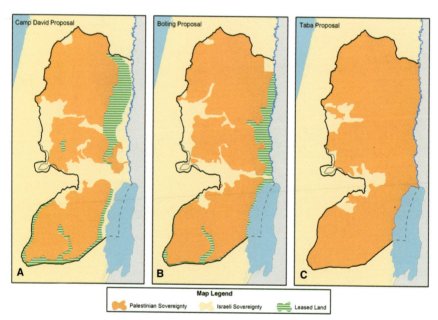

**Map 2** Israeli Territorial Proposals for the West Bank, 2000–2001
A: Camp David, July 2000
B: Bolling AFB, December 2000
C: Taba, January 2001
Courtesy of Samih al-Abed, Ministry of Planning, Palestinian Authority

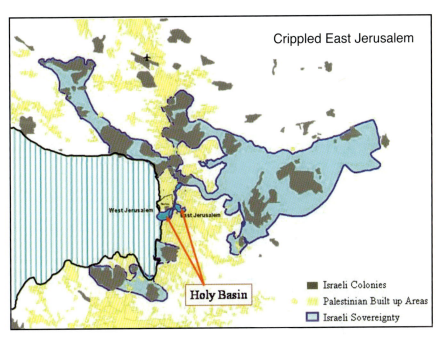

**Map 3** The Israeli Proposal for East Jerusalem from
the Palestinian Perspective
Courtesy of Samih al-Abed, Ministry of Planning, Palestinian Authority

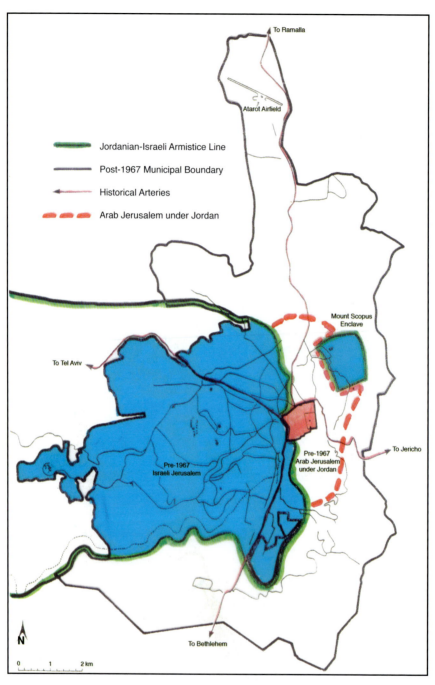

To Ramalla

Atarot Airfield

Jordanian-Israeli Armistice Line

Post-1967 Municipal Boundary

Historical Arteries

Arab Jerusalem under Jordan

Mount Scopus
Enclave

To Tel Aviv

To Jericho

Pre-1967
Israeli Jerusalem

Pre-1967
Arab Jerusalem
under Jordan

N

0    1    2 km

To Bethlehem

**Map 4**  Changing Municipal Boundaries of Jerusalem
Courtesy of Israel Kimhi, the Jerusalem Institute for Israel Studies

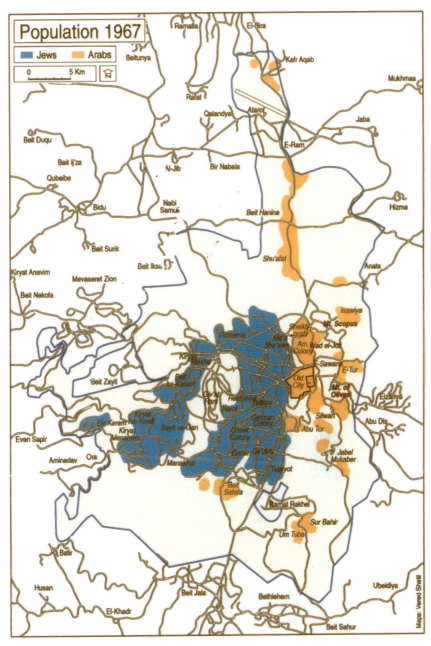

**Map 5** Jewish and Arab Populations of Jerusalem, 1967
Courtesy of Israel Kimhi, the Jerusalem Institute for Israel Studies

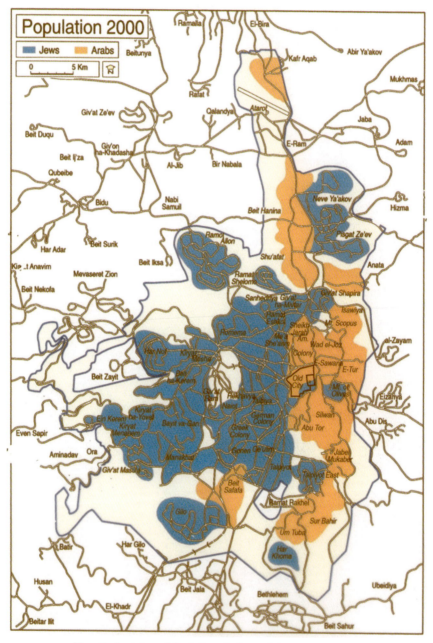

**Map 6** Jewish and Arab Populations of Jerusalem, 2000
Courtesy of Israel Kimhi, the Jerusalem Institute for Israel Studies

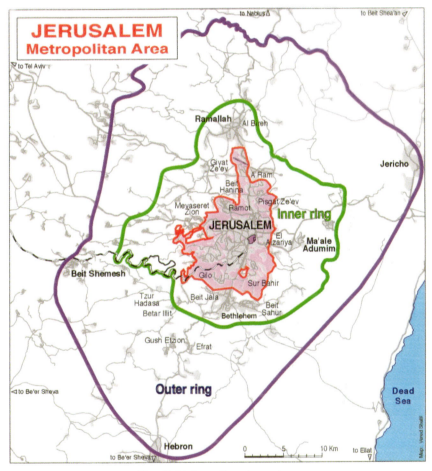

**Map 7** Metropolitan Jerusalem
Courtesy of Israel Kimhi, the Jerusalem Institute for Israel Studies

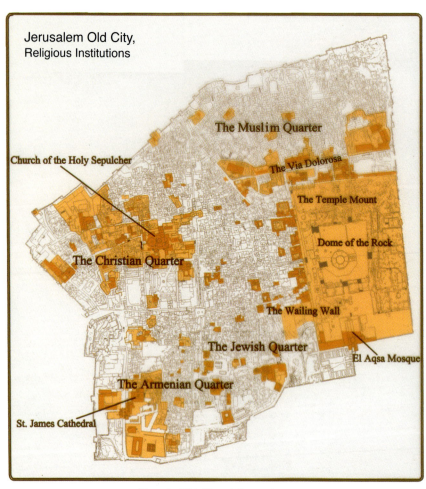

**Map 8** Old City of Jerusalem
Courtesy of Israel Kimhi, the Jerusalem Institute for Israel Studies

or trade freely within their own state without Israeli permission, and Israel could close the main routes at will.

When the refugee issue, which was barely discussed between the two sides, was raised, the Israelis only mentioned that they would offer a satisfactory solution, but the Palestinians were never informed what that would entail. Regarding land swaps, they were far from being on a basis of equality. In exchange for fertile West Bank lands that contain most of the region's sparse water aquifers, Israel offered at Camp David to give up a piece of its own territory in the Negev Desert – including a former toxic waste dump – about one-tenth the size of the land it would annex. Israel would have also retained under its sovereignty a network of so-called bypass roads that would crisscross the Palestinian territories, further splitting the West Bank. The territorial waters offered in the Dead Sea could hardly be utilized. Israel would have maintained security control for an undetermined period over the Jordan Valley, the strip of territory that forms the border between the West Bank and neighboring Jordan. Regarding international access, Palestine would not have free access to its own international borders with Jordan and Egypt, putting Palestinian trade, and therefore its economy, at the mercy of Israel.

Under such circumstances, Arafat could not sign an "end of conflict" agreement stipulating that the decades-old war with Israel was over and that the Palestinians waive all further claims. In Palestinian eyes, Prime Minister Ehud Barak's posture at Camp David was seen as an attitude of, "We are not here to negotiate with them, but to confront them." They felt that that his was an attitude of, "I always win, you always lose, what is wrong with that?" Thus, to the Palestinians, the "generous offer" was an illusion in the mind of those offering it.

Here the role of the third party was crucial. By blaming Arafat for the failure of the negotiations, President Clinton tilted the blame scale to the Palestinians. The Israeli journalist and peace activist Uri Avnery indicated that by doing this, Clinton broke his word to Arafat. Before the summit, Clinton had promised that if it failed, he would not blame the Palestinians. Only on this condition did Arafat agree to come to the conference in spite of the fact that he was convinced that it convened without proper preparation. At the end of the conference, however, Clinton judged the failure to be the responsibility of Arafat. He would have been better advised, as a mediator, to reserve his judgment for a later time. His statement directed the public discussion to the issue of "who is to blame," assigning the Palestinians and Arafat in particular, the greatest share of the blame.

To sum up, negotiations at the Camp David summit were not coherent and important aspects of them were not clear in the minds of the negotiators. Most issues were highly complex, and information was vague and inadequate. The third party was not sufficiently aware of the negotiators' perceptions of each other, or of their different perceptions of its role. Mutual mistrust was not dispelled. Top negotiators resented each other, thus affecting the style and content of the negotiations and their mutual expectations. There was not adequate understanding of the effects of the issues being negotiated on the parties' national security needs. The way agendas for sessions were set – a highly significant factor in the process of moving complex negotiations toward agreement – failed to encourage trade-off deals. The level of expectations of each side was too high, making it difficult to reach an agreement.

What are the main lessons to be learned from Camp David? I would summarize them in six points.

(1) The more a conflict is protracted, the more complex its issues become, and hence a more imaginative approach is required from the negotiators. This conflict started as one-dimensional: religious. After that it became two-dimensional: religious–political. Then it became three-dimensional: religious–political–historical. Subsequently it became multi-dimensional, adding more elements: sociology, economics, psychology, geography, demography, culture, archaeology, even semantics. At Camp David, an "arithmetical" dimension was added. Hence, a student of the Arab–Israeli conflict today has at least ten times more material to master than he would have needed some twenty years ago. In such a situation, without innovative ideas negotiations are fated to fail.

(2) If one or both parties are not happy with the role played by the third party, then they ought to convene a bilateral summit.

(3) Negotiators should avoid the "blaming game" and focus instead on working out genuinely viable, acceptable, rational and practical solutions.

(4) Negotiators ought to put behind them the clash of historical narratives. Discussing it is premature. Eventually, a narrative acceptable to both parties will emerge.

(5) In successful negotiations, the first stage is denial and the final stage is acceptance. The question is what needs to be done so that the interval between the first stage and the final stage is the shortest possible.

(6) Negotiators must avoid any personalization of the conflict. The problem is not the singer, but the song; not the person, but the issue. Negotiators should deal with the issues as objectively as they can. There

is also the danger that personalities will be misperceived. Arafat believed that Bush would give him a better deal than Clinton, and thought that dealing with Sharon would not be worse than dealing with Barak. Time proved him wrong on both points.

The well-known Egyptian journalist, Muhammad Hassenein Heykal, wrote a book entitled: *Madha Jara fi al-Sharq al-Awsat?* ("What Happened in the Middle East?"). He wrote it in the late 1950s, a period of turmoil, bloody revolutions, upheavals, wars, social unrest. Yet, his concluding remark in answering the question of the title was, "Nothing happened in the Middle East, life is going on as usual." What he meant was that for ordinary people the requirements of daily life prevail. Indeed, despite what happened at Camp David and after it, for ordinary people in the Middle East life is basically going on as usual. We have become accustomed to violence, turmoil, upheavals and conflicts. But let us not forget how much prosperity, tranquility and happiness peace can bring.

# American Participants

AARON DAVID MILLER

# The Effects of the "Syria-First" Strategy

IT SEEMS COUNTERINTUITIVE TO BE HOLDING A CONFERENCE on the permanent status issues discussed at Camp David, given the current environment
in the region. But at the same time, what transpired at Camp David, and the
lessons learned, will be extremely important when Israelis and Palestinians
eventually return to these issues.

As I survey the debate and the literature on Camp David, the pull of the
historian nags at me once again, as do the numerous difficulties of writing
and commenting on what I would call "current history," which is a bit of an
oxymoron. Current history presents many challenges: there are problems
with sources and problems with participants writing about the events they
lived through. There is also the tendency toward self-justification, particularly in a politically charged environment such as this one.

Camp David was not a morality play; it did not pit the forces of good
against the forces of evil. It was a terribly complex event, a watershed event,
and needs to be taken seriously, analyzed and evaluated. The issue of "who
lost Camp David?" may well be important, but I would argue that it is not
the critical issue.

Sadly, I am a professional historian no more; in fact, I have not been a
professional historian for the last 25 years. I have refrained up until now
from presenting my views on Camp David. Some of my colleagues have
already presented theirs, and others will do so in forthcoming books. I
thought I would take advantage of this conference to offer some observations – a point of view, if you will, not a serious history. That may well have
to await the emergence of someone who, with the benefits of documentation, distance and perspective, can in fact write the history of this period.

My approach is somewhat different. I look at Camp David not as a discrete event but as a process of failed peacemaking, in which all parties bore a measure of responsibility for the absence of an agreement. In my view, the Palestinians deserve tremendous criticism for their lack of responsiveness, their passivity, and their failure to negotiate in any meaningful sense of the word. About that, I think there is no doubt. I was there, and I think that is evident, certainly to those Palestinians who were honest and critical of their own actions. But at the same time, I would argue that the year before Camp David was the critical period, not the eve of the summit, but the twelve months before Camp David during which Israelis and Americans played roles of their own in creating a set of circumstances that minimized the prospects for success.

In fact, my thesis is very simple. In order to understand the aims, the motivations, the logic of Camp David and the reasons why it failed, do not look at the twelve to fourteen days of the actual summit, though it is clear they have to be evaluated in their own right. Look at the twelve to fourteen months that preceded the summit. In particular, although this is an arguable proposition, examine the elusive quest for what we jokingly referred to – though I mean this not as a joke – as the "other woman": the Israeli–Syrian agreement.

It proved to be a very bitter and cruel joke, because the pursuit of an Israeli–Syrian agreement in the year that preceded Camp David seriously minimized the prospects that Camp David would succeed in producing a breakthrough. As far as the "other woman" is concerned, we do not have to go through a long saga of "the ups and downs" of that story. Damascus and Hafez al-Asad have mystified every US president and every secretary of state since 1973, beginning with Henry Kissinger. Suffice it to say that an Israeli–Syrian agreement was pursued as a strategic challenge, a transformational event, not a transactional event, one that would fundamentally transform the region.

An Israeli–Syrian agreement was believed to be achievable. After all, here was a strong, practical leader who could deliver, who had respected the disengagement agreement that Kissinger had negotiated. The Golan Heights, unlike the West Bank, was not such a divisive issue in Israeli politics. Solve the security issues, so the theory went, and you could convince most Israelis that the Golan could be returned in total. This logic drove three Israeli prime ministers, Rabin, Peres and Netanyahu, to pursue seriously, though in some respects, only half-seriously, an agreement with Syria. Hence, it is not surprising that a fourth Israeli prime minister, courageous as he was, would seriously engage in the pursuit of the "other woman."

I believe that this was a dangerously alluring strategy, adopted by Israel and enabled by the US. Between July and October 1999, that strategy sought to pacify and stabilize the Israeli–Palestinian track, and between October

1999 and March 26, 2000 (the date of the failed Geneva summit), the goal was an agreement with Syria that would in effect be transformational. It would (a) create a rational and disciplined basis for withdrawal of Israeli forces from southern Lebanon; (b) be easier to "sell" in Israeli domestic politics; and (c) reduce Palestinian leverage and expectations, so that once the Israeli–Syrian deal was completed, it would be easier to reach an agreement with the Palestinians. By the end of 2000, arguably, you could attain not one peace treaty, but three – Lebanon, Syria and the Palestinians – all of which could be presented to the Israeli public, either in a referendum or through some other politically sanctioned mechanism, to create the grand peace.

This was a truly bold and comprehensive vision. Sadly, the theoretical analysis that held that this was possible could not match the reality. Asad, crafty, clever, decisive leader that he was, was also the "Frank Sinatra" of the peace process. He chose to do the peace process "his way," and in doing it his own way during the last three years of his life, he priced himself out of the market. In fact, Asad defied the three basic political laws of gravity that had governed every other agreement that Israel had reached with its other neighbors, Egypt, Jordan, and the Palestinians. One was secrecy. All of those agreements had employed secret diplomacy in an effort to demonstrate intentions and allow leaders, through their empowered representatives, to get a real sense of what the other side was prepared to do. Second, there was public diplomacy, grand gestures to create a constituency for peace building. Of course, there was also the US role, on which all three of those sets of negotiations had depended.

For Asad, however, secret diplomacy of a meaningful kind was simply never an option. Public diplomacy, on the other hand, was perceived to be some kind of benefit of normalization ahead of peace. Therefore, Asad relied almost exclusively, indeed I would argue totally, on the American role. Given his niggardly view of peacemaking, the American role was simply not enough.

I, for one, do not fault Israel's position on territory, with respect to Syria. Frankly, the Syrians did not deserve better. Asad refused to allow his foreign minister to shake the hand of the prime minister of the State of Israel; Asad continued to run a proxy war against Israel in southern Lebanon – and for this, he was to be offered almost everything he wanted. That is not my complaint, however. My complaint is that the pursuit of the "other woman" constrained and undermined the chances for reaching an agreement on the one track upon which Israel's quest for peace, security and preservation of its identity *vis-à-vis* its Arab neighbors truly depended.

This happened in three ways. First, with respect to time, it left the US with less than six months to try to mediate the Arab–Israeli conflict's single most complex set of issues. In fact, someone argued that it left the US with only three months, because by September, with the American electoral campaign underway, it was quite clear that a deal with the Palestinians would have had to be concluded by then. Second, it truly generated a sense of urgency on the part of both the prime minister of Israel and the president of the United States.

As Martin Indyk has said, if negotiations succeed, they succeed because of the sense of urgency among the protagonists. Arafat, however, was not in a hurry. Part of the reason he was not in a hurry was that he knew that *we* were in a hurry. The one thing you never do when you go into a negotiation, if you have any doubts about your interlocutor's sense of urgency, is that you betray the fact that you yourself are in a hurry, that you want an agreement more than he does. Arafat's reaction, I think, was the reaction of the weakest party in the negotiations. It was as though he was saying, "Having ignored me for eight months, the Israelis now want a deal, and I'm not so sure I want one right now. Let's see what I can get."

This response, combined with Arafat's personality, and the fact that he did not comprehend why the Israelis, enabled by the Americans, had pursued the Syrian track for the previous eight months, resulted in the absence of any real incentives for Arafat to agree to a deal. Although I am mindful and respectful of the extraordinary offer the Israelis put on the table, from Arafat's perspective, the only Arab leader who had ever been to Camp David was Anwar Sadat. Sadat had received one hundred percent of his territory, and look what happened to him. So, with no real sense of urgency, terrified of being manipulated into some sort of American–Israeli trap, and faced with an offer in the low nineties (the percentage of West Bank/Gaza land being offered), Arafat was not going to budge on territory. His transgression was not that he did not accept the offer; his transgression was that he failed to respond to it.

The third way in which the pursuit of the "other woman" skewed the negotiations was that it elevated to a level of prominence, both inside and outside the negotiating room, the principle of June 4, 1967. If there was any Palestinian flexibility on the June 4, 1967 borders, I think it was stripped away by the fact that Arafat saw Israel prepared to give 99.9% of the Golan Heights to Syria, to a man who refused to play by any of the rules or conventions of normal peacemaking.

Finally, there is the matter of trust. This was supposed to be a leaders' summit. By hermetically sealing Camp David, which was the American strategy, by putting leaders in the throes of a negotiation, maybe, just maybe, they could find their way to a breakthrough and reach one another at some level to make a deal. I am not here to write a brief, legal or otherwise, for Arafat's behavior, but I think the pursuit of the "other woman" did, in fact, create a sense in Arafat's own mind that, to some degree, this was "payback" time.

I sat with Arafat, as Dennis Ross did, in Ramallah when President Clinton made the announcement that he was inviting Prime Minister Barak and Syria's Foreign Minister Faruq al-Shara' to Blair House. And I remember distinctly the reaction of all of Arafat's colleagues. They were incredibly excited. Why? Because they believed that Hamas and Islamic Jihad would thus be undermined, that Damascus would reassert its control over the "nay-sayers." Moreover, the principle of withdrawing to the June 4, 1967 lines would now provide a kind of unified negotiating framework, the basis for a kind of all-Arab coalition. They could not have been happier. I was sitting next to Arafat, and he said nothing during this happy scene; in fact, he rarely said anything. I asked him what he thought. His reply was short, "Mr. Barak should not take me for granted."

Finally, history is full of unknowns and contingencies. I do not have an answer to the question of whether the result would have been different if in June, or even September 1999, Israelis and Palestinians had pursued a negotiating process on a twenty-four hours a day, seven-days a week basis. But I do know that had this been the case, the proposition that Israelis and Palestinians could in fact reach an agreement would have been subjected to a much more sustained, credible and serious test. The rest, as we say in the trade, is history.

I would like to try to link Camp David to the current perspective. I do not believe that there is a kind of metaphysical mystery in the Israeli–Palestinian track. I do not believe that it is impossible to reach an agreement between Israelis and Palestinians. The two agreements that Israel has reached with its neighbors and that have lasted, the "permanent status" agreements with Egypt and Jordan, were based and continue to be based on a balance of interests, not on a balance of power. The key to the Israeli–Palestinian process of peacemaking must be symmetry between Israelis and Palestinians.

The imbalance of power is skewed in both directions. Palestinians wield the power of the weak. We should never forget that the power of the weak is a formidable one, because it enables the Palestinians to say, "I'm not responsible for this, I'm under occupation, I have a long list of grievances, the Israelis are doing this, this and this. Therefore, I can acquiesce in suicide terror or, if I'm truly devious, orchestrate any number of violent or terrorist acts against Israel because I wield the power of the weak." Israel, on the other hand, wields the power of the strong. It has the capacity to act unilaterally in any number of ways: settlement activity, housing demolitions, bypass roads and land confiscation. Most of these actions may well have nothing to do with Israel's security. But it seems fairly clear to me that the question for the Road Map, ultimately, is whether or not a way can be found to create a balance of interests in the Israeli–Palestinian negotiations. Negotiations, frankly, are not much different from good marriages, good business propositions or good friendships. If each side gets what it needs, then negotiations will be consummated, agreements will be reached, and maybe even one day the result will be an Israeli–Palestinian peace.

---

## Remarks during the Discussion

---

I may be too much a prisoner of the past, but I do believe that the instruments that were used to resolve the negotiations with the Egyptians and the Jordanians need to be looked at in a more systematic way in order to address this set of negotiations. That is to say, there was secret diplomacy with respect to Oslo; there was secret diplomacy with respect to permanent status issues as well. However, it might not have been the kind of organized, authoritative secret diplomacy that was necessary to set the stage for a high-risk summit like Camp David.

On public diplomacy, all I hear nowadays is that publics have to be prepared, that constituencies need to be molded in order to support the bold and courageous decisions that leaders take. I think there is a large measure of truth in that. Arab–Israeli peacemaking has largely been transactional; it has been about business propositions. There has to be a transformational aspect to Arab–Israeli peacemaking as well.

And then there is the US role: How could the US have played a more effective role, given the circumstances that we confronted? When the president of the US asked, *after* the invitations to Camp David were issued, whether or not it was a good idea to go, my response was more or less the same as all of my colleagues, which was, "Mr. President, you have to go. If you don't go, there will be violence, and no one will ever be able to understand how you couldn't have spent the last six months of your administration trying to help Israelis and Palestinians, based on what we thought might be achievable."

But I knew that in fact, if we were going to go to Camp David, we had to have a successful outcome. It is not the "going" that, to this day, haunts me. Rather, it is the question of why we did not create an alternative scenario enabling me to write a briefing for Arafat, Barak and Clinton, which would have turned this summit into a negotiating success.

It did not have to turn out the way it did. And I would simply say that politics and psychology are critical, but you have to begin with diplomacy, because how Israelis, Palestinians and Americans organize themselves will determine whether or not the deal ultimately gets done. Secret diplomacy, public diplomacy, and a different kind of US role – all are requisite components of success.

# MARTIN INDYK

# Sins of Omission,
# Sins of Commission

THERE IS SOMETHING THAT IS NOT GENERALLY WELL KNOWN about Camp David, but worth bearing in mind. Just as there were divisions within the Israeli negotiating team, and very strong divisions within the Palestinian team, so too was there a long-standing and strong-willed division within the American team, between what we called the "Syria-firsters," of whom I was obviously one, and what we called the "Palestinian-firsters," which included Aaron Miller and Robert Malley. While both sides acknowledged that the president was determined to pursue a Syria-first approach, nevertheless there was tension throughout the Clinton years between the proponents of these two different views of America's strategic interests.

The issue of preparation for the summit has come up on several occasions. Shimon Shamir has stated that the lack of preparation was a mistake, a point we need to learn from. I think it is important to understand why there was, in fact, a lack of preparation. From the American perspective, I think that we were guilty of a number of sins, of omission and commission alike. The central sin of omission was that we could not do better in terms of getting the parties, through pre-negotiations, to the point at which the summit would simply be a matter of leaders making the final decisions and the final compromises. That was because of the structure of the negotiations. In order to move the issues to the point where the leaders could make the final compromises, there needed to be secret diplomacy. Indeed, there was, in Stockholm, and the Stockholm negotiations actually made progress because of their secrecy. But there were leaks very soon afterwards, and once that happened, the secret negotiations came to a halt. This happened not just because the parties no longer felt assured that the deliberations would be kept confidential, but also because Abu Mazen, who was supposed to be in charge of the negotiations from the Palestinian side, discovered that the Stockholm talks were going on behind his back. He also learned that one of the participants was Hassan Asfour, at a time when Abu Mazen believed that Asfour was trying to undermine him, organize demonstrations against him and create obstacles to his efforts to succeed Yasser Arafat.

On the Israeli side, there was a similar inability to proceed with the secret negotiations once the Stockholm talks had leaked, because Prime Minister Barak found himself constantly exposed politically as a result of the leaks, causing serious erosion in his political support and in his coalition. In sum, we simply did not have the ability to conduct talks in secret. Compounding matters further was the fact that the Palestinian negotiators believed that whatever they said would become public. Hence, they were simply unwilling to demonstrate any flexibility on the core issues – Jerusalem, refugees and the Right of Return, territory, settlements – for fear of being accused by their public of selling out Palestinian national rights. As for the Israeli side, the Barak government's concessions, once made public, became politically damaging. Hence, it was simply impossible to deal with these issues in the kind of pre-negotiation that was required in these circumstances. It was a big problem, and we had no solution. Finally, given the assessments of all three parties that the absence of a breakthrough would lead to a violent confrontation, the president concluded that it was better to try and fail than not to try at all. I believe that all of his advisors shared this view.

Our sins of commission were, I believe, a product of that quality of American diplomacy called naïveté. The peace process benefits from it, because otherwise we would not keep coming back for more. At the same time, the process suffers from it, because the US becomes open to the manipulations of both sides, since the Americans do not fully understand the exact nature of the games being played. What was important in this regard, beginning during the run-up to Camp David and continuing through the conference itself, was that a power struggle over the succession to Arafat was taking place among the Palestinians. This had begun in 1998 following the agreement on the Wye Plantation Memorandum, when the Palestinian people reacted adversely because of what they considered to be a bad deal on prisoner releases. By the way, the people who made the deal on prisoner releases, and I have a photograph to prove this, were the people who quickly shifted the blame to Abu Mazen, who was not in on the prisoner deal.

Hence, a dynamic was created on the Palestinian side, one that had been building for a long time, between what I call the "Abus" and the "Muhammads." The "Abus," Abu Mazen and Abu Ala, considered themselves the rightful heirs to the throne, while the "Muhammads,"

Muhammad Dahlan and Muhammad Rashid, were maneuvering to take power. Ironically, Dahlan and Abu Mazen later became allies against Yasser Arafat, but in those days there was a bitter dispute between them. Our first sin of commission was that we managed to insert ourselves, unaware, into the middle of the Palestinian succession maneuvering by inviting Muhammad Dahlan to the White House. When he was in Washington for his usual meetings with the CIA, he had a meeting with Sandy Berger in the White House. This convinced Abu Mazen that we were engaged in promoting Muhammad Dahlan at his expense. Hence, Abu Mazen, whose influence on Yasser Arafat was second to none, came to Camp David believing that the exercise was directed against him and he reacted accordingly, taking himself out of the game (at one point, he was even absent physically, attending his son's wedding). Throughout, his behavior at Camp David was entirely passive.

President Clinton made our second sin of commission. Angered by the unwillingness of the Palestinians to put forward any position regarding territory, he attacked Abu Ala, actually started screaming at him, in the presence of the Israeli delegation. That humiliation of Abu Ala, who is a very proud man, took him out of the process as well, and he turned passive, or negative. Hence, the two key people who were in a position to influence Yasser Arafat at Camp David were simply not willing to cooperate. Despite or perhaps even because of the efforts of Dahlan and Rashid to get an agreement, the "Abus-versus-Muhammads" dynamic among the Palestinians played an important role in the paralysis and passivity that many have remarked upon.

An important sin of omission was our failure to ensure Arab participation in the negotiations, particularly that of President Mubarak, but also of the Saudis and the Jordanians. At the last minute, when we were already at Camp David, we decided to reach out to them, to try to generate some Arab cover for the compromises that Arafat would need to make. However, they were simply not prepared to cooperate.

From my perspective, the US praxis at Camp David contained two problems, The first was that we did not prepare a fallback option in case of failure, and the second was that although we had a strategy, it changed on an almost daily basis. I think that our inability to stay on track with a particular approach contributed to the problems that developed.

The Palestinians thought that they were being dragged into an Israeli–American trap. This view was a product of the fact that the US and Israel, not just at Camp David but basically throughout the peace process, coordinated their policies. People will recall how the Egyptians were offended when everything that Jimmy Carter put forward seemed to have been coordinated with the Israelis in advance. They used to say it was not an American plan that was being tendered but an Israeli plan. That was certainly the Palestinian perception at Camp David as well.

There is a reason for this: the US is not an even-handed mediator. We have our interests and allies, and Israel is an ally of the US. The approach that successive administrations have taken to Arab–Israeli peacemaking has been that the only way to move forward effectively is to get behind Israel in what it wants to do. Sometimes this approach came from desire and sometimes out of recognition of reality. We are obligated to Israel because of our commitment to its security and well-being.

It is also a political reality that Israel is the party with the cards. Particularly when it comes to negotiating with the Palestinians, Israel holds nearly all of the cards in its hands. To get Israel to give up its cards, the US has to provide Israel with guarantees, reassurance and various forms of assistance. Inevitably, in any negotiation that has succeeded, as well as those that have failed, the US and Israel engaged in what the Palestinians regard as collusion, but what I would argue is the only way in which we can achieve a successful outcome. Nevertheless, there was this perception at Camp David, that we were following Israel's script, that we were colluding with them, which contributed to the sense of Palestinian paranoia about what exactly was going on behind closed doors.

Then there was the problem of the "end of conflict" requirement. Here we had an impossible situation. From Prime Minister Barak's point of view, the only way he could justify to the people of Israel the far-reaching concessions that the Palestinians demanded in order to reach an agreement was to be able to stand before them and say, "It hurts, but that's the end of it. There will be no more claims; there will be no more conflict. It's over." Amos Oz described this at the time as a multiple amputation, not in stages but in one go, like a leg and an arm together, in one last surgical procedure. From our perspective, this was an entirely justifiable position. We had great admiration for the courage that Prime Minister Barak was prepared to show at Camp David, but it was courage that was based on a political calculation, namely, that he could sell it to the Israeli people if he achieved an "end of conflict."

The problem with the Israeli need for "end of conflict" was that it produced a Palestinian need to resolve all the issues to their satisfaction. This forced the negotiations away from the issues that I think could have been resolved at Camp David and afterwards, the issues of territory and security, and toward the issues that had barely been touched before Camp David, the issues of Jerusalem and refugees.

People have concluded that Camp David broke down because of the Right of Return, but that is simply not the case. Refugees were hardly discussed at Camp David. The issue of Jerusalem was the one on which the negotiations broke down twice: before the president left for Okinawa, and after he came back, at the end of the summit. We simply did not have a way of reconciling the competing Palestinian and Israel requirements for sovereignty over the *Haram al-Sharif*/Temple Mount. Various formulas were put forward, but it simply was not possible to agree on any of them.

In our view, the Israeli proposal on Jerusalem went far beyond what we had imagined a prime minister of Israel would tender. Thus, we were very sympathetic and supportive of Prime Minister Barak, regarding his move as extraordinary. But because it did not deal with the issue of sovereignty over the *Haram al-Sharif* in a way Yasser Arafat could accept, we were stymied. In essence, though there were many problems that contributed to the failure at Camp David, I believe that the Temple Mount issue, irresolvable at that juncture, was at the core of the failure.

Because we were working for an "end of conflict" that required a deal on Jerusalem, it became impossible to introduce a fallback plan for negotiations on territory and security. I believe that we could have reached an agreement in those areas. However, once the issue of Jerusalem had been put on the table, nobody could walk away from it and simply defer addressing the subject, as in the past. In retrospect, we should have gone into Camp David trying to work for the fallback, not trying to resolve all of the issues, but that is the wisdom that comes from hindsight.

The final point I want to stress is that Camp David was the beginning of the negotiation process, not the end. There is a conventional wisdom, in both Israel and the US, that Camp David was the "be all and end all" of the process, and the failure at Camp David brought it to a halt. In fact, this was not the case. The negotiations continued all the way up to the Taba talks in January 2001. However, December was the climactic month, at least for the American role, when the Clinton Parameters were presented. Thus, discussion about which party was at fault, or what went wrong, needs to take account not just of what happened at Camp David, but what occurred thereafter.

I can understand why Yasser Arafat said "no" at Camp David. He did not have a satisfactory solution at that point for Jerusalem and his negotiating tactics dictated a need to see what else he could get. One must also give him his due, in that he made some important concessions at Camp David on the question of the Jewish suburbs of Jerusalem coming under Israeli sovereignty and on the question of settlement blocs, thus displaying some flexibility regarding borders. Where I fault Arafat is that after Camp David, he willfully sought to escape the trap in which he imagined he was being placed, by allowing the violence to flare, refusing to bring it under control, and trying to use the violence to improve his position.

To be sure, objectively speaking, Arafat was successful in this regard.

During the months after Camp David, leading up to the Clinton Parameters in December, the Israeli and American positions evolved significantly in Arafat's favor. President Clinton's December proposals constituted much more than was offered to Arafat at Camp David: Israel's withdrawal from 95% to 97% of the West Bank and all of Gaza, with territorial swaps as compensation for the West Bank areas remaining under Israeli control, a just and fair solution to the refugee problem, sovereignty on the surface of the *Haram al-Sharif* for the Palestinians, and sovereignty over the Western Wall and what lay behind it, below ground level, for the Israelis. Yet, the Palestinian leader said "no."

Arafat was asked to accept the Clinton Parameters as a basis for negotiations, not as the final deal. In response, he sent Sa'eb Erekat to Clinton to deliver his 52 objections to the American proposal. My indictment of Yasser Arafat is for his failure to respond positively to the Clinton Parameters, not for his having said no at Camp David, and I believe that his own people should feel the same way.

There are many lessons to be drawn from the Camp David experience, but I will limit myself to three. First, I believe it was a mistake to try to resolve all the issues there. It was very clear, and continued to be clear right though to the Clinton Parameters, the Taba negotiations and up until the present, that we do not have a solution to the issues of Jerusalem or the Right of Return. It is possible to see how the issue of the Right of Return can be resolved to the satisfaction of both Israelis and Palestinians. I do not, however, see a solution to the Jerusalem problem that will be acceptable to both sides. If we should try to resolve those issues in the process that is getting underway now, we will arrive at a continued impasse. It was possible to resolve the territorial and security issues at Camp David, it is possible to resolve them today, and I believe that it is important to try to use diplomacy for what is possible, not the impossible.

That means that the process outlined in the Road Map for developing an agreement on a Palestinian state with provisional borders is the one that now holds out the most hope. This is where the parties should focus their efforts, precisely because it defers those very critical issues of Jerusalem and the Right of Return. Some on the Israeli side insist that the Right of Return should be dealt with as part of the process creating a Palestinian state with provisional borders. However, they are making a big mistake, because such a demand will foreclose the possibility of achieving an interim solution, which is inimical to Israel's interests. Finally, a lesson that I think we can draw not so much from Camp David but from what happened afterwards, is that violence cannot be part of a process of peacemaking.

## Remarks during the Discussion

From the Israeli point of view, there was a political justification for demanding "end of conflict." Actually, there is a better way of approaching this, which is to focus on ending *claims* rather than ending the conflict. If we had focused on ending the claims, it would have made dealing with each issue easier; you could end the territorial claim by resolving the territorial dispute, without raising all the other issues involved in ending the conflict. This is, I believe, an important lesson.

As for blaming Yasser Arafat, it was a mistake at the time. In fact, if you look at the president's statement at the end of Camp David, he was very careful. Although there was some criticism of Arafat, it was not really blame. The blame came in an interview with Israeli television, where he really laid it on the line. Here again I go back to the point that the US is not an objective mediator; we are bringing our influence to bear. The president was then, as he is today, probably the best politician in America, and also a very human politician. Clinton was deeply concerned about the fate of his partner in this process, Ehud Barak, after Barak had made all of those concessions to which Arafat had not responded. By contrast, President Clinton did not feel that he owed anything to Arafat at that point. In fact, he was angry with him. So basically, Clinton's public pronouncements, particularly in that interview, were directed at helping Barak politically. But given that Clinton was a mediator, and especially because we were still in the process of trying to get a deal, it would have been better not to have blamed either side at that point. That is another lesson about mediation. There was plenty of opportunity to blame Arafat afterwards, as it turned out, and that is probably the way we should have handled it.

I believe that it is time that Israelis take a hard look at the question of the territories, and question the mainstream Israeli assumption that the territorial cards cannot be relinquished without resolving the other issues. First of all, the really important question Israelis need to confront is whether the West Bank is an asset for Israel or, as Shabtai Teveth called his book, "a cursed blessing." The consequences of holding on to the Territories as a bargaining chip are profound for Israel.

In addition, it is time to question whether it is possible, with these final status issues, to effect trade-offs. We thought, in the Clinton Parameters, that we could exchange the Right of Return for sovereignty over the Temple Mount. But I think that was the heart of the reason that Arafat said "no." The *intifada* was raging, while Palestinian minds had been inculcated for decades that the Right of Return was their fundamental right. Arafat was simply not prepared at that point to stand up in front of his people and say, "Listen, we got a great deal on Jerusalem; you refugees, sorry, you've got to give up your Right." Indeed, I question now, in retrospect, whether it is possible for any Palestinian leader to have the courage to stand up in front of his people and make that kind of statement. We see, for example, that Abu Mazen today takes a harder line on the Right of Return than even Arafat ever took.

ROBERT MALLEY

# American Mistakes and Israeli Misconceptions

THE CONTINUING INTEREST IN THE CAMP DAVID SUMMIT IS SURPRISING. After all, the substance of this event was rapidly declared "null and void" by the US President; the three main protagonists no longer are in office; neither the current Israeli Prime Minister nor the current US President want anything to do with the event; and the summit has been superseded by years of horrific violence. Moreover, if one is to believe the story that was told immediately after Camp David, there is little to say about it other than, "We came, we saw and Arafat failed."

If there is so much interest, it is not primarily because of what actually happened at Camp David. Rather, it is because of the political use that has been subsequently made of the summit by all sides. Camp David has become a slogan, a convenient sound bite in the conflict between Israelis and Palestinians – and also among Americans. It has become, as it were, a metaphor with much wider implications about what Israel and the Palestinians are pursuing.

In my view, the largely one-sided accounts spread in the period immediately after Camp David have had a very damaging effect, not only on Israeli public opinion but also on American foreign policy. I believe that was already clear at the time, and has only become clearer since. Moreover, those one-sided accounts have been widely discredited over time. One is now compelled to conclude that we are *all* Camp David "revisionists," if measured against the "orthodox" narrative that emerged immediately after the summit (using the categories suggested by Professor Rabinovich). Hence, the question today is whether or not these revised views will influence public opinion in the places where it matters: here, among the Palestinian people, and in the US.

The "orthodox" narrative that emerged immediately after the summit consisted of the following core notions: (a) Camp David proved that the Palestinian leadership was incapable of reaching a peace agreement. The supporting evidence for that proposition was the alleged existence of a generous Israeli offer, more generous than anyone could have contemplated, and Arafat's peremptory rejection of it. (b) What the Palestinians wanted, what Arafat wanted, and what the Palestinian leadership desired at the time was not a two-state solution but a one and one-half state solution, with a Palestinian state existing alongside a bi-national state.

What others and I have tried to do is deconstruct those simplistic propositions and one-dimensional accounts of the summit. I have tried not to defend one side or another but to probe beneath the surface. The reason I have done so is because of the heavy political costs associated with the view that ascribes to the Palestinians a position that is inimical, hostile to, and inconsistent with a two-state solution.

The factors that have been listed by participants to explain why Camp David might have failed include the following:

(1) The conflictual situation on the ground, a situation that predated Oslo but continued thereafter, involving extensive Israeli settlement expansion and land confiscation, continued Palestinian incitement, and a proliferation of armed Palestinian groups that engaged in violence. To put it simply, there existed a vast gap between what was happening on the ground and what was occurring at the negotiating table.

(2) The issue of timing. For various reasons, there were only roughly six months to reach a deal on the most complex of all issues in the Arab–Israeli nexus.

(3) The lack of trust between the two leaders, Arafat and Barak.

(4) The lack of preparedness of constituencies on both sides. That certainly was true on the Palestinian side. Indeed, one of the reasons why Yasser Arafat did not want to come to Camp David was that he did not feel that his public, and particularly the relevant political constituencies, were prepared for what had to take place. This was true in Israel as well. Indeed, at Prime Minister Barak's request, the issue of Jerusalem was not discussed prior to Camp David, precisely because he felt the Israeli public was not yet prepared to hear some of the things that were needed to be said.

(5) The internal Palestinian divisions that Martin Indyk has referred to, namely, the disputes between Abu Mazen, Muhammad Dahlan, Abu Ala and others.

(6) The other factors: the withdrawal from Lebanon, the pursuit of the Syrian deal, etc.

Let me be clear: I am not saying that all of these necessarily played similar roles in the summit's failure or even any role at all. But some, if not most of them, almost certainly did.

One more point that deserves mention has to do with the behavior of the parties during the Camp David negotiations. All three sides are to be indicted for their conduct but particular responsibility must be attached to the Americans. The US lacked a sense of direction coming in, a coherent plan once there, and a fallback position coming out.

If you had asked the half-dozen members of the American team on the eve of the summit what they thought the substantive outcome of Camp David was likely to be, you would have received six different answers. Indeed, this was probably true during the summit as well, right up to the last day. The fact of the matter is that, at the outset, the Americans had no clear idea about how the summit would turn out.

Of course, we could not have known precisely where it was going to go. But what we should have had was a clear notion of what the ultimate substantive outcome ought to have been. This also was true with regard to tactical issues. We too often reversed course; so often, in fact, that we jokingly referred to our approach as "bumper car diplomacy." When we bumped into an obstacle, we shifted directions, which is why we never had a strategy that could carry over for more than a day, sometimes even to the surprise of the party that we were hoping to accommodate. I remember vividly what happened when we floated a proposal on the second or third day of Camp David. The Israeli delegation reacted very negatively, and so we promptly withdrew it. Only then did we discover that they had not actually expected us to withdraw the proposal. Their negative reaction was a mere negotiating ploy, in order to make the point that this was as far as they would go and no further. We thus got off to a pretty bad start, for we had demonstrated to the parties that if they objected to our proposals, we would retreat.

In a way, our approach was not crystallized at Camp David. Rather, it was the product of seven years of nurturing a peace process by President Clinton and his team, one in which we became so invested that we indulged the parties and overly accommodated them.

Another problem at Camp David was the Palestinians' suspicion that the US was coordinating everything with the Israelis. That too was a legacy from the past, and one that is explained by very good reasons. But it came with a very real cost. Every time we took a position on something, even if it was accommodating to the Palestinians, the Palestinians automatically assumed that it was an Israeli position, and pocketed it. They then expected us to put forth an even more accommodating position, in order to reach America's, and not Israel's, bottom line. The end result was to devalue the role of what all sides recognized as the indispensable party, the US. We came to Camp David imagining that we would get close to Israel's bottom line, we would then give it to the Palestinians, receive a counter-offer, bring it back to the Israelis and clinch the deal. That strategy took a few wrong turns: we never got to Israel's bottom line, we never received a counter-offer and, obviously, we never achieved a deal.

The final matter to be discussed is the issue of substance, the actual content of the American-backed Israeli offer at Camp David. If there is one myth that has to be put to rest, it is that the deal was something that any Palestinian could have accepted. One should not excuse the Palestinians' passivity or unhelpful posture at Camp David. But the simple and inescapable truth is that there was no deal at Camp David that Arafat, Abu Mazen, Dahlan, or any other Palestinian in his right mind could have accepted. That has become far clearer in hindsight. What was put on the table was not a detailed agreement but vague proposals: nine percent of the West Bank would have been annexed by Israel with a one percent swap of Israeli territory in return, a satisfactory solution to the refugee problem, a custodianship for the Palestinians over the *Haram al-Sharif*/Temple Mount, Palestinian sovereignty over the Muslim and Christian quarters, and a hybrid arrangement for the rest of Jerusalem in which some areas would fall under Palestinian sovereignty and some under functional autonomy. When the Palestinians came to us and asked, "Why the 9:1 ratio?" we had no answer other than the fact that those were the numbers that we were transmitting from Israel. When they asked us which neighborhoods would be under Palestinian sovereignty, we had no answer. When they asked us what the satisfactory solution on the refugee problem would be, again there was no answer. In all instances, the best we could do was to explain that this was the best that Israel could do, which is no answer at all.

Hence, those who would like to argue that the single explanation for the collapse of Camp David is that the Palestinians were not prepared to make a deal on terms that Israeli could live with, would have to dismiss all that we now know. They would have to say that everything, including the atmospherics and the context that preceded Camp David, as well as the tactics that were employed, had absolutely no impact on the behavior of the Palestinians. This is a very difficult argument to make, given that we know how important atmospherics, tactics and context were to Prime Minister Barak. Indeed, Barak had made very cogent arguments along the way about (a) how "we can't discuss Jerusalem at this time because we will lose Israeli public opinion"; and (b) how "we need to continue with settlement activity because otherwise we are going to lose some sections of public opinion." Why is it so difficult, then, to understand that the Palestinians, and Arafat in particular, also faced political constraints beyond the substance of the deal being presented? If Barak could not ignore all the background noise, why was Arafat expected to ignore it?

You would also have to dismiss the argument that what Arafat had in mind was to implement the salami-like tactic of pocketing concessions in order to attain additional ones at the next stage, because if that was his intention, he had ample opportunity to do so at Camp David. President Clinton suggested to him at one point to defer the issue of Jerusalem and deal with other issues. Arafat could have said to himself, I will take the offer and I will live to fight for a better day and a better deal. I do not have a perfectly coherent explanation for Arafat's behavior, and I am not sure that anyone does. But it stands to reason that his approach was inconsistent with the so-called salami tactic.

Finally, one would have to explain the fact that it was not just Arafat who said "no," also many of the people around him, including those who today we identify as carrying the hope of a peace deal between Israelis and Palestinians, had the same position. Many of them were not only as obstinate and stubborn as Arafat, but perhaps more so. And the truth is, for those who say that they should have accepted the deal at Camp David, that there is a simple retort from a Palestinian perspective: promptly accepting what was offered would have made them guilty of diplomatic malfeasance, since on almost all the issues, the US and Israeli positions ultimately moved closer to theirs.

If there is one lesson to all this, it is that a little modesty is in order regarding how we interpret what happened at Camp David, the responsibilities we assign and the blame that we cast. This was a complex process, with a complex history. Ultimately, the explanation for "what went wrong" lies there, not in the mythical image of a generous Israeli offer peremptorily rejected by non-compromising Palestinians. Yes, it was a generous offer from an Israeli perspective, measured against past Israeli positions. Indeed, Israel's relative generosity highlights the fact that this was the first time that Israel made such moves, the first time that Israel talked about dividing Jerusalem, and agreed to territorial swaps. It also shows how early in the process we actually were. Yes, the US team did not know how far this was going to go, but I am not sure the Israeli delegation did either. Certainly the Palestinians did not know where this was headed, and they kept an attitude of, "We are just here to listen, we are not here to do much else."

It is too early to try to draw hard lessons about Camp David. Nonetheless, there are some lessons to be learned about the overall process, which can be summarized in four points. The first point has to do with the question whether negotiations are based on a "balance of interests" or a "balance of power," something that Aaron Miller has referred to. The second has to do with the unique process of de-occupation that this conflict requires. The third has to do with the role of third parties, particularly the US. And the fourth with the issue of politics and public opinion.

(1)   Regarding the first point: this was a negotiation based on an assessment of the balance of power. Neither side came to Camp David with a clear definition of its core needs, its vital interests. On the one hand, the Israelis were thinking more about how much they could get away with and less about how much they had to hold onto. On the other hand, the Palestinians were thinking about how much they could attain, not how much they really needed. So neither side came with a sincere, genuine sense of their core needs. At Camp David, in fact, the Israeli side began to grapple with its core interests – whether with regard to Jerusalem, territory or other issues. The Palestinian side had only a vague notion of its core interests, but it too began taking important steps, agreeing to the lines of June 4, 1967 with territorial modifications, and Israeli sovereignty over the Jewish neighborhoods of East Jerusalem and the Wailing Wall. These may seem like minor moves, just like Israel's concessions may seem minor to the Palestinians. In both cases, however, they were fundamental moves from the perspective of the party making them, and they reflected a move toward defining each side's core interests.

(2)   Regarding the unique nature of the process of ending the occupation: what strikes me as a principal difference between the Israeli de-occupation of Palestinian territories and various Third World de-colonization movements is that Israel cares deeply about the nature of the Palestinian entity that will succeed it in the territories it evacuates, whether regarding security-related matters, holy sites, or other subjects. This renders the negotiations extremely difficult. France, by contrast, did not care at all about the kind of regime that would succeed French rule in Algeria. Some of the ideas that have since emerged, including Martin Indyk's idea of a trusteeship and Shlomo Ben-Ami's idea of an international "envelope," illustrate that this is not a classic case of simply withdrawing from territory, without concern for what is to come afterward.

(3)   Regarding the subject of third party intervention: we have realized since Camp David that a third party role is even more important than we thought at the time, because only a third party can provide assurances about the nature of the emerging Palestinian entity, and compensate for the mistrust between the two sides.

(4)   As for the role of public opinion: neither the Israeli nor the Palestinian publics were properly prepared for an agreement. Conversely, one can ask whether the political leaderships were adequately prepared for the kinds of concessions that were necessary to achieve an agreement. What we saw at Camp David was that there are certainly infirmities in the

Palestinian political system, but also in the Israeli political system, making it difficult to take critical political steps. Sometimes, it may even be easier for the publics than for the leaderships to take action. Consequently, it is now time to consider holding a referendum, not one that would endorse an agreement already reached, but a referendum that would precede an agreement. Its purpose would be to apply pressure on hitherto inflexible political systems, rendering them more capable of concluding a final status agreement.

A few concluding words are necessay regarding the role that Camp David has played in the political debate between Israelis and Palestinians, and in shaping and constraining US foreign policy. Camp David was not supposed to be, and should not have been about, "unmasking Arafat." Camp David was not, and should not have been, about a black and white choice between a path of peace and a path of all-out war. It was a stage in a process – not, as we wrongly thought, the end of the process, but a stage, one that was arguably far closer to the beginning than to the end. Like so many times in the past, the very people who first rejected some of the ideas put forth at Camp David may well eventually embrace them.

As a member of the American team at Camp David, I acknowledge that we made mistakes. However, having been there, I also believe that the accomplishments, legacy and possible future role of Camp David are under-rated. It would be wrong to reduce this experience to a simple story of Palestinian negation of Israel's right to exist, and to conclude that the only remaining available choice is confrontation. Camp David deserves better that that, as do all those who inspired it and were behind it, not to mention the Israeli and Palestinian peoples themselves.

# The Barak Version

# EHUD BARAK

# The Myths Spread About Camp David Are Baseless

I AM STRUCK BY THE CONTINUING INTEREST GENERATED by the Camp David summit. Four or five books have already been written about it and more are in the pipeline, not to mention long television documentaries screened around the world in almost every language imaginable. I am not sure why there continues to be so much interest. Perhaps it is because Camp David was a formative event, even though it did not succeed in achieving peace.

The Camp David summit was indeed the first time that anyone tried to address the deepest and most painful roots of one of the bloodiest and most difficult conflicts in the world. It was a determined attempt to prevent a tragedy of the kind that is unfortunately taking place now. Moreover, Camp David continues to be relevant: after several years of violence, the Palestinians understand that Israel will not give in to terror; Israel has once again learned the limits of power; and the Americans realize that a global conflict cannot be managed, let alone resolved by remote control. If and when Palestinians and Israelis once again sit together and try to resolve the conflict, they will find themselves going back to the same principles and same points that were on the Camp David agenda.

Peace was not achieved at Camp David because peace – like tango and a marriage – requires two willing partners. At Camp David, the other side was not a willing partner capable of making the necessary decisions. As this conference has demonstrated, the Camp David summit and its offshoots were extremely complex, and as we know, any complex phenomenon can be explained, certainly in academic conferences, in many ways. A given scientific conference can probably explain how a butterfly fluttering its wings in China started a chain of events that eventually led to fierce rains in Israel. Still, the most straightforward, common sense explanation would be

117

that which was given by a comedian when asked why is it raining – "because it's winter." To deal with complex subjects one must have not only courage and capability, but also keep touch with one's common sense. Before delving into the myriad secondary and tertiary interpretations of the *gestalt* that is our life, one must put one's finger on the straightforward explanation.

Arafat did not have the making of President Sadat or King Hussein. Had he possessed their fortitude of character, then peace between Israel and the Palestinians would have been a reality by now. I am deliberately giving the example of these two persons. The older people among us still remember burying thousands of young men who were killed in wars with the armies of Sadat and Hussein. But when these two leaders concluded that the time was ripe to make the required decisions for peace, they did not look for approval from half or three-quarters of their people. They did not check whether every extremist in their societies was cheering them on. They displayed leadership.

President Mubarak gave me a vivid description of how Sadat had made his decisions, and this description exemplifies the difference between him and Arafat. Sadat did not consult his men, or prepare them, before taking his decision to go to Jerusalem, and most of them were indeed deeply shaken by that decision. There was not a single member of the Egyptian leadership, on record, who agreed with Sadat's move. Some were stammering and others were sweating with fear, and even the vice-president (Mubarak), who eventually realized he could not afford to oppose the move, tried to stall. He said, "Mr. President, we cannot do this without talking to Asad first. He withstood the test of the war with us." The vice-president was convinced this would dissuade Sadat, but the president looked him in the eye and said, "Husni, you are right. Let's go to Damascus." Sadat went indeed to Damascus, but proceeded with his journey to Jerusalem. That is leadership. Arafat, however, did not have the character and historical insight that enable leaders to make decisions of this magnitude. Therefore – and in response to various analyses we have heard here – I emphasize that the summit was a story of leadership failure.

Is it really important to scrutinize the specific positions that would have been taken in the talks between us and the Palestinians, had such talks seriously commenced? The basic fact is that Arafat refused, time and time again, to accept the proposals made to him – mostly by the Americans – as a basis for serious discussion. This is why the negotiations never actually took off. It would have been frustrating, painful and annoying, but still legitimate, if the two parties were to have conducted genuine discussions and yet failed to bridge their differences – but this is not what happened there. What happened at Camp David was that one side made a deliberate decision not to accept as a basis for further negotiations any of the offers that were being put forward, as far-reaching as they may have been, and instead opted for terror. This clarifies the crux of what happened much better than any sophisticated explanation that is being offered in retrospect, and it also places responsibility where it rightfully belongs.

Summing up my observations during the year and a half I served as Israel's prime minister, when I had the opportunity to see Arafat up close, and the preceding and ensuing years during which I followed him from a greater distance, I conclude that Arafat simply and fundamentally refused to recognize Israel as a Jewish state, period. He was, of course, familiar with the Jewish faith, which is mentioned in the Koran, and he was well aware that throughout history Jews lived in all the Arab countries, but he did not acknowledge the existence of the Jewish people. The fact that he did not recognize Israel as a Jewish state was congruent with his rejection of our demand that he give up the insistence on the Right of Return. It also determined his perspective on the vision of "two states for two peoples." When we Israelis talk about this vision, we talk about a Palestinian state that expresses the identity, history, personality and aspirations of the Palestinian people, alongside a Zionist and democratic State of Israel, which expresses the same things with respect to the Jewish people. Arafat's vision, however, was quite different. He envisaged the same Palestinian state I described, alongside a state by the name of Israel, whose democracy and tolerance would be exploited over the years to gradually create a bi-national state and, subsequently, an Arab state that contains a Jewish minority. This would be achieved through the implementation of the Right of Return, the demographic growth of the Arab population living inside Israel, and the unfolding of what he believed are the broad historical trends. In this respect, Arafat's vision was fundamental and, from the Palestinian perspective, even legitimate. However, it was a vision of a perpetual clash, and as such it did not leave room for peace. I differ here with Rob Malley, who believes that a peace agreement with Arafat was achievable.

President Mubarak was the first to mention to me the argument that Arafat could not sign a peace agreement with Israel because he feared he might be assassinated. I said to him, "Mr. President, if you were the one to raise this, it would have made sense. After all, while Sadat was murdered for a whole list of reasons, peace with Israel was one of them. If I were the one to raise it, it also would be a legitimate concern. Yitzhak Rabin was assassinated because he led a peace process that the extremists in Israeli society were unprepared to accept. But show me a single Palestinian that was murdered because of any type of progress toward peace with Israel. One Palestinian assassinated was Issam Sirtawi, but he was not engaged in any formal peace process, and that was 20 years ago."

The Palestinian who declared several months ago that the tragedy of the Palestinians was that they did not have a Ben-Gurion of their own was right. He meant it in two senses. The first sense is that they had no one like Ben-Gurion, who was prepared to accept the partition plan even though the Jewish state it offered consisted of just three cantons with narrow links connecting them, without Jerusalem and without any corridor leading to Jerusalem. Ben-Gurion made this difficult decision in order to attain what was possible. He was torn inside and did it with a heavy heart. He did not give up the dream, but he did give up in practice his maximalist political goals, provided that the other side accepted the arrangement as well (which it did not, and I will return to this later). The other sense is that Ben-Gurion was ready, in the midst of Israel's War of Independence and the bitter battles over the road to Jerusalem, to instruct young soldiers of the newly established IDF (among them Yitzhak Rabin) to open fire on Jews even though they had brought badly needed arms and munitions. They intended them for use by a paramilitary organization fighting alongside and within the IDF but separately, and this was unacceptable. His purpose was to make it crystal clear that the first and foremost attribute of a lawful government is the maintaining of monopoly over carrying and using weapons, and that no entity, as patriotic as it may be, may carry arms for any goal, no matter how essential, except on behalf of, and under the orders of this legitimate government.

In all fairness, this is indeed the Palestinian tragedy. Abba Eban was right when he said on several occasions that the Palestinians never miss an opportunity to miss an opportunity. This has repeated itself ever since 1948, and unfortunately, this is also what happened at Camp David.

The summit did accomplish several things. Although peace was not achieved, several substantial and irreversible accomplishments were nevertheless registered. Without these accomplishments, most of us would probably not keep our interest in that summit, and we would not be holding this conference.

First of all, for the first time in the history of the conflict, the parameters for a permanent status agreement were defined. These parameters will be valid even if such an agreement is only reached in five, ten or fifteen years. When we once again reach that moment of truth somewhere down the road and negotiate an agreement, it will take a magnifying glass to find the differences between the agreement that will be discussed then, and the one that was on the table at Camp David.

The second accomplishment was that Arafat's true face was exposed for all to see, that face which I have just described. My use of the passive voice is not unintentional. He was exposed, and it was not we, or me personally, that exposed him. It was not our initial intention to do so. We did not go to Camp David planning to expose some hidden face that we knew Arafat had, and which we had been unable to unveil in any other way. We went there to make a *bona fide* peace agreement, and I think that the issues we agreed to put on the table at Camp David speak for themselves. We came to make peace and were ready for concessions that went far beyond the consensus back home, or at least had not been expressly discussed within Israeli society. We were willing and ready to make decisions and take risks. But it turned out that Arafat was not willing to do the same. The British have a saying that might be relevant here, "If it looks like a duck, quacks like a duck, and swims like a duck, it's probably a duck." If Arafat looked like a terrorist, acted like a terrorist and talked like a terrorist, then maybe he was a terrorist. This diagnosis has ramifications. Arafat's formidable mistake at Camp David marked the end of his historic role.

The third important result of the summit was that it generated a shock which made both the Left and Right in Israel abandon their ideological dreams. The right-wing abandoned its fantasies and the left-wing its wishful thinking. They came face to face with reality, which is always painful. As with any pains of growing, one has to abandon the normal stage of, "Daddy, I want this," and learn to deal with complex realities. The Israeli Right realized that the dream of Greater Israel – which many of us who are not right-wingers also find alluring – is just that: a dream, and not a politically viable option, and that there is no choice but to accept the principle of two states for two peoples. The Left understood that no angel had descended from the heavens to embrace a "New Middle East," and that we should accept the fact that we live in a rough neighborhood. We live in the Middle East, not the American Midwest. What we have on our borders are not Canada, Mexico and two oceans, but a Palestinian people fighting for its interests and dreaming of making us disappear one day. They may accept our presence as an accomplished fact, but they do not accept our people-hood. Let me stress that I am not talking about the Palestinian friends present with us today, whose depth and breadth of understanding are exceptional within their society. I am referring to the general Palestinian population, which after many years of brainwashing and incitement does not accept Israel as a legitimate neighbor living on this land alongside the Arab nations.

The disillusionment on both sides of the political spectrum in Israel has led to a more mature and responsible perspective and served, to a great extent, as the foundation for the unity we see today. Political views are now much more uniform than in the past, and there is greater overlap between the positions of parties that used to be left-wing and those that used to be right-wing, so much so that everyone agrees that we must fight terror with all our might and at the same time wait for a Palestinian leadership that will be ready, like King Hussein and President Sadat, to make painful decisions. I do not accept the myth that the Israeli electorate has veered to the right; it stayed put. This is a healthy electorate. If and when the Palestinians have a leadership that is prepared to make the necessary decisions, Israeli society will rise to the occasion and start moving toward implementation of agreements and separation from the Palestinians.

Professor Rabinovich, in his presentation yesterday, classified me with the holders of the "orthodox" narrative. But what he calls "orthodoxy" is simply a matter of common sense. Those in the Left who failed to comprehend this following the summit paid a dear price at the polls during the February 2003 elections. Leaders often lag behind their public. The electorate of the Left, which realized a long time ago that the refusal of leaders in the peace camp to support Ariel Sharon made no sense, penalized the Labor and Meretz parties for their obstinate rejectionism, while rewarding Shinui. Israel's sensible left-wing voters asked themselves how the leaders of prominent parties in the peace camp could agree to sit with Arafat yet refuse to sit with Sharon. It defies any logic. Decent, reasonable Israelis were asking themselves, Where were these people in the last two years? Are they delusional? The outcome of those elections, a broad-based center-right coalition led by Sharon, was nothing but common sense in action.

Yesterday we watched here a documentary on Camp David (*Shattered Dreams of Peace*) in which most of the protagonists were interviewed. I missed there President Clinton, whose version has been classified in this conference with the "orthodox" group. Clinton voiced the sharpest reaction I have ever heard to the narrative of the "revisionists" (by the same classification), the first wave of which emerged two years ago in a long article in *The New York Review of Books* by Rob Malley and Hussein Agha. I was vacationing in Europe at the time, when President Clinton called me and said, "What's all this about, all this nonsense? Imagine the two of us convening a press conference and admitting even 50 mistakes. How could all those mistakes be compared to the one cardinal, crucial mistake that Arafat made?"

Indeed, for the first time in the history of this conflict, the Palestinians were offered – in return for ending the conflict, giving up the Right of Return into Israel proper and acknowledging Israel's security needs and its historic link to the birthplace of the Jewish nation – an independent, contiguous state in more than 90% of the West Bank and in 100% of the Gaza Strip, access to the neighboring Arab countries, the Right of Return for Palestinian refugees to any place in the Palestinian state, massive international assistance and even a hold in a part of Jerusalem that would become the Palestinian capital. Arafat refused to accept all this as a basis for further negotiations, and deliberately opted for terror. That is the whole story. The rest is gossip. Although gossip has some merit, it is still no more than gossip.

Whenever Palestinian spokespersons argue, "It is all the occupation, occupation, occupation," I say, "It is not the occupation, it is the terror." And how do I know? I know because I was there, in the year 2000, placing an offer on the table. If the issue were indeed the occupation, we could have now been deep into the implementation of peace agreements. The person who made the conscious decision to reverse the scenario fully understood the meaning of his actions. He was a very sophisticated individual. It has been said that Arafat had certain limitations, but no one has ever said that he was not intelligent or did not understand reality. He fully did.

For national leaders, serving the national interest, no decision is illegitimate, even if it may be unacceptable from the perspective of the international community and, of course, from that of one's adversary. Experience has taught us all that seeking a solution to a conflict by stating the truth is a painful process. I do not want to patronize, but I am not sure that the Palestinians are better off dealing with the truth and with reality as it is, because this will require them to draw some very hard operative conclusions . . .

Let me say a few words about what was called here the "determinist" narrative. I have been in contact with Dr. Henry Kissinger (who was mentioned as a representative of this school of thought) throughout the decade. He should be credited for consistency in his worldview and for the eloquent articulation of his positions. He was involved in securing interim agreements with both Syria and Egypt. Based on his experience, it is only natural for him to choose this approach. However, the cases of Egypt and Syria cannot be compared with the Palestinian case. Israel held at the time assets that Egypt wanted, and still holds ones that Syria wants. It successfully traded assets for peace with Egypt and can potentially hold on to its Syrian assets for as long as it pleases. In these cases it makes sense to move toward conflict resolution through interim agreements.

The Palestinian case is entirely different. Our two nations live inside one another, we are intertwined, and time is pushing us forcefully in the direction of the Bosnian or South African predicaments. This is a real threat that will certainly materialize unless we take action and change the situation. Hence, politically and historically it would be wrong to conclude that the only proper strategy to solve the conflict with the Palestinians is a series of gradual agreements that defer the solution far into the future. This would be evading the crux of the matter, even though some may find this formula comforting because it lowers the volume of internal discord.

Therefore, Dr. Kissinger's "determinism" is irrelevant to the Palestinian case. As for the "determinism" of the intelligence community, mentioned by Professor Rabinovich, even if it is correct, the State of Israel had no choice but to continue trying, certainly when we were after the Madrid Conference and deep into the Oslo process. But now we must state unequivocally that we tried and discovered that there was no partner on the other side and that the other side was not ready for progress. This is why we abandoned ship and let it take its own course, even if this meant that it would inevitably be wrecked and sink.

As for those who belong to the "eclectic" school, they are motivated by a genuine desire to find their way. But finding your way if you tell the truth is sometimes hard, and it is thus easier to manipulate the truth in the hope that it does not get in your way.

Some of the die-hard Israeli left-wingers empathize so deeply with the Palestinians and their grievances that they are prepared to see Israel give up everything, concede everything. They want the Israelis to bury their head in the sand, let the storm blow past it, then raise their head and say, "Oh well, so be it." They are ready to make big concessions, even such that might jeopardize Israel's very existence.

This is not the way. Israel has an urgent, compelling need to separate from the Palestinian population. This is a logical strategic choice that will lead to immediate positive consequences. Ten million people live between the Jordan River (only a few tens of kilometers to the east of this campus) and the Mediterranean Sea (a couple of kilometers to the west). They consist of six and a half million Israelis, and three and a half million Palestinians. If only one sovereign state, Israel, continues to rule this piece of land, the state will become, by necessity, either undemocratic or not Jewish. If the Palestinians are allowed to vote in such a state, it will turn into a bi-national state, *par excellence*. If they are not allowed to vote, this will be an apartheid state, *par excellence*. Either way, this is not what the Zionist dream was all about. Concerns for Israel's future and nature therefore make it imperative for us to implement the separation. We must create a border that will involve minimum land annexation coupled with a maximum number of settlers, and maximum security. The minimal land annexation will guarantee a Jewish majority for generations to come. The failure of the Israeli Right to recognize this strategic reality, and the danger posed to the whole Zionist enterprise, has been its gravest mistake. Recently, some of its leading spokesmen have actually admitted to this failure.

In light of this demographic–strategic imperative, Israel must be proactive and take steps to implement the separation of the two states. Israel must not waste any time. It must act before Palestinian society is swept away by other strategies that today are still marginal, but can already be clearly discerned. The day after the Taba meetings, some Palestinians argued in the *Financial Times* that the concept of two states for two peoples was no longer viable. They said that it transpired that one of the two projected states would not be contiguous. Even if the West Bank in itself is territorially contiguous, they asked, how could contiguity with the Gaza Strip be accomplished? The two communities, they argued, are living together so closely that even diseases can easily spread; they also share the same aquifers. Accordingly, these Palestinians called for establishing instead a unified state, on the condition that this state is "compatible with the norms of the 21st century," namely – democratic, secular, and tolerant, and follow the principle of one-man one-vote. Does this remind you of something? Well, this may become the future Palestinian strategy unless we take action without delay.

It is this insight that drove Rabin, Peres, Netanyahu (albeit reluctantly) and myself to advance the process. The Oslo process was not wrong, although just like any other practical project, it too involved mistakes and pitfalls, some of which I had warned against when I was still in uniform. But the strategy underlying the process was well founded. The Jewish state could not start the process of separating from the Palestinian population with a unilateral move without first honestly and seriously trying to do it in agreement with the Palestinians. However, the Jewish state, which was founded after so many years of yearning, after undergoing trials and tribulations, many of them in the past century alone, cannot afford to lose its lucidity. This state cannot lose its head and must not lose its footing either. Israel must look reality in the eye and say that we shall be doing everything we can to reach a settlement, and we are prepared to go a very great distance to achieve this – if we can only find a partner that agrees to end the conflict under reasonable terms for both sides, or at least be prepared to discuss the possibility. Otherwise, we will not let the absence of a partner paralyze us, but will act on the basis of our understanding of reality, as painful and brutal as it may be.

Our relationship with the Palestinians has been on a collision course for years because of the basic fact, which the incumbent prime minister Ariel Sharon has recently noticed as well, that we cannot continue controlling another nation. (At long last, a truly astounding revelation . . . ) I had publicly cautioned against this drifting toward a collision course years before I became prime minister. I contacted members of Likud-led cabinets, one by one, Natan Sharansky, Ariel Sharon, Rafael Eitan, Itzik Mordechai and others, saying to them, "Surely you can see where things are headed; it is impossible that you do not understand."

Anyone who says that the current wave of violence is the result of the Camp David summit should know that the summit was in fact the last attempt to *prevent* the collision toward which we had been consistently racing for years. Israel would have suffered a great calamity had we collided with the Palestinians without having first made a genuine and visible attempt, on behalf of the young people in Israel, and in face of the whole world, to prevent this tragedy. The result would have been the tragedy of a country finding itself in the midst of a violent conflict without the world recognizing the justness of its cause, and without domestic unity. We were liable to find ourselves in an intolerable situation: burying our dead, isolated on the international arena and torn from within. This is the tragedy we wanted to prevent.

Granted, the Oslo process suffered from some structural shortcomings, not just technical failures here and there. The full, true story of Oslo will be told at some time in the future. But in Oslo, too, we had on our side players who were in effect striving to initiate a process in which we would first hand over our assets and only then check whether we had a partner to work with or not. I recall long talks with Rabin when I was still in the military. I asked him, "Yitzhak, why are you making a concession here?" And he said to me, "Ehud, we still have a safety margin, we have no choice . . . Arafat has nothing at all."

As I stated, Israel holds all the assets, and since we wanted to transform Arafat from the terrorist leader he obviously was into a head of a state that is a member of the family of nations, we had to give. Along the road we had to part with some of the assets, as painful as that may have been. It was nevertheless clear all along that the time would come for us to call a spade a spade, to ask ourselves in all honesty whether the process was headed toward peace or not, and to be able to give ourselves honest answers, even if they did not fit with our expectations.

While the Camp David summit was a determined, painful, necessary and genuine attempt to make peace, accompanied by a sober realization that the attempt might fail, there are those who view the summit just as the direct cause of the *intifada*. The argument that the failure of the summit to bring peace is to be blamed for the *intifada* is tantamount to saying that the willingness of Ben-Gurion to accept the 1947 UN partition plan was to be blamed for the 1948 War. At first, the Palestinians thought that the desire for Jewish sovereignty was dying, that Ben-Gurion was wavering. Only later did they realize what a historic challenge it was, and started a war against us. Of course to blame Ben-Gurion is nonsense. Ben-Gurion was prepared to make tough decisions, and he understood the painful consequences just as well as anyone.

Why does the radical right-wing in Israel claim that Oslo and Camp David were the cause of the violence? Because the alternative explanation of the *intifada* would be that the mistake was not the Camp David summit or the Oslo process, but rather the extension of the settlement enterprise beyond the metropolitan area of Jerusalem and the security zones into areas densely populated by Palestinians. This was a grave historic mistake by the right-wing leadership. We may go back to the first Camp David summit and the ensuing Egyptian–Israeli peace treaty (1978–79) and analyze how it all started there. The Israeli government gave back the entire Sinai, undergoing the trauma of uprooting settlements, but believed that this would ostensibly enable Israel to retain its hold on the West Bank, which was, of course, an illusion even then. So I understand why the extreme Right clings to the argument that the Oslo process and the Camp David summit are the roots of violence. If not for them, the finger would have to be pointed at the settlement expansion throughout the West Bank, mostly since 1977.

I also understand why some of our friends among the Left find it hard to swallow realities. For if Arafat was not a partner, this means that they wasted many years of their lives and much of their political energy investing in a concept that now turns out to have been an illusion. They must find it hard to justify the positions they held over this long period of time. It reflects on their judgments and perceptiveness.

I know how Yitzhak Rabin was turned by the public into a virtual dove after his assassination. He was an honest man, strict with himself, and doubtful about Arafat. Yet he realized that he must move ahead with the process and give it a *bona fide* try, not out of affection for Arafat but because of his sense of historical responsibility.

The question "what went wrong" has some underlying assumptions that are in my mind logically false. First, an underlying assumption of this question is that something was not done correctly. When you are building a house and you have a good plan, mix the cement properly and lay the foundations in place, the house will look exactly like in the plans; if it does not come out as planned, it means that it was not built right. But conflict resolution just does not work that way. The fact that an agreement did not result from Camp David does not mean that we – especially we – should be ridden with guilt for not having done our job right. We know that we honestly did everything we could to achieve an agreement. It is perhaps simplistic, but an agreement of this kind cannot be attained unless both parties are prepared to undertake all of the complex, necessary steps for achieving it. Unfortunately, we did not have a partner of this kind.

The second incorrect assumption underpinning the question of "what went wrong" is that every development is the logical consequence of whatever came before. This is not the case.

The third implied assumption, which is baseless, is that which maintains that one should follow the rule, "if you're not sure that you can fix it, you shouldn't try." This may sound like simple common sense, unless – and I have been saying this for years – you realize that your country is heading toward collision and disaster. When you travel down a road or cross a long bridge having only one lane, and you see in front a vehicle approaching at full speed, you must be very naïve to assume that the driver of the other vehicle would not crash into you, and an absolute fool not to try to stop it – even if you cannot be sure that you will succeed. The fact that a collision is likely does not exempt anyone, certainly not a national leadership, from making a genuine and determined effort to try and prevent it, and take all the necessary risks. What was involved in this attempt was not issues to be discussed at symposiums, but the danger of the loss of human life.

What was the situation with the Palestinians when I became prime minister? We were eight months after the Wye Accord and a few months before the additional further redeployments (FRDs), which threatened to lead to an almost certain clash. Netanyahu thought he had convinced the Americans that everything would work out beautifully if the third FRD would include only one additional percentage point of West Bank territory. By contrast, the Palestinians' understanding of Oslo II, and even the 1978 Camp David Accords, was that they should receive the remaining areas of the West Bank, except the settlements, specified military locations and areas "related to the permanent status issues," which everyone interpreted as referring to Jerusalem. The situation was not simple because the Palestinians were contemplating a unilateral proclamation of the founding of an independent Palestinian state, and the Europeans had promised them that they would be able to do this in February 2000, regardless of whether or not Israel gave its consent. Even the President of the US made a statement pointing in this direction.

Syria was also in the picture. A few months before I came into office, there had been negotiations between Netanyahu and the Syrians. I had taken part in the talks under Rabin and Peres, and was familiar with the details. When Netanyahu needed to submit maps to Damascus, he had no choice but to brief his ministers. That was the first time he updated Itzik Mordechai and Ariel Sharon, who then blocked him from making any further progress. Maybe it was the NIH ("not invented here") syndrome – namely, whoever cannot be credited for the move will oppose it. In my mind it would have been irresponsible in practical terms to ignore the situation that had been created and not pursue the Syrian track at that point. My rationale was not just strategic, although I admit that years earlier I belonged to a group of officers in the General Staff who believed that securing a peace agreement with Syria first was the best strategy.

Concurrently, Lebanon was a lingering tragedy. The so-called security zone was useless. As early as 1985 I opposed the security zone concept, because I knew it would never stop Katyusha rockets but would turn into a battlefield, generating more and more hostilities. True, there were times when we did not expect to achieve any political agreements and told both others and ourselves that we had no choice but to stay there. But when the babies that were born when we first went into Lebanon in the late 1970s joined the army and started getting killed there, without us having any need or claim to a single inch of Lebanese soil, and without the security zone fulfilling its *raison d'être*, I thought – and I am proud of it – that this must be stopped. We did not do this before the halt in talks with Syria or after, or before or after any stage in the negotiations with the Palestinians. There was no connection. I had announced the withdrawal a year and a half earlier, in plain Hebrew. I do not think that anyone in the Arab world or among the Palestinians doubted my sincerity.

The picture was as follows. The Palestinians were racing toward a violent conflict with us, which was liable to turn into a tragedy if Israel did not make a genuine attempt to reach an agreement. It was a moment of historic opportunity to strike a deal with Syria. In my mind it would have been irresponsible on the national level not to pursue this opportunity as long as Hafez al-Asad was still alive. Concurrently, our presence in Lebanon was a bleeding tragedy in and of itself. So we were facing "two and a half fronts," as Danny Yatom said here.

We had to deal with all these issues together. Imagine a very sick man suffering from gangrene in one place, blocked blood vessels in another and cholera to boot. Who says that you should not treat the cholera before the gangrene heals or the blood vessels are opened? From day one I had been explaining to Arafat that because of Israel's considerations of historical responsibility, we felt that we must talk with Asad as well. Rabin, Peres and Netanyahu had all done the same. I promised him he would be in the loop and would be fully informed of all moves; that we had no ulterior motives and did not even know whether the talks with Syria would succeed. We have no intention of pulling a fast one on you, we told him. I spoke with Arafat about this on more than one occasion, and also with all the Arab leaders with whom we had direct or indirect contact.

When the Palestinians rejected the 1947 UN resolution, even as a basis for negotiations, this was the first opportunity that the Palestinians lost. Sounds familiar, doesn't it? Instead, they mobilized the Arab world to try and annihilate Israel. Therefore, when the war ended as it did, Israel had the stamp of approval of the international community to retain the territory it had taken in that war, a legitimacy it holds until this very day.

The main consideration in Israeli statesmanship, of which I have long been aware, is that the State of Israel cannot collect the political benefits of any operational or military victory unless two conditions are met: first, Israel must occupy the moral high ground and be regarded by the international community as having a just cause; and, second, Israeli society must be united. These conditions were met in 1948 (a war in which we lost one percent of our population), which is why we were able to win the war and retain our territorial gains.

In 1956 we joined a British–French operation. It was seen as exploiting an opportunity, riding the back of two dying empires, and consequently our role in the war did not enjoy support from the international community. Nor did it have unanimous support at home. Hence, Eisenhower and Bulganin needed only three weeks to convince Ben-Gurion to withdraw from Egyptian territory and it took Ben-Gurion just another four months to do so.

In 1967, although we were the ones to fire the first shot, the world saw us as trying to free ourselves of strangulation by our neighbors. The international community had failed to meet the commitments it had undertaken in 1956, and our war therefore enjoyed broad legitimacy. We also managed to uphold internal unity. The outcome was that we still control portions of the territory taken in that war.

In 1982 we conducted an operation that pushed us deeper into Lebanon than the 40-kilometer buffer zone originally declared as our objective. Hence, Israel was unable to secure either the support of the international community or domestic unity. Therefore, even though our success was unmistakable – we reached the heart of an Arab capital, the peace agreement with Egypt did not collapse, and no Arab army was deployed at our border – it was clear that this operation would yield us no political benefits. The two basic conditions were not met.

We must apply this analysis to our conflict with the Palestinians as well. Unless we make sure that both the international community and Israeli society – including the young men who are demanded to put their lives on the line – know that we did whatever we possibly could in a genuine effort to prevent a confrontation with the Palestinians, we will not have done our job. Of course, it is realized that even if we make all these efforts, we will not be sure that we would be able to stop the other side from escalating toward the crash, because peace takes two whereas one party is enough to start a war all on its own.

Without Camp David, then, we would currently have no foundation for internal unity or for the support we receive from portions of the international community. When President Bush or Secretary of Defense Donald Rumsfeld were asked why Arafat was no longer relevant, they did not say it was because he had been effectively isolated at the *Muqata'a* (his Ramallah headquarters compound). Rather, they explained that, in 2000, Clinton and Barak made an offer to him that by any logical standards he should have accepted as a basis for negotiations, and he refused to negotiate on that foundation and opted for terror. Arafat made it clear that he was no partner for negotiations. He finished his role, even if the Europeans did not share this view.

On the eve of the elections that I lost to Sharon, and at the end of Clinton's term, I described the right strategic conclusions that Israel should draw from the Camp David summit and its aftermath. I said that given the present situation, Israel's strategy should consist of the following three elements: (1) War on terror – any time and anywhere; (2) Unilateral separation by a fence that would surround Israel proper, the large settlement blocs around Jerusalem, the bloc in the center of the Samarian hills, and a few other small areas. This would comprise in all 12% of the territory. Adding a security zone in the Jordan Rift, held until an agreement is signed, it would bring it up to 25% of the territory. These measures are needed for our security, but also as a clear political signal that we are determined to separate from the Palestinians and to stop controlling another people. (3) At the same time we must clarify that we do not wish these measures to remain unilateral and that the door is still open to the resumption of negotiations, based on the principles laid out at the Camp David summit, without any prior conditions except for the complete cessation of violence.

That was the right strategy that I laid down at the time for Israel – a nation that was deeply shaken by the renewal of violence. Particularly shaken was the Left, which had not yet recovered from the loss of credibility of the

Chairman (Arafat) – their darling. But this is the very same Left that (as I remember from my childhood) found it so hard to recover from the shock of discovering what Stalin had been doing to his own people in the Soviet Union. After the start of the *intifada* it was hard for the Left to recover from the blow, and Sharon won the elections.

I respect the people's choice. Time will judge whether Sharon has lived up to his promise of security and peace. However, my view is that we are headed for a harsh awakening. Meanwhile we have already buried about a thousand people. I am convinced that a good many of them would still be alive today had we built the fence immediately, as a national emergency defense project. It is because of domestic political reasons that the fence has not been completed yet, to avoid admitting that we can no longer control another people and that this separation is needed for our security.

How can we be sure that the fence will be a success? In Gaza there is a primitive old fence that (Maj.-Gen.) Matan Vilnai insisted on building, and would not relent until he was allowed to complete it. This fence surrounds the Gaza Strip, home to one million Palestinians and the headquarters of Hamas and Islamic Jihad. No one can argue with the facts, and the facts are that no suicide bombers have penetrated into Israel through this fence. Granted, the fence does not protect us against many other problems, such as Qassam rockets and attacks inside the Strip itself – but no terrorist has yet made it into Israel.

Now that we have finally decided to build the fence, we still have to pay the price of our earlier blindness. It turns out that in the present circumstances, President Bush picks up the phone and complains that the fence prejudices future agreements. There is heavy international pressure. Now it is up to us to prove that the fence is designed primarily for security and does not mark the final alignment of the border, so that if an agreement is reached in the future that demarcates a different line, we will relocate the fence according to what will be agreed.

Let me comment on points that were made here previously:

Regarding Martin Indyk's observations on the negotiations with the Syrians.

The facts are correct, but the interpretation is not. Perhaps the fascinating visit to Damascus with Madeleine Albright and Dennis Ross has led Mr. Indyk to judge reality differently than we did. At Shepherdstown, we found the Syrian leadership's basic approach unchanged from the time of the US-sponsored negotiations during Rabin's term – and I had worked closely with Rabin, Peres and even Netanyahu on the Syrian track, *mutatis mutandis*, as jurists say. An agreement with Syria was not reached, not because we could not agree on a controversial stretch of land by the Sea of Galilee, as many people think, and not because we could not agree on the difference between the international border and the June 4, 1967 line. An agreement was not reached because the Syrians had a fundamental condition, for any negotiations, that Israel makes a direct, documented and irrevocable political pledge to accept all the demands Syria will make in the negotiations. Anyone who would even entertain accepting a condition of this kind, regardless of the guise under which it appears, would be well advised to steer clear of national leadership. It is preposterous, but this is what the Syrians wanted.

Rabin insisted on the "deposit mechanism" (according to which he "deposited" the territory-for-peace formula with US Secretary of State Warren Christopher) in order to make the Syrians understand what they could receive, without making any prior commitment. We were prepared to go even further, and at some point we tried to communicate with them directly. For years, the talks had been conducted through the Americans only because there was no possibility of talking with the Syrians directly, except for meetings with certain "go-betweens" and with Asad's biographer (Patrick Seale). We talked endlessly with the Americans. We felt that if a core understanding could be created that would serve as a basis for a solution, the Egyptian and the Jordanian scenarios could be duplicated. In other words, we were trying to create a channel of direct, noncommittal, undocumented covert talks to build some common ground. One of the motivations for this strategy was our awareness of the problem faced by Arab leaders, for whom even commencing negotiations is a serious risk. They therefore want to know beforehand what they are getting into. On our part, however, we cannot afford to give them everything they want even before negotiations begin and as a condition for initiating negotiations. Hence – a back-channel. At the time, I pressed for convening such preparatory covert talks, following the example of the first Camp David meetings. I argued that it made no sense that the greatest power on earth cannot convene five persons from each side without any information leaking out. I even made some technical suggestions how to do it, but to no avail.

Finally, we managed to meet at Shepherdstown, which was not exactly what we planned. What was it that hindered the negotiations there? At the most critical moment a document leaked out that made it appear as though the Syrians had already given up some of their demands, which was of course most embarrassing to them, while in reality they had given up nothing and made no move whatsoever. This leak instantly made them non-cooperative. The subsequent investigation indicated that it might have been an American official – one of those described by Indyk as "pro-Palestinian" – who had innocently shared his impressions with an Israeli friend, who then took the information to a friend from the media, who had it published. This is how we lost the Syrians. That is the whole story.

It is a distortion to claim that the Palestinians stepped up their demands when they realized we were prepared to discuss with Syria the borders of 1967. First of all, they already had the precedent of full withdrawal in the Egyptian and Jordanian cases. Did anyone ever think things would work differently with Syria? Second, the Syrian dispute is entirely different from the Palestinian one. In the former, our natural reference is the international border, but with the Palestinians we have no such reference. We had the armistice lines of 1949, according to which two Arab countries controlled the Palestinian territory for 18 years. A Palestinian state was never created on that land. Israel occupied the West Bank and Gaza after it was attacked, and once again it won. As I told Clinton and Arafat many times, both before and at Camp David, we will never apologize for our victory in 1967. All this created a situation that was different from the precedents with Egypt and Jordan.

A word about gradualism, as laid down in the Road Map. I truly hope this strategy works, although I am not convinced at all. Under international law, a provisional Palestinian state is for all intents and purposes a state, and as such it has rights. Israel might find itself with a serious problem if it agrees to provisional statehood. It seems that the decision on such a state, an amorphous entity with only a remote chance of ever materializing, was hastily made, and the particulars of the plan have not sufficiently been discussed. Most Israelis probably think that this stage of temporary statehood is planned for a remote future, while in fact it is meant to materialize in just a few months. I can only hope that my concern will be proven wrong.

To sum up, I think we must nevertheless adhere to the basic approach I have outlined. First, we fight terror. Second, we are prepared to enter negotiations based on the principles defined at Camp David. We may now dub them the "Bush–Sharon–Abu Mazen" principles, but they would essentially be the same; there are no other. And third, we are ready to separate unilaterally, even if we face opposition, because any other alternative would lead us to a still more dangerous situation. After all, there are quite a few people in the world who would be happy to see Israel turn into a modern-day version of what South Africa used to be.

Let me try to refute some of the myths concocted mostly in the "revisionist" camp.

One such myth is that Arafat was forced into the summit. It sounds almost like an oxymoron that Arafat, a Nobel Peace Prize laureate, would be dragged, howling and kicking, into a peace summit that is designed to resolve a conflict. This concept seems odd to me. Then there is the complaint about the timing of the summit. It is said that Arafat did not want the summit to take place in July. Clinton's head of the National Security Council, Sandy Berger, once asked me, "Why doesn't Rob Malley tell the other side of the story too? Arafat agreed to hold the summit at the end of August." Now you must ask yourselves in all decency: in a 100-year conflict that has claimed so many victims, what is the difference between mid-July and the end of August? The only things that occurred during those six weeks were the conventions of the two main political parties in the US, which nominated their respective candidates for the November presidential elections. The incumbent president, whose term was drawing to a close, would naturally be weakened by the nomination of his eventual successor. If weakening Clinton was the reason for Arafat's insistence on waiting until the end of August, then indeed we had a problem. Otherwise, the choice between July and August was meaningless.

The second myth is that Barak did not serve the baklava with his right hand but with his left . . . I think this myth is out of date, although yesterday I once again heard someone speculating what would have happened if Barak had held his head this way or that way, before or after dinner, etc. I cannot see how such a conflict, which goes to the core concerns of two nations, can be decided by these factors. Well, over the course of my 60 years, I have learned to appreciate personal relations. I have never raised my voice, and I believe I spoke with Arafat warmly and appreciatively. I confess that I find this analysis offensive. It is also disrespectful to the other side. Arafat and the Palestinians are serious people. They fully understand their own interests, which naturally often conflict with ours. It is the interests that guide them, not inter-personal chemistry, external manifestations of respect or level of human warmth, as important as those may be. I strongly suggest we completely drop this way of thinking .

The third myth is that the summit was not properly prepared. Was this in fact the case? We were nearly nine years past Madrid and seven past Oslo, with reams of reports and working papers in our archives. We had met with Palestinians in every corner of the globe except perhaps Antarctica and the North Pole. In my fourteen months in office prior to the summit we had held hundreds of hours of discussions with them. In fact, I do not think that any other Israeli prime minister had dedicated so many hours during his term in office to discussions with Arafat and the Palestinian leadership. When I was Chief of Staff I visited the southern tip of South America, whose waters have been a bone of contention between Chile and Argentina. After many years of dispute, they told me, they mobilized none other than the

Vatican to mediate. It took the Vatican two years to study that conflict. What is it that we still needed to learn before the summit? Was there anything we did not know yet? What are all these fairy tales? After burying hundreds and thousands of human victims throughout the Middle East, a region in which we know every road bend and every wadi, and are familiar with every problem, are we not ripe to sit down together and resolve our disputes? Was insufficient preparedness really the reason for the failure of the summit, or is it just an excuse given after the fact? The way I see it, the summit was prepared meticulously and carefully.

The fourth myth is that Barak did not propose anything; the Americans made all the proposals. All right, it was a US offer that was put on the table. But we were ready to adopt the principles as a basis for negotiations, even though we had reservations, while the Palestinians were not. This is the basic truth of the matter.

The fifth myth is that "Barak said: all or nothing." This is a legend. The concept of a framework agreement, worked out together, was created specifically in order to overcome this hurdle, since no one seriously thought that a 100-year conflict could be resolved by one stroke, in two weeks. We therefore suggested to follow in the footsteps of the 1978 Camp David summit – namely, that we first draft a framework agreement. We told the Palestinians explicitly that the particulars would not be deter-mined in advance but by negotiations. Regardless of whether the framework document would consist of eight, eighteen or eighty pages, what mattered was that it would cover the essential issues, those on which we could agree at that point. This would make it possible to fill it later with agreed details, even if it took a whole year to formulate them. In the process with Egypt it also took a half-year after the Camp David summit of 1978 to translate the framework accord into a detailed peace treaty, and another three years to implement it.

Moreover, when we reached the core issue of Jerusalem, the Americans at some point proposed deferring the discussions on it by two years or, alter-natively, deferring discussions on the Holy Basin by five years. It was not an easy decision for us to make, since for Israel it meant that despite all the concessions we would have made, the Palestinians could still legitimately bring up claims about Jerusalem, and we would have to re-open the existing agreements. And in spite of that, out of a historic sense of responsibility, we agreed to accept this plan as a basis for negotiations, provided that the Palestinians would agree as well. Do you know what they said? They said they did not like it. When the Americans asked them why, they pointed to the precedent of the Pakistan–India conflict, where in 1947 the two sides agreed to leave the Kashmir issue open for another two years. Since then, three wars have been fought and hundreds of thousands of people killed, both countries acquired nuclear bombs, and Kashmir is still an open issue. That is what the Palestinians said. This gives us some food for thought about the difference between a gradualist approach and a strategy of decisive moves to resolve all the issues in one go.

The sixth myth is the claim that "what Barak was proposing to the Palestinians amounted to just another Bantustan." That is absolutely baseless. A map that includes more than 90% of the West Bank and 100% of the Gaza Strip cannot possibly be seen as a Bantustan. True, these two areas are not contiguous, but we searched for ways to solve this, the construction of an overpass or some other plan. The Palestinians did not have to approve the demarcation lines that we proposed, and this was perfectly legitimate, but if so they should have come to the negotiating table and declared at least acceptance of the proposal as a basis for negotiations, bringing up their reservations. They could have said, for example, "We do not want the Ariel enclave to extend all the way out here; instead we want the line to be demarcated over there," and so on. That would be a legitimate debate. If we had differences, we could discuss them. Had Arafat agreed to negotiate, Clinton would not have been furious at him and would not have blamed him even if ultimately the negotiations failed. Such failure to reach an agreement may be regrettable, but it is legitimate.

The seventh myth is that "Barak wanted to discuss everything right there and then." I have already explained why this was not true.

The eighth myth is that "Barak was not talking with Arafat." Actually he did, quite a lot in fact. Precisely because I had talked with him so much I knew, to my chagrin, that at Camp David no amount of talking would have helped. Actually, it might have even been harmful – creating another myth to the effect that the summit failed because of what happened at that meeting. In fact, we did meet for two hours socially, with Abu Mazen also participating, eating cookies and baklava, but admittedly this was not much. We did not meet to talk about substance. Why? The reason was that to do this, both leaders must be prepared to discuss substantive matters and Arafat was not. Arafat had no appetite either for small talk or for serious discussion about matters of substance. It simply was not easy to negotiate with him directly. I was waiting to see whether there was any breakthrough, and in that case, I thought, when the time comes for the leaders to make final decisions, I would be there, ready and willing to meet the Palestinian leader face-to-face.

Moreover, in retrospect, did Begin and Sadat do much person-to-person talking at the first Camp David summit? Did Nixon talk with Giap? Did De Gaulle talk with Ben Bella? Did the fact that such leaders did not communicate much ever come in the way of resolving historic conflicts between nations? Is this the decisive factor? Where there is a will and a political leadership, there is a way. When they are lacking, things just do not happen. That is the basic fact. The niceties are no more than marginal.

The ninth myth concerns the failure to withdraw from the villages of Abu Dis and Azariya. These were supposed to be confidence-building measures, and needed to be true to their name. On the same day that I asked the Knesset to approve the handover of these villages to the Palestinians – which many in the Knesset fiercely opposed, as some of you remember and others can surely imagine – the first shots of the *Nakba*-day were fired. Not the day before, but on that very same day. One day earlier we had submitted the bill to the Knesset to give members an opportunity to review it. When the discussion of the bill was held in the Knesset, I stood on the podium exercising my authority not just as prime minister but also as a former Chief of Staff with professional expertise in military matters. I said to the Knesset, "Don't tell me about Palestinian shootings, I shall deal with them, I am also the defense minister. From you I demand an approval of the bill." However, as I was getting the Knesset to approve these confidence-building measures, Musa Arafat and his unit, as well as members of other Palestinian security forces, started firing at Israeli soldiers. That evening I said to Clinton, "Since building trust is what we are talking about, this was broken today, and until I am convinced that today's events will not recur, I will not hand over Abu Dis and Azariya, even though I have the approval of the Knesset to do so."

I remember that as Chief of Staff I had to explain why we were giving the Palestinians guns. We said that without them they would be unable to eradicate terror. The right-wing and some of the settlers warned us that at the moment of truth the Palestinians would be turning these guns at us. Indeed, the Palestinian guns that we allowed them to obtain have become the litmus test for the sincerity of the Palestinian Authority. We can argue about the militias that the Authority hardly controls, but if the forces of the Authority itself initiate violence, the confidence-building measures collapse.

Of all the trends in the public debate in Israel, my least favorite is that which I dub "sophists" – those who, no matter what happens, always say that if the opposite had been done, things would have been better. Life is nothing but a wide range of possibilities. In real life, each and every one of us, leaders included, are continually making choices, always leaving endless possibilities untried. This opens a wide scope for complaint: on the individual level, one can say, "If only I had been there, everything would have been different"; or on the collective level, "If only the government had done things differently, everything would have been better." These complaints are useless.

The tenth myth is that of the percentage game. The critics ask, "How is it that Barak had originally spoke of 75% of the Territories, then 80%, and at Camp David he said 89% and then 91%? How do you expect the

Palestinians to accept Israeli offers if they see that as time goes by the offers tendered to them only improve?" I know these critics. Had I proposed 93% from the start, they would have accused me of not understanding the norms of bargaining in the Middle East where a deal always begins with offers that are not taken seriously. We opted for the method that in my mind was the most effective.

The eleventh myth concerns Jerusalem. I am being asked, "Why did you bring it up so suddenly at the end, without proper preparations on the Israeli side?" First of all, I did prepare myself on this issue, and very thoroughly. I had spoken with every expert who had ever dealt with Jerusalem, and read the works of those whom I had not consulted directly. Second, I felt that the issue of Jerusalem should not be brought up at the beginning of the meetings because then the whole summit could collapse. Imagine if we were to have raised this issue at an early stage and the talks had ended abruptly, then the very same people would have accused me of being rash. They would have said, "Didn't you realize that once Jerusalem was on the table everything would collapse?"

The twelfth myth is that of the settlements: Why did we continue construction there? A few days after I became prime minister, I met with Arafat and informed him that my cabinet had decided not to build any more settlements in the West Bank. I also told him that we had decided to dismantle all unauthorized settlements – not as a gesture to the Palestinians but because we have a law-abiding administration. However, as such, the administration must honor contracts that were already underway, signed and approved by our predecessors. Most of them were in large towns such as Ma'ale Adumim and Givat Ze'ev, and the remainder inside existing settlements. I told him that I understood what the Palestinians must be feeling when they look at all the construction that has taken place around them over the years and at all the settlers who have moved to the Territories, which – as one of the Palestinian delegates had put it – created facts on the ground that changed the situation. However, I said, this is not the time to raise the issue. We now have an exceptional opportunity to end the conflict in a year and a half, while Clinton is still in the White House, and we should focus on that.

I said to Arafat, "In Israel it takes more than a year and a half to build a house. In other words, no new houses on top of those you see now will be finished before we sign an agreement." I said to him, "If we sign an agreement and a specific neighborhood or particular home eventually end up in a Palestinian area – and this may happen with entire settlements – you will be able to use those facilities to house relocated refugees, or you may do with them as you please. If other settlements end up in Israeli-controlled areas, according to a mutual agreement, what difference does it make to you that construction there is underway?" And so, the Palestinian argument about construction, which had previously made some sense, lost much of its weight when there was a serious intention to conclude a comprehensive peace within a year and a half.

Those critics who have said that I was under the pressure of time are wrong, rest assured that I was not. The only time element that I did have to take into account was the approaching end of Clinton's term. He had invested seven years in attempts to broker a solution to our conflict and the next president would require a year and a half just to study it. Who could know if by then we would not find ourselves in the middle of a tragic blood-bath? The need to save lives was the only pressure I felt.

Before I conclude, I would like to underscore two additional important matters. First, Lebanon. We hear people arguing that terror was enhanced by our withdrawal from Lebanon. In my mind, this is nonsense. I remember how as Chief of Staff during Rabin's term, exactly ten years ago, I was watching burned-out buses that looked exactly like the burned-out buses we see today, with dozens of bodies scattered around the wreckage. And at the time we were nowhere near withdrawal from Lebanon. So how can one argue that the pullout is to be blamed for terror? I remember a very serious wave of terror during the term of Shimon Peres in which one hundred people were killed, while we were still present in Lebanon. So what has this got to do with the withdrawal? I also recall a terrible suicide bombing in the pedestrian mall in Jerusalem, another one at the market in Jerusalem and another at the Apropos Café in Tel Aviv – all during Netanyahu's term. Palestinian terror killed 59 Israelis during those years, and we were still in Lebanon. And in addition we had to bury 140 dead who were killed in Lebanon, including 73 in a helicopter crash.

When we went into Lebanon in 1982 – I was already a general then – the locals threw rice at us as a sign of welcome. Amal existed, but Hizballah was not even in the making. Hizballah emerged because of our presence in Lebanon, not because of our withdrawal. I have already said that even back then I believed that the security zone should have been organized in a completely different way. There is a big difference between Lebanon and the Territories, because we have no claim to any part of Lebanese land. Yet, the way we chose to deploy there was as though it was part of the Territories made no sense. The Palestinians know that we have a claim to part of the Territories, and they use this claim as justification for their terrorism, unre-lated to Lebanon. For us, of course, there is no reason to accept this justification: it is a bogus rationale for terrorism that cannot be condoned.

Moreover, had we stayed in Lebanon, during Operation Defensive Shield in April 2002, we would have had to deal with Katyusha rockets fired from Lebanon at Migdal Ha'emek and Zichron Ya'akov. Those rockets were already in Hizballah's hands and were not acquired after the withdrawal, as some of the critics allege. Had we stayed in Lebanon, those "sophists" would have said that we were out of our minds to be involved in two fronts simultaneously, when there was nothing to keep us there.

Second, Taba. No negotiations were conducted at Taba. What was the situation? Elections were about to take place. There were no negotiating teams. I did not agree to hold a plenary meeting. I did not athorize meetings between the delegations. I did not allow minutes to be taken. I did not allow the Americans to be brought into the room. What I did allow was for a group of our leaders to meet with a group of Palestinians leaders for unofficial talks, with the sole purpose of checking whether there would be any room for discussion after the elections. We were trying to find out whether Arafat had had a last-minute change of heart. Aided by several Israelis, the European observer Miguel Moratinos fabricated the so-called "Taba Understandings." As Israel's prime minister at the time, I suppose I would have been familiar with any such understandings, had any been reached. Since I am not, I can assure you that no such understandings ever existed.

Clinton's Parameters are very good as a basis for final status talks, but cannot replace what we did at Camp David. However, we never even got to the stage where we could discuss these parameters. They were presented to both sides. We were prepared, albeit with a heavy heart, to accept them as a basis for further negotiations. The Palestinians, on the other hand, were not. Hence, as previously agreed, the parameters melted away. We do not delude ourselves into thinking that these parameters have been forgotten, but as a binding document it did become void, from the moment that the Palestinians rejected them.

Finally, I would like to share with you a short description of a meeting held at the Oslo residence of Israel's Ambassador to Norway, the late Joseph Harmelin, just less than one year before the Camp David summit. Attending were Arafat, Abu Mazen, Abu Ala, Clinton and some of his team. It was the sixth anniversary of the Oslo Accords. I was sitting beside Arafat, and the atmosphere was strained. Nevertheless, we fondly remembered the late Yitzhak Rabin. I said to Arafat:

Mr. Chairman, we may be dealing with the most complicated conflict on earth, but we can't look to the heavens for a solution. This conflict can only be resolved by human beings, on this earth, and these human beings are you and me. The decisions that must be made are not easy for either of us, but if we do not have the courage to make them, we will be burying thousands of people. Moreover, they will have died needlessly, since either we ourselves, or our successors, will eventually reach the very same situation and be resolving the very same problems . . . Mr. Chairman, the toughest part of the decisions you will have to make will be those that will compel you to face not me but your own people. And the toughest decisions I will have to make will be done not facing you but facing my people. I am prepared to make these decisions; I understand what they involve. But there will be no agreement unless you too are prepared to make these decisions on behalf of the Palestinian people.

Harmelin's apartment was on the fifth floor, and we were sitting right across from the window. I said to Arafat, "Try to see our situation in these terms. Imagine that we are standing on the ledge of the window and both of us must jump. We have small parachutes; your hand is on mine and mine is on yours, and if we don't jump, innocent people now walking the streets of Gaza, Ramallah, Hebron, Tel Aviv and Jerusalem will die."

Although Arafat nodded his head with a solemn look and declared that yes, he understood, Rabin was his friend, he had promised him to pursue peace, and would do whatever it takes – in fact he never was ready to take serious, responsible action in the spirit of what was said in that room.

I am often asked how, looking back, I see the overall picture of what happened. Some people ask me why I do not get up and confess to all of my many mistakes and get that load off my chest. Let me answer by concluding with a few words that Winston Churchill said in Parliament on November 12, 1940, only a year into World War II, after ten years in which Churchill had had no contact whatsoever with day-to-day British politics:

It is not given to human beings, happily for them, for otherwise life would be intolerable, to foresee or to predict to any large extent the unfolding course of events. In one phase men seem to have been right, in another they seem to have been wrong. Then again, a few years later, when the perspective of time has lengthened, all stands in a different setting. There is a new proportion. There is another scale of values. History, with its flickering lamp, stumbles along the trail of the past, trying to reconstruct its scenes, to revive its echoes, and kindle with pale gleams the passion of former days. What is the worth of all this? The only guide to a man is his conscience; the only shield to his memory is the rectitude and sincerity of his actions. It is very imprudent to walk through life without this shield, because we are so often mocked by the failure of our hopes and the upsetting of our calculations; but with this shield, however the Fates may play, we march always in the ranks of honor.

## Remarks during the Discussion

I was asked whether, if I were prime minister today, I would oppose the plan known as the "Road Map to Peace." Considering my opposition to the creation of an independent Palestinian state with provisional borders, my response is that although the Road Map is very important, it contains contradictions whose resolutions depend on conditions and outcomes. If the Palestinians do not implement all the reforms that Bush has called for, I think Israel must not make even the slightest gesture, except for dismantling unauthorized settlements and taking humanitarian steps to make life for Palestinian civilians easier. However, if the Palestinians do implement these reforms, there is no reason to wait and let a handful of extremists torpedo negotiations again. We should have the responsibility and courage to go ahead and resolve our problems. Time will not make it any easier, only harder.

In this context I feel that our leadership was wrong not to inquire as to the meaning of "statehood with provisional borders." Creating such a state would be a mistake. In this I agree with (Transport Minister Avigdor) Lieberman and Netanyahu that if this is the case it would have been even better to have advanced directly to negotiations. This kind of statehood simply means that you are handing over your assets to the other side, because the only provisional element in the so-called provisional state is the borders, and in the matter of borders, the international community fully supports the Palestinians. A state, even with provisional borders, has inherent rights. It does not have to ask for permission to do anything. You cannot enter with your forces the major cities of such a state – even if its borders have not yet been finalized – in order to respond to terrorist attacks that were carried out against you, because this would be regarded as no less than an invasion. There is, therefore, a catch in this kind of statehood. Otherwise, the Road Map as a whole is very important, and we must do everything to guarantee its success. Following the UN resolution in 1947, Ben-Gurion was ready to accept partition, painful as it was. Of course there are always those who say that it was not a big concession because he knew for a fact that there would be a war that would change the map. No one can know in hindsight what really was in Ben-Gurion's mind, but there is no doubt he had made the right move for the State of Israel that was soon to be born.

I have been asked why I waited for six months to say out loud that no agreement could be reached with Arafat, instead of saying so immediately when I had realized this, in July 2000? And why did I send Sher, Ben-Ami and Beilin to post-Camp David talks with the Palestinians, if this was my evaluation? Well, in statesmanship it is not enough that you are convinced, because it is not a personal process that is at stake. In statesmanship you are dealing with the international arena. Because of the reasons I enumerated earlier, the State of Israel must hold the moral high ground internationally and remain united from within. The prime minister's conviction alone is therefore not enough.

As prime minister, I never concealed the fact that I had found Arafat an "unsuitable partner at this time," as I phrased it. I realized that if we voluntarily dropped out of the Camp David process before the end of Clinton's term, within a few weeks we would find ourselves isolated in the international community, and the world would blame us for the collapse of the talks instead of seeing that justice was on our side, as it really was, and pointing the finger at Arafat. By consenting to further talks with the Palestinians we convinced important segments of the international community to acknowledge that the decisions we took were legitimate decisions made by a country pursuing its responsibility and its rights.

If we had not delayed our decision to abandon the talks, within a few weeks we would have found ourselves inundated by criticism from the members of what we now call the Quartet (the US, Russia, the EU, and the UN) and, possibly, even from members of the Clinton administration. They would have charged that my decision was motivated by personal political survivalism, since I was trying at that time to set up a national-unity government. They would have argued that although a democratically-elected leader is entitled to use his discretion, Israel is responsible for the decisions that its leader makes. Some would have even said that Barak is nothing but a megalomaniac: he gave a two-week shot at resolving a 100-year conflict, he failed, and decided he had had enough. This is no way for a responsible leadership to conduct itself, they would have said. Therefore, as hard as it was, in the few months until the end of Clinton's term, we had no choice but to continue negotiating Clinton's Parameters. I did not like that choice, but there was no other.

Why did we not put these parameters to a cabinet vote? Had we done so and they had remained pending, it would have appeared as though Israel had rejected them. If Israel had been seen as rejectionist when the *intifada* started, the outcome would have been the situation I described earlier: burying our dead, ostracized by the international community and torn from within.

Some may question how I can be so sure that this would have been the outcome. Suffice it to point out how effective the "revisionists" – including those who ask these questions – have been at convincing themselves, and quite a few others as well, in the aftermath of the Clinton Parameters and Taba, that their approach was correct. The same is true of the right-wing. I used to say to Sharon, "It's no good; there will always be some right-wing radical who will say to you, 'if you had only done this one little thing, everything would have worked out just as we wanted.'" Unfortunately, I had a similar experience with the Israeli Left and the pro-Palestinians in international diplomacy. So we had to continue. No matter what we did, as long as Clinton was in office, it could always be claimed that there was just that one more thing that could still be done to make everything fall into place. Therefore, at some point, my common sense told me that although our efforts would all be in vain, we could not afford, because of the overall considerations, to let it look as though Israel were responsible for the discontinuation of the process before the end of Clinton's term.

It was mentioned that Arafat proposed allowing 150,000 refugees to come to Israel every year, for a total of 1.5 million over 10 years. Well, I do not recall ever hearing these figures or any such demand made by Arafat. To be sure, the Palestinian Right of Return was one of the main causes for the failure of the Camp David summit. Once we understood that Arafat was not willing to give up the Palestinian insistence on letting refugees return to sovereign Israeli territory – something we realized at Camp David and Yossi Sarid later realized at Taba – we told Clinton and Arafat that although we would be willing, like previous Israeli governments, to accept thousands of Palestinian refugees under the humanitarian umbrella of family reunification, we could not accept Arafat's version of return to Israel. Neither I nor any other Israeli prime minister would be ready to take in a single refugee based on the political principle of the Right of Return, because that would undermine Israel's *raison d'être*.

I was asked why we did not put the talks on hold three months before they ended in failure and hold a referendum about an agreement, since it was clear that once the talks had ended, we would lose both public support for the process and the elections. Well, we discussed this question many times. It was clear that in order to survive, the government could have followed a different course of action; however, such measures would have spelled great danger for vital Israeli interests. We could have saved our own skins at the cost of a national tragedy. The choice was explicitly discussed: what should we favor – politics or history? I am proud that our decision – which we made consciously, being aware of the obvious personal price we would have to pay – was that history means more than politics.

I was asked how could I compare the decisions that President Sadat and King Hussein had to make for peace to the fateful decisions and painful concessions that Arafat had to make, which in his case amounted to giving up core national interests. I think that the person who asked me the question and I are in agreement. Indeed, the decision with which Arafat was faced was, in essence, more difficult than those faced by Sadat or Hussein. Still, it was a decision without which there could be no peace. What I had told him face-to-face in Oslo still holds true, "There is no one else who can make this decision, and we cannot look to the heavens for a solution. This is a decision that only leaders can make, and we are those leaders. We are fully responsible. If we do not make this decision, we will both be burying our dead."

I was asked how we imagined making such a quantum leap to a comprehensive agreement at Camp David, after the joint Israeli–Palestinian team, which had been discussing the issues of the political framework for several weeks before Camp David, had finished its work without making progress on the pivotal issues of security, refugees and settlements and without even addressing the issue of Jerusalem. My answer is that I had no way of telling how things would evolve. I am a realist, and the only thing I knew was that if we did nothing, nothing would change. I calculated that Israel could not afford the luxury of standing passively without making a genuine attempt to achieve peace. Suppose we had reached an agreement, or even just partial agreement on two or three issues, this would still have been a good outcome. The actual outcome, which God already knew but we were yet to learn, was unforeseen. Our decision should be seen in the proper context. We were facing the threat of being obliged to hand over assets in line with international resolutions, receive nothing in return and find ourselves in a tragic situation. It was our duty to actively prevent tragedy, and attempt to negotiate even when we did not know the ensuing results. I never deluded myself that a successful outcome was assured, and tried not to delude the Israeli public either.

One of the lessons I learned at Camp David was that in the future the public should perhaps be better informed of risks and pitfalls. But there is a problem here: had I shared my doubts with the public before Camp David, present-day "sophists" would have said that I was deliberately preparing the ground for failure.

In spite of the failure of the back-channel preparatory talks, I decided that we must assume full responsibility and move ahead with the summit, not letting that failure deter us. Who knows why those back-channel talks failed? Perhaps Arafat was holding his cards close to his chest and did not want to reveal his real positions beforehand. Perhaps he was unwilling to delegate authority to the participants in the preparatory talks, to such persons as Abu Mazen and Abu Ala. Or perhaps these individuals were unwilling to assume responsibility because they were afraid that Arafat would abandon them and withdraw his backing. We had to find out for ourselves.

And what did we have to lose? Once we understood that a catastrophe was imminent, that two forces were moving toward each other on a collision course, we were determined that nothing should stop us. There was nothing to lose by making a last-ditch attempt to save the situation, even if propaganda and superficiality sometimes make it appear like the opposite. The collision was bound to happen anyway, it was not the result of trying to *prevent* the collision. This is why we exercised responsibility throughout.

We did not encourage illusions. We tried to explain to the Israeli public, through journalists who were asking us about the chances of reaching a peace agreement, that the chances were only fifty-fifty. That was my answer to them not because there was something I knew that others did not, but simply because common sense held that there were two possibilities: the process would either succeed or fail, and I really did not know which one would it be. The only thing I knew for sure was that it was our duty to try. I used to say to the media, and through them to the public, "Lower your expectations, lower your expectations." However, when the aim is to change the reality that has prevailed in the last hundred years, the possibility of failure should not deter leaders from doing what they think is right. Our true responsibility and accountability is to the public. I was driving through Israel's streets and those of the Palestinian Authority, observing innocent people and their families, living their lives and dreaming their dreams, not knowing – still not knowing – that they might die because irresponsible leaders were unable to make tough decisions.

# The Barak Version:
## *The Critics*

RON PUNDIK

# The 1967 Lines Should Have Been the Basis for Negotiations

I THINK THE COMMENTS MADE BY FORMER PRIME MINISTER Ehud Barak deserve a response, especially in the context of what I would like to focus on: the issue of territory and the "percentage game."

It seems to me that at the Camp David summit, Barak was looking for his equivalent. He wanted to find a "Barak-compatible" to negotiate with, but found the exact opposite – Yasser Arafat. Barak is a man of details, while Arafat only sees the bigger picture. Barak talks in specific terms, Arafat makes generalizations and talks about symbols and gestures. Barak was the principal negotiator on behalf of the State of Israel, while Arafat always wanted others to do the negotiating for him. This interface was very charged to begin with, and a conflict was almost unavoidable. Preparations should have been made to soften the impact of this polarity and circumvent such conflict, but they were not.

Barak ignores these facts. He dismissed the need for personal dialogue and disregarded the recommendations to negotiate with Arafat face-to-face. To this day he believes that letting the other leader feel he is respected hardly plays any role in negotiations.

Apart from that, one of the main problems was that the preparations for the summit, which the Israelis perceived as an all-or-nothing game, were very rudimentary and completely insufficient, especially on the Israeli side but also on the Palestinian one. Tragically, the Americans as well came almost empty-handed.

In order to create a media spin and make the public believe that the Palestinians were entirely to blame – thus substantiating the Israeli explanation for the roots of the *intifada* and the escalating violence – Barak has been consciously contradicting himself and thus confusing his Israeli audience. He now portrays Arafat as though he had planned the violent clash from the outset and as though his strategic objective has been to gradually do away with the State of Israel. Moreover, according to Barak, as long as Arafat "had even a grain of influence on the ground," no agreement could be reached. But this unequivocal statement does not jell with the fact that after the summit, when ostensibly Barak had already realized "the truth about Arafat," Barak still instructed his chief negotiator, Gilead Sher, to continue communicating with the Palestinian delegation for several months in dozens of secret meetings. There is no way to reconcile the statements he now makes in retrospect with the fact that he himself enabled, and some even say instructed, his people in those meetings to offer the Palestinians much more generous terms than those offered at Camp David. The truth is that from the day after Camp David up until the Taba talks, Barak tried everything he possibly could to reach a settlement with the very same leader whom he now says had already been "diagnosed" as an enemy of peace.

An examination of the negotiations over the issues of territory, what I call the "percentage game," makes the problem with Barak's *ex post facto* interpretation of the facts even more obvious. His statement that the Israeli offer at Camp David was the final one and that when the Palestinians rejected it, this revealed the true face of Arafat and proved he did not genuinely want peace, is incongruous with the progress of negotiations before and during the Taba talks. As mentioned, after the summit at Camp David, the Israeli cabinet, with partial backing from Washington, blamed the Palestinians for the failure of the talks, claiming that they had rejected Israel's territorial offer. At the same time, Israel continued to conduct secret negotiations with Arafat's representatives. For these talks, Barak sent at first his personal envoy Gilead Sher, then his foreign minister Shlomo Ben-Ami, and finally an official Israeli delegation with senior ministers and expert negotiators equipped with maps and other paraphernalia. Today, in hindsight, Barak argues that all of this was designed to prove beyond doubt that there was no real partner on the other side. But in real time, Israel continued to negotiate with the Palestinians for six months, discussing new proposals and thus proving to the Palestinians that they were right to be entrenched in their positions at Camp David and that Israel's so-called final offer was not final at all. Barak allowed his representatives to revise the "generous" offer of Camp David, which included an annexation of 11% of the Territories, and the American plan offered at Camp David, which spoke of Israel annexing 9%. In the post-summit talks they agreed to reduce the figure to an annexation of 6% and a leasing of another 2% for a limited term.

Moreover, various sources in the negotiating teams indicate that at Taba, Mohammed Dahlan received an offer – although not in writing – that Israel would make do with an annexation of 4–5%, and on top of that give the Palestinians an area inside the Green Line that equals the size of 2% of the Territories. Incidentally, every percentage point equals approximately 55 square kilometers.

These proposals that Israel eventually made could have served as a serious basis for the permanent status agreement. But the talks at Taba were discontinued, and not because the delegations chose to stop them, or because of an impasse reached in the discussion of major issues – Jerusalem or territory. Rather, they were terminated because the parties were forced to put them on hold due to the elections in Israel. At Taba, the parties continually narrowed the gaps between them on all fronts. For example, the drafts pertaining to territory included an Israeli consent that the border between Israel and Palestine would be "based on the line of June 4, 1967." In answer to a question from an Israeli journalist as to whether peace was really within reach at any time, Dahlan said, "Only at Taba." Barak's statement to the effect that no negotiations took place at Taba and that all he did was just send a ministerial delegation to see for itself that there was no one to talk to, thus seems tainted by ulterior motives. Responding to Barak's statements, Yossi Beilin wrote that at Taba the differences between the parties on all the permanent status issues were substantially narrowed. Both parties announced officially that an agreement could be reached within a relatively short time. It was agreed that Barak would meet with Arafat even before the elections and ratify the agreements reached that week at Taba. It was further agreed that immediately after the elections the delegations would meet again to sign the framework agreement.

The conclusion is simple. If the full implementation of Security Council Resolution 242 is the fair basis for a permanent status agreement, Israel's territorial proposal at Camp David was not generous at all. It was only generous compared to the traditional position of Israel's right-wing, which never seriously wanted peace, or to Barak's opening position in the talks which, as even he himself subsequently realized, was unrealistic. It now transpires that Israel's approach to the negotiations on permanent status was based on a strategic miscalculation. In my opinion, it should not be attributed to reluctance to reach an agreement, unfairness or malice. Rather the sources of this miscalculation were the following: (a) a failure to understand the reality of the negotiations; (b) insufficient knowledge of the details and inadequate preparation; (c) a condescending attitude toward the Palestinians; and (d) a notion of asymmetry of power that set the tone of the talks with the Palestinians. Only an Israeli proposal based from the outset on 100% of the Territories could have been seen as truly generous. Israeli politicians can go on misrepresenting the facts and claiming that Israel had offered the Palestinians 97% of the territory and another 3% in a land swap, but even a novice historian can easily establish that this was not the way it happened.

The "percentage game" is an Israeli manipulation. Some people use this data knowingly as a political tool, while others rely on it simply because they are unaware of the true facts and have bought the media spin that followed the summit.

At the same time, I have serious reservations about the Palestinian policies, the way the Palestinians conducted themselves at Camp David, and the dynamics within their negotiating teams. They were clumsy and sometimes even foolish, and every now and then they shot themselves in the foot, as though it were not their own future that they were discussing. But their shortcomings did not entitle the Israelis to exploit the situation and push the process off a cliff.

Israel had two choices when it entered the negotiations after Barak was elected. One was to say that UN Security Council Resolution 242 does not apply to the West Bank and Gaza (although it is mentioned in the Oslo Accords and in all the documents that Israel subsequently signed with the Palestinians). Israel, according to this choice, would consider the West Bank and the Gaza Strip to be an area under dispute, which should be divided – in agreement – between the Israelis and the Palestinians. The second option was to recognize that the negotiations with the Palestinians were not conducted in a vacuum. They emerged from developments that had taken place since the beginning of the Middle East peace process, or, to be more precise, since 1978, when Menachem Begin signed the Camp David Accords. These developments required the application of Resolution 242 and the acceptance of the borders of June 4, 1967 as the basis for the territorial settlement between the two sides, subject to negotiated arrangements that, among other things, would guarantee Israel's vital security needs.

Israel should have said from the outset that if an agreement were reached, it would include the establishment of a Palestinian state. Instead, the Israelis chose to hide behind such terms as "a political entity." Barak himself used this term in the beginning of the talks, which only made the Palestinians feel that Israel did not mean statehood and did not genuinely wish to reach a settlement of the dispute. Israel should have said from the outset that a Palestinian state would be established, based on the borders of 1967 (with the necessary mutual adjustments), because Israel perceives the Palestinians as rightful partners for peace, just like the Egyptians, Jordanians, Syrians and Lebanese.

Barak's misguided strategy set the ground for the failure of the talks. He should have put on the table the principles for a solution – especially regarding the issues of self-determination and territory – at the very first stages of the talks. This would have motivated the Palestinians to continue the negotiations vigorously and enabled their leaders to tell their people – who were suffering under the yoke of the occupation – that there was a light at the end of the tunnel. Instead, Barak chose the first option. He endorsed the interpretation of the right-leaning Attorney-General, who said that Resolution 242 does not apply to the West Bank and the Gaza Strip, since they do not constitute territories under occupation, but are only territories under dispute. Israel's opening offer was withdrawal from most of the Gaza Strip and from 55%–60% of the West Bank. Barak procrastinated and used the bargaining techniques of an oriental bazaar. Moreover, for many months after the talks began, the prime minister strictly forbade his negotiators, some of whom opposed this policy, to talk about a Palestinian state and only permitted them to mention an "entity."

Abu Mazen, the Palestinian architect of the Oslo Accords who wanted to lead the final status negotiations, personally advised Barak to declare from the outset his endorsement of the principles involved in the second option, namely the principles of 242. Had Israel agreed, this would have turned Abu Mazen into a strategic partner who could have pushed the negotiations ahead, as he had done previously with great success when he talked Arafat and his other colleagues into accepting the Oslo Accords. (Professor Nusseibeh has even dubbed the Oslo process and the permanent status negotiations "Abu Mazen's peace project".) This is also how Abu Ala, the engine and the "fixer" in all the negotiations between Israel and the Palestinians, understood the situation. In an interview with *Ma'ariv* on October 28, 2001, just a little more than a year after the Camp David summit, he said:

> We have agreed to settle for the borders of 1967. To us this means that we get to keep only 22% of the historic land of Palestine and you hold on to all the rest. We have recognized Israel and agreed to its demands for secure borders, security arrangements and cooperation and coordination in security matters. You did not consider this to be a concession on our part. As far as you are concerned, it is all yours, as though we never existed. You pocketed this incredible historical concession and made more demands. You wanted massive settlement blocs that would have turned us into a state of cantons, with no access anywhere. This is a situation in which no one would agree to live. We agreed to border adjustments, subject to land swaps. You did not make any concessions, while we accepted border adjustments on both sides, as land swaps.

Barak refused to accept this approach, hoping that his strategy would give Israel control over more land without any need for reciprocal territorial concessions. He was also unnecessarily apprehensive about showing his cards too soon. According to Shlomo Ben-Ami, Barak was convinced that his initial first map – an expansion of Yigal Allon's plan that offered the Palestinians around 66% of the Territories – "made perfect sense," and he tried to persuade Ben-Ami that anyone who sees it will understand that this plan is an absolutely reasonable offer. Ben-Ami says that Barak's comment – "look, this is a state" – reflected a well-intentioned yet a patronizing and wishful-thinking attitude. The Israeli negotiators did not realize that if no principles and guidelines were laid down, then no agreement would be reached, whereas a clear statement of such principles and guidelines could motivate the Palestinians to work hard for an agreement; it would also have strengthened the pragmatists, who until this day maintain that a permanent status agreement with Israel is achievable. The tragic outcome was that when Barak eventually disclosed his relatively moderate position toward the end of the talks, it was too late, for he had already lost credibility. Moreover, by failing to define basic principles and by conducting the bargaining the way he did, he weakened Israel's standing and was repeatedly forced to concede some of his opening positions without getting anything in return.

Contrary to the perceptions that have now taken root due to the Israeli spin, the Palestinians actually did display during the negotiations understanding for Israel's needs and interests. Their condition was, however, that these needs would only be met as part of a just agreement based on a deal involving 100% of the territory, including land swaps.

One such crucial interest was that concerning the settlements. Personally, I believe that the Israeli settlements in the Territories are a disaster for Israel and compromise its vital and existential interests. Continuation of the settlement activities might lead Israel to a point where a "surgery" separating areas inhabited by the Israelis and Palestinians would no longer be possible. There would be no choice but to annex the Territories *en bloc*, and this would lead within a very short time to a situation in which an Arab majority will be living under a Jewish apartheid regime. However, as long as it is still possible to reach an arrangement that would keep those settlements that are close to the Green Line intact, with minimal border adjustments and without undermining the viability of the Palestinian state, the principles of *realpolitik* should be heeded. The fact that more than 400,000 Israelis live outside of the Green Line, including 200,000 in the West Bank and Gaza and 200,000 in East Jerusalem, cannot be ignored. The Palestinians are aware that it is unrealistic to demand that Israel disregards this reality and withdraws to the exact borders of 1967, which is why they were prepared to discuss the annexation of some of the settlements, subject to land swaps.

Therefore the Israelis should have said to the Palestinians, let us discuss these interests and find a way to safeguard at least most of them. But Barak adopted a different approach. In his initial proposal to the Palestinians –

submitted by Oded Eran in the form of the so-called "schematic map" – he went as far as offering them less than 60% of the West Bank. Even if he thought that starting with such a low figure was a good bargaining gambit (which was a mistake by itself), and even though subsequently, at Camp David, he raised the offer to much higher percentages, it still reflected his basic misunderstanding of the situation. Barak is a courageous and determined man who has Israel's best interest in mind, but it was his genuinely mistaken perception of the meaning of the 1967 lines that led him to believe that such a proposal could serve as a basis for negotiations. When the Palestinians ignored this offer, he could not understand why. Barak never realized that what he was offering the Palestinians was not much short of an insult.

Barak refused to accept the fact that the Land of Israel/Palestine is the subject of a historic dispute between two legitimate national movements – the Zionist movement and the Palestinian national movement – each of them believing that it is rightfully entitled to the entire country. Barak also dismissed the argument that from the Palestinian perspective, they had already made the biggest historical concession when they accepted the principle of partition and agreed to acknowledge the State of Israel not on the basis of the partition plan of 1947 but on Resolution 242 and the borders of June 4, 1967. These borders give the Palestinians only 22% of the land between the Jordan River and the Mediterranean Sea. Granted, Palestinian ideology does not recognize the legitimacy of Zionism as an ideology, nor does it endorse the way in which Zionism staked its claim. Palestinians accept the presence of Israel in this region primarily as a *fait accompli*, and not on the basis of Zionist tenets. This acceptance was prompted mainly by Israel's strength, the backing it has received from the US and the international community, and the ethical norms it upheld since 1948 – which are gradually eroding in the course of the occupation. Deep down inside, many of them would have preferred not to have the Israelis around, just as many Israelis would have preferred not to have the Palestinians around. But ever since the Oslo Accords, the Palestinians have adopted a "Ben-Gurionist" way of thinking. This time around, it was they who applied *realpolitik* and pragmatism, not the Israelis. This time it was Arafat who said it would be better to receive less but get started on the historic road to statehood. He understood that claiming the whole territory was not realistic and the best thing for the Palestinian people at this point would be to enter negotiations and make a historic concession that would get them sovereignty, even if only over 22% of British-Mandated Palestine west of the Jordan River.

This was how the Palestinians began the territorial negotiations. However, Ehud Barak's response sounded to the Palestinians as though he was saying, "Twenty-two percent? No way, you can make do with half of that; that's a state too." To Barak, enclaves under dubious sovereignty connected by bridges and tunnels, with fingers of Israeli territory criss-crossing the West Bank, with Kiryat Arba, Beit El, Ofra and Tapuah deep inside the Palestinian territory and with the area east of Jerusalem toward Jericho in Israeli hands, constituted a reasonable offer.

One of the allegations made against the Palestinians was that they were extremely rigid in the territorial negotiations. It seems, however, that Israel's negotiating strategy left them no choice. For example, when the Israelis started their negotiations, as mentioned above, with the far-reaching suggestion of annexing more than 40% of the West Bank, the Palestinians responded with a demand for 100% of the territory. When Israel became more flexible and offered the Palestinians higher percentages of the territory, the Palestinians did not budge, and of course were portrayed as rigid and as though they were not truly prepared to negotiate. Israel should have applied the Egyptian precedent at the first Camp David summit as a model. Had Menachem Begin made the same offer to Anwar Sadat as Ehud Barak made to Yasser Arafat, even the more far-reaching offer in the later stages of Camp David, Begin's offer to the Egyptians would have amounted to a pullout from only 90% of the Sinai, with the towns of Yamit and Ofira remaining in place, and the peace agreement with Egypt would have never been signed. Barak was looking for a Palestinian leader of the stature of President Sadat or King Hussein, who would make decisions similar to theirs, but this was a mistake, because the cases were essentially dissimilar. King Hussein indeed showed courage but it should be noted that in the Israeli–Jordanian peace agreement he received a one-for-one land swap. Over the years since 1949, Israel had annexed various parts of the Jordanian portion of Wadi Araba/Nahal Ha-Arava, but in the 1994 agreement, Israel gave Jordan parts of the Israeli portion in return. Both sides felt it was a fair deal, and no one in Israel charged that the cabinet had violated the "sanctity" of the Israeli borders. For the Palestinians this was a precedent, and they did not see why they should deviate from it.

The Palestinians themselves, of course, did not perceive Arafat as a hard-liner in the negotiations. Arafat was not alone in his opposition to Barak's territorial proposals at Camp David; the moderate Abu Ala, the pragmatic Abu Mazen and many other Palestinian leaders whom Israel has not ruled out as partners for negotiations, felt the same way.

The Palestinians were dragged to the Camp David summit against their will. Arafat did not want to go there, not because of the reasons simplistically put forward here by Barak, but because he considered the Israeli position, as presented to him the day before the summit, far from being fair and reasonable. On the eve of the summit, Israel told the Palestinians, "This is the map you can get; you will be getting no other map, and the borders of 1967 are not even an option."

The conclusion drawn by the Palestinians was well-founded. It is a fact that an adequate groundwork for the summit had not been laid, nor had the Americans done their homework. The Palestinians felt that unless the summit was fully prepared as a genuine leaders' summit with three, four or five remaining topics marked out in advance for discussion by the heads of state themselves, there was no point in participating. Nevertheless, this does not exempt them from the charge that once they arrived at Camp David, they should have conducted themselves in a better way.

About four days before the end of the summit, the Palestinians submitted a map of their own. To Israeli eyes, this map seemed illogical and jarring. But it introduced new principles that could have served as a platform for progress. Israel chose to ignore this map, which was far removed from Barak's position, but in retrospect it seems that the Palestinians were the first to suggest a concept that may eventually serve as the blueprint for an agreement. In this map, which represents an approach of *realpolitik*, the Palestinians agreed to let Israel annex all the Jewish neighborhoods around Jerusalem, as well as settlements that are near the Green Line, based on the principle of annexing only the minimal areas necessary to create settlement blocs and avoiding the annexation of any Palestinian villages. For every square kilometer annexed by Israel in the West Bank, the Palestinians expected to receive an equivalent area inside the Green Line, the understanding being that Israel's vital interests should not be compromised.

I believe that the proposals that were formulated after the summit at Camp David, and before and during the Taba meetings, brought us close to an agreement. This perception leads me to believe that if negotiations are resumed and a far-sighted "Ben-Gurionist" leadership leads the Israeli side as well, a peace agreement that will put an end to the conflict can be achieved.

# The Strategy of Creating Facts on the Ground Impeded Peace Negotiations

WHAT FOLLOWS IS MY UNDERSTANDING OF THE REASONS for the failure of the Israeli–Palestinian peace process as a whole. I agree with Aaron Miller that the Camp David summit should be seen as the climax of a year-long process, rather than just another milestone. My main argument is that the Israelis approached the process from two entirely different perspectives: there was the above-board diplomacy, and there were the underlying currents and developments. Although the two approaches may not be diametrically opposed, the tension between them created so many problems that there was simply no way for the Camp David summit to succeed.

The first approach seeks international legitimacy. It is symbolized by UN Security Council Resolutions 242 and 338. The spirit and the letter of the various existing agreements between the two sides are based on this approach. The second approach seeks creation of facts on the ground. In the past, this approached served the Israeli interest well. In 1937, the Peel Commission proposed giving the Jews in Palestine only 17% of the land west of the Jordan River. However, by 1949, the Jewish community managed to attain control of 78% of the territory. A good part of this was achieved through the creation of facts on the ground. The settlement of isolated areas (such as the overnight construction of eleven settlements in the Negev in 1946) influenced the territorial demarcation of the Jewish state by UN General Assembly Resolution 181 – the partition plan of 1947. It also helped Israel win its defensive War of Independence and thus reach the lines confirmed in the 1949 armistice agreements.

All Israeli cabinets after 1967, including the period after Oslo, have maintained the same approach, unfortunately avoiding a reassessment and continuing to believe that the permanent borders will depend on the map of settlements. This explains why the number of settlers in the Territories has risen from 125,000 in 1993, when Israel signed the Declaration of Principles, to almost 250,000 today, despite the fact that politically, Israel was supposed to implement Resolution 242 and withdraw from the bulk of the Territories. This was regrettable, as it contradicted the intention of the Oslo process to resolve the conflict by dividing the land west of the Jordan River into two states. Naturally, the settlement activities carried out by Israel after 1967 did not win the stamp of approval from the international community.

These two approaches collided incessantly and impeded the progress of the peace process. Even after the signing of the Declaration of Principles in September 1993, Israel needed eight months to reach the Cairo Agreement regarding the transfer of Gaza and Jericho to Palestinian control, as the first step in the agreed five-year interim period. The "facts-on-the ground" approach, which derived from the worldviews and collective consciousness of the Israelis (and existing among Palestinians as well), was incompatible with the spirit of these agreements – namely, with the "legitimacy" approach mentioned earlier.

The post-1967 war diplomacy yielded UN Resolution 242 which neither party was prepared to accept for many years, but it became the foundation of legitimacy in this dispute. Israel, however, continued pursuing the creation of facts, albeit with decreasing international approval.

Any analysis of Israel's post-1967 policies shows clearly that the settlement activities in the Territories failed to change the demographic balance there. This is true even in the Jordan Valley, from where a large flight of Palestinians took place immediately after the June 1967 war. Apart from a very few specific areas covering no more than 200 square kilometers – such as the Jerusalem environs, the Etzion Bloc and the western edge of the Samaria hills – Israel has been unable to establish territorial contiguity or a demographic balance that would serve as a basis for annexation.

The Palestinians refused to acknowledge the outcome of this policy of creating facts on the ground, to which they themselves had contributed over the years by refusing to recognize the State of Israel and by waging war against it. The continuing settlement activities, even after the mutual recognition in the 1993 Declaration of Principles, was strongly protested by the Palestinians.

The contradiction between these two elements in Israel's policies was brought to a head at the Camp David summit, which could not accommodate the two contradictory approaches simultaneously.

Israel needed time to become accustomed to the idea that the starting point for negotiations would be the June 4, 1967 lines. Before the Camp David summit, Israel repeatedly talked of giving the Palestinians just over 40% of the territory – namely, those areas that they had already received in 1995 as zones A and B (marked by full and partial Palestinian control, respectively), and whatever additional parcels of land that would be agreed upon. The Palestinian demand on the eve of the Camp David summit was that they should receive 100% of the land, or perhaps slightly less if a compromise was needed. Here, then, were the two competing views: "40% plus" vs. "100% minus."

The Palestinian position was clear. They were saying, "Let us agree that we are talking about the borders of 1967, recognizing the heavy price we have paid in giving up 78% of historic Palestine, and start negotiating about real needs that may require amendments to these boundaries."

The most prominent example of Israel's demand to recognize the outcome of its decades of settlement construction is to be found in the Jerusalem area. Before 1967, the territory of East Jerusalem was six square kilometers, including one square kilometer (roughly 245 acres) of the Old City. Today, the united city of Jerusalem, which Israel wanted to keep united, spans over 123 square kilometers, 71 of them in the West Bank. At Camp David, all the areas where building activities had taken place were claimed by Israel. During the negotiations and in unofficial meetings – in which I continued to participate – the Palestinians kept asking, "What is so sacred about the new neighborhoods of Neve Ya'akov or Gilo? The Temple had nothing to do with these areas."

Let me give you another example of the results of the strategy of creating facts on the ground. After the 1993 Declaration of Principles, leaders on both sides moved to the sidelines, making room for the professionals to take over. The Israeli cabinet invited the Defense institutions to prepare proposals, and it submitted what was known as "the map of essential interests." This map, which covered a vast part of the West Bank, was nothing more than an operative tool for Oslo's upcoming five-year interim period. It included the metropolitan area of Jerusalem, the "seam line" (that is, the area contiguous to the Green Line separating pre-1967 Israel from the West Bank), the Jordan Valley, and the blocs of Israeli settlements and the roads leading to them. The map, which received extensive media coverage, led both the political leadership and the general public to believe that those areas represented interests "essential for Israel's security" and therefore could not even be the subject of negotiation. This fixation shaped both public consciousness and official actions from the moment Israel began to implement the stages of "further redeployment." The map drew lines that no one was allowed to cross. This absurdity climaxed when Netanyahu's government adopted the map as a cabinet resolution, officially delineating

Israel's essential and non-negotiable interest areas. The prime minister and his cabinet thus committed themselves to interests defined by the Defense establishment, reflecting the contours of the established facts on the ground. These perceptions of "vital interests" – although in time they were narrowed down – impeded the negotiations with the Palestinians.

To conclude, I fully agree with Martin Indyk that the Camp David summit marked the beginning of a negotiating process, not an end. I would sum up my vision for the future in the following way. Both parties must put down the whips they have brandished throughout the years, and brought with them to the negotiating table. Israel's whip is that of settlements and the other facts created on the ground, while the Palestinian whip is that of terror. Both parties must lay down their whips and come to the negotiating table with clean hands. Our guiding principles should be that once we enter the process, we must bring it to a successful end. I do not recommend complicated recipes, but rather the endorsement and implementation of the letter and spirit of what we signed in 1993. The simplest expression of this formula is this: Israel give up its dream of controlling the Territories, the Palestinians must give up the dream of returning the refugees into Israel. The two sides should be able to meet the real needs of the other. The Camp David negotiations should have been conducted on this basis.

# The Input of Experts

## REUVEN MERHAV

# Planning for Jerusalem

THERE ARE NO EXPERTS ON JERUSALEM; there are only students who try to better understand the complex set of Jerusalem-related problems and perhaps find ways to ameliorate the situation, as part of a multifaceted solution for the Palestinian–Israeli conflict. Such "students," from both the government and non-government sectors, were employed in seeking to formulate a Jerusalem policy for the negotiations.

Important work was done by the Economic Cooperation Foundation, a Tel Aviv-based, EU-funded NGO. I myself, in a personal capacity, was involved in the work done by the Jerusalem Institute for Israel Studies on Jerusalem, since 1994. The work of that institution was congruent with the desire of the Israeli government, under the leadership of Ehud Barak, to try to have the Jerusalem question addressed and even resolved at the Camp David summit.

This was quite unusual in itself, because when governments try to deal with such sensitive and substantial matters, they normally have their own professional and intelligence organizations do the preparatory work for them. It is quite rare for them to call on an external institution for assistance. This particular cooperation resulted from the fact that the lack of preparation, or the belatedness of preparation by the government of Israel, on the eve of the summit meeting, was never so marked as on the Jerusalem question. There was a very simple explanation for this, namely, the unique character of the public discourse on Jerusalem since 1967. There have been very few, if any, issues besides Jerusalem in which there has been such a major discrepancy between the importance of a subject, on the one hand, and the paucity and shallowness of the public discourse on that subject, on the other hand. Surprisingly, there is great ignorance about the details of the

Jerusalem issues. If asked to identify on the map two particular neighbor-hoods that are part of Jerusalem, many Knesset members, government officials and members of the press would rarely be able to do this, nor would they have ever been there.

Jerusalem became the capital of Palestine when the British occupied the country and created the Mandate of Palestine in the wake of World War I. Early on, from the 1920s, the Arabs, under the astute leadership of Haj Amin al-Husseini, made Jerusalem into the amalgamated symbol of their religious and national struggle. That marked the start of an aggravated contest for Jerusalem, and the attempts made up to 1947 to find some kind of *modus vivendi* were rarely successful. That year, as part of the partition plan, the United Nations resolved that Jerusalem become a 200-square kilometer *corpus separatum*, to be governed and administered by the UN; after ten years, a referendum was to determine its future. The partition plan was rejected by the Arab side, resulting in armed hostilities, and at the end of the war Jerusalem was divided between Jordan and Israel. The ceasefire line of November 1948 became the Armistice Line of 1949, and hence the accepted *de facto* border between Jordan and Israel.

In 1967, the late King Hussein of Jordan joined the Arab belligerents in the Six Day War, at the end of which Israel found itself in control of the whole of the West Bank, including East Jerusalem. A series of decisions, not planned in advance, all taken haphazardly, determined the municipal contours of Jerusalem for years to come and brought us to the present-day situation. There were many other contributing factors, but the main factor influencing the decisions on Jerusalem was the security paradigm, resulting in the annexation of some 70 square kilometers – including the six square kilometers of Jordanian-Arab Jerusalem – to the existing 30 square kilome-ters of West Jerusalem (**Map 4**).

Israel's security paradigm derived from the experience of the 1948 War of Independence, during which Jerusalem was under constant siege for almost a year, shelled from the surrounding hills. Therefore, the idea in 1967 was to create a buffer zone to distance the artillery of the Jordanian Army. The prevailing expectation at the time was that within a month, two months, or at most a year or so, Israel would receive a telephone call from King Hussein, peace would be negotiated, the West Bank would be returned but Jerusalem would have a security zone to defend the city against the recur-rence of the trauma it had experienced during the siege of 1948. No telephone call came, history rolled on, and the Israeli discourse on the ques-tion of Jerusalem became more and more rhetorical.

I do not speak as a UN observer. I am an Israeli, a Jew and a Zionist, and for me Jerusalem is as important as for every Jewish Israeli Zionist. The word "Zionist" comes from "Zion," which is one of the many designations of

Jerusalem. It is holy for many, yet for all other nations and creeds it is, at best, in second, third, or fourth place. For us, it is the one and only. Over the years the public discourse on Jerusalem has been mantra-like, in the sense that we would over and over again acclaim "united Jerusalem, forever." By doing so, we were trying to solidify and perpetuate borders that had in fact been artificially demarcated – seeking to attain as much security as possible, with as few Arab inhabitants as possible.

In 1967, the territory of the 70 square kilometers that Israel annexed had a population of approximately 70,000 Arabs (**Map 5**). Between 1967 and 2000, the Jewish population of Jerusalem doubled, increasing from about 200,000 inhabitants to over 400,000. At the same time, its Arab population tripled, from 70,000 inhabitants to over 200,000 (**Map 6**). This is a major factor that should be kept in mind in any consideration of the Jerusalem problem.

Another determining factor was the decision by Moshe Dayan to return the Temple Mount/*Haram al-Sharif*, to the control of the Islamic *Waqf* (endowments) authorities. The Israeli flag, which flew there for less than a day, was removed, and in August 1967 a cabinet decision was taken directing those who wanted to pray on the Temple Mount to the Western Wall – otherwise known as the Wailing Wall. This perpetuated and actually guaranteed Arab control of the *Haram al-Sharif*. The cabinet decision was followed by a rabbinical ruling that reiterated a long-standing warning to Jews not to enter the Temple Mount, since in our time the exact location on the Mount of the forbidden Holy of Holies (the holiest spot in ancient times) is unknown. All these factors created a confluence of interests, leaving the *Haram al-Sharif* in the possession of the Arabs, administered through the *Waqf*. This has remained so, and aside from some isolated, very deplorable incidents, peace, albeit tense at times, has prevailed on the Temple Mount/*Haram al-Sharif* up to this day.

The Jordanians used to be deeply involved for many years in the management of the *Haram*, but now the Palestinian Authority is in control, and the Jordanian role is marginal and residual.

Paradoxically, the fact that a site in the heart of Jerusalem, the holiest place for the Jewish people religiously, nationally and historically, and the site of the ancient Jewish temples, has remained in the hands of the Muslims, has created the potential for a future settlement of the Jerusalem problem. Conversely, a unilateral change of this arrangement would preempt any chance to reach a future accord on Jerusalem.

What was the situation prior to Camp David, as far as the public discourse is concerned? All Israeli governments had declared that Jerusalem would be eternally united. Prime Minister Barak himself, a month or so before Camp David, on Jerusalem Day, repeated the same statement. When someone tried to soften his text, Barak reverted to the original one. Any politician who would have said so much as, "We have to rethink the future of Jerusalem," would have committed political suicide.

In the 1993 Oslo Accords, it was agreed that the five big issues – refugees, security, borders, Jerusalem and the settlements – were to be dealt with only in the final status negotiations. This was endorsed by the government and the Knesset, and later reaffirmed by the Netanyahu government.

Nobody dared to deal with the Jerusalem problem. If anyone in the Foreign Ministry, the Prime Minister's Office or the Israel Defense Forces had so much as mentioned the idea of addressing this question, he would have immediately been silenced. It thus happened that some non-governmental groups, prominent among them the Jerusalem Institute for Israel Studies – where I am a fellow – undertook to work on the Jerusalem question quite early on, already in 1994. Our team chose to concentrate on the whole metropolitan issue, not seeking solutions but rather developing options. By doing so, first of all, we managed to overcome political difficulties within the group. Secondly, we produced a solid corpus of knowledge for the public sector, to serve future governments and decision-makers as well as the public at large.

On all the other four final status subjects, the government had prepared over the years a huge data base. On Jerusalem, however, there was complete silence. When we presented our findings to consecutive prime ministers and cabinet ministers, they would all say that the work we were doing was very important and then try to hush us up. For a long time, officials tended to conceal the fact that they were meeting with us. In particular, I remember one meeting with the late Prime Minister Rabin in his office. For an hour and a half, the team presented its work to him, while simultaneously I was exchanging notes with a senior aide about ways to conceal the very fact that such a meeting ever took place. Rabin, mind you, had just come from the Knesset, where he upheld the notion of "Jerusalem forever."

When Prime Minister Barak appointed Ambassador Oded Eran to head the Israeli team for the permanent status negotiations, four committees were formed to deal with the other four subjects on the agenda, but there was no Jerusalem committee. At that stage we approached Eran, and through him Barak, and told him that we had done some work on Jerusalem and were ready to place all of it at his disposal. We said that he does not have to reinvent the wheel: the database and the outlines for all possible options are there.

In Hebrew we say, *Be-Yisrael shoom davar lo ishi, hakol personali,* which means roughly, in Israel everything is personal. People know one another intimately and trust depends on personal acquaintance. Barak, who was of course very wary about the subject, asked who was involved in this project.

When told, he was satisfied that we were credible and discreet. A joint team was formed, comprising government and Institute people, and I had the privilege of heading it. During the months of November and December 1999, we prepared a number of papers detailing the basic understandings upon which any settlement for Jerusalem should be based. Those were as follows:

➤ Israel faces a grave demographic problem in Jerusalem. If the political–territorial status quo is maintained, by the years 2033–2035 Arabs may constitute a majority within the existing municipal boundaries.

➤ We must "de-sanctify" most of the area of the annexed parts of Jerusalem. Dealing with these areas simply as real estate, as non-urban suburbs or villages, will minimize the problem and it will be possible to deal with them on a pragmatic level.

➤ There must be some kind of special status for the Old City, a special regime that will recognize its importance to two billion Christians, over a billion Muslims and of course to over 15 million Jews for whom Jerusalem is, as I mentioned, "the one and only." The question of sovereignty will have to be addressed in a creative way, to facilitate the acceptance of an agreement on Jerusalem by all of the international community. Moving forward in this way will enhance progress on all other pending issues.

➤ The strategic Palestinian lifeline from north to south, from Jenin to Hebron, should pass through East Jerusalem.

➤ The 200,000 Arabs in Jerusalem are not thin air. They have their identity, traditions and aspirations. Israel has accepted the fact that they have a special status regarding education, residence and citizenship (most of them had retained their Jordanian citizenship, while also holding Israeli identity cards), as well the right to vote for the Palestinian Authority, to which they are closely linked.

➤ Most importantly, the Temple Mount/*Haram al-Sharif,* which is in the hands of the Muslims, should remain so. Concurrently, there would have to be an acknowledgment of the fact that we, as Jews, have a special affinity to it.

This, in broad lines, is what was prepared for Prime Minister Barak, with the additional observation that Jerusalem is the heart of a large metropolitan area, and this has important ramifications.

With regard to Jerusalem's municipal boundaries and the hasty drawing of the annexation lines in June 1967, a number of facts are worth mentioning:

➤ The bulge that juts out at the northern end of the city's expanded boundary includes the Jerusalem airport Atarot (Qalandiya). These lines were drawn by a committee comprising IDF officers Shlomo Lahat and the late Rehavam Ze'evi , as well as three civilian experts – Messrs. Terlo, Shmu'eli and Salman. The secretary of the committee was a jurist from the Ministry of Justice. The reason why this airport – which occupies land that was expropriated from Jews by the British back in the 1930s or 1940s – was annexed to Jerusalem is an interesting one. The authorities believed that since many immigrants would come to Jerusalem, an airport was needed for them. This, of course, turned out to be pointless, since Atarot cannot accommodate large aircraft and Israel's major airport is quite close anyways, only 50 kilometers away. On the other hand, the airport could be very useful to the Palestinians, perhaps in cooperation with Israel.

➤ The annexation lines were drawn to include as few Arabs as possible and to give as much security for West Jerusalem as possible. In demographic terms, the metropolitan city can be seen as consisting of three concentric circles (**Map 7**):

(a) In the center is the Old City and the inner urban circle, where today over 600,000 people live. This is the nucleus of the metropolitan area.

(b) The second circle adds another 400,000 inhabitants to metropolitan Jerusalem.

(c) With the third, outer circle, Jerusalem has a million and a quarter inhabitants.

➤ Since 1967, extensive Israeli development took place in the outer circle, including new suburbs, which the Arabs call settlements. At the same time, aerial photos show that the amount of Arab development around Jerusalem was no less than that of Israeli development; it was just not as systematically planned. The 40 percent principle, namely the percentage of developed land allocated for public purposes, does not exist on the Arab side, and this has extensive future ramifications for the environment. The fact remains that the Arab population within Jerusalem's post-1967 extended municipal boundaries tripled, whereas the Jewish population only doubled. Based on all these facts, we need to adopt the comprehensive metropolitan approach and redraw the lines inside the metropolitan circles. This area has living place for everyone, but no place to satisfy everyone's respective ambitions. This is the framework in which the contours for a resolution may be drawn.

In the prevalent situation there is a fact that has great political significance. From 1967 to 1999, no secular Israeli political institutions were built in the Old City. Earlier, between 1948 and 1967, Israel had established almost all of its secular state institutions in the western part of Jerusalem: the Knesset, the Supreme Court, the President's Residence, the Prime Minister's Residence and almost all of the various government ministries. After 1967, except for a very short-lived attempt to build a residence for the deputy prime minister in the newly-annexed Old City, the Old City was left devoid of any built symbol of sovereignty.

The same should be true for the Arabs, we recommended. The Old City should be left as a center for all three religions – Judaism, Christianity and Islam – for pilgrims and visitors, with no political affiliation and no political institutions. That is why when it was suggested prior to Camp David that the Palestinian Authority and Arafat personally be given a political base on the Temple Mount, most of us opposed it vehemently; we thought that in this respect there should be symmetry in the Old City between Israel and the Palestinians.

Later on, at Camp David, the subject came up again in a meeting with Prime Minister Barak and Foreign Minister Shlomo Ben-Ami. I spoke to them passionately against giving Arafat any kind of a political representation or foothold on the *Haram al-Sharif.* I pointed out to them that nowhere in the Islamic world, neither in Iran, Saudi Arabia nor anywhere else, is there a combination of a religious shrine and a political capital. Even the Umayyads, when they took over Palestine in the seventh century, established their administrative center in Ramla, leaving Jerusalem for the service of God. Hence, allowing the Palestinians to establish a political presence on the *Haram al-Sharif* would be a grave historic mistake, to be avoided at all costs. Moreover, it would not even be to the liking of the Muslim world, which did not want to see Arafat's stature grow out of proportion. The fact that we Jews and Israelis have avoided establishing official institutions in the Old City makes it possible to create there a special regime defined, for example, as a World Heritage site under the auspices of, and in cooperation with, UNESCO.

At Camp David, the idea was that the whole metropolitan map could be redrawn, and certain parts of East Jerusalem that have nothing to do with its urban fabric – such as al-Sawahra in the southeast, or Kafr Akab in the north – could revert to the Palestinian Authority. There should be close municipal cooperation between Arabs and Jews, and a Palestinian supermunicipality, with close links to the Palestinian Authority, should operate alongside the existing municipality. All these points could serve as a basis for negotiations. Indeed, this was put on the table by the Israeli team at Camp David. In addition, there arose the possibility of a territorial swap, a notion floated for the first time in December 1999 as a "personal idea" of negotiator Oded Eran under the direction, or tacit approval of Prime Minister Barak.

As these ideas became public, the sky did not fall down, as we say in Hebrew, and public opinion surveys, which until then had shown total support for the mantra "eternally united Jerusalem," suddenly reflected a new mood: the majority favored a redrawing of the metropolitan lines. It was clear that we could swap territories and make other new arrangements without too much public resistance. It seems that these options became the basis of the subsequent Clinton Plan.

Two problematical ideas emerged concerning the Old City. When things in Camp David became entangled, the idea of dividing the Old City was floated. I thought at the time that the Americans had suggested it, but actually the idea came from the Israelis, namely from Barak himself. From the moment I heard of the idea, I utterly opposed it. I argued that the Old City was a vibrant, interwoven entity, where communities, arteries, public utilities, commercial centers and major religious sites are all interlinked. It is impossible to divide a car in motion. It would be a fatal mistake, not to say a tragedy, to divide it. A divided Old City would not be able to function and would be totally unacceptable to all concerned. The idea is a non-starter: the area of the Old City is less than one square kilometer, and of these 187 acres, almost 100 acres are religious property – Muslim *Waqf*, Christian and Jewish establishments (**Map 8**); accordingly, it must remain one unit in order to retain its importance and significance. Besides, I asked, who says that the Christian world wanted Arafat as a master and sovereign within the Old City? There are different voices in the Christian world, and a large part of the Christian community in Palestine, which mostly seems to have supported Arafat, was actually very apprehensive of him.

A second idea, floated later, suggested that Israel would have sovereignty under the Temple Mount and the Palestinians above it. I saw this as even more futile. I maintained that all these matters of sovereignty should be placed where the late King Hussein declared them to belong: in the realm of the Divine. One could live with the questions of sovereignty left open. This will be the only basis on which an agreement may be reached.

For the Old City and the area called the "Holy Basin," which together make up about two and one-half square kilometers, we suggested some kind of an international monitoring system for which special security provisions would be needed. It would have to be under Israeli supervision as long as no proper security arrangements are made with the Palestinians. The arrangements made when the Pope visited Israel in April 2000 could serve as a model.

Finally, when things became really messy, what emerged was a clash of narratives: The Palestinian position was to deny any Jewish link to the Temple Mount in history. This put the Israelis up in arms, because if you tell even the most secular Israeli that there is no proof that there had been a Temple on that site and that the whole Jewish-Israeli narrative is false, the response will be fierce and there will be no more place for negotiations. After Camp David, I went to the (now late) Feisal Husseini and said to him, "If you want to push the process forward and eventually convince the Israeli electorate to accept new arrangements in Jerusalem, you must acknowledge the link of the Jews to the Temple Mount. It may be agreed that due to existing political constraints the Jews will not actualize this link, but the link itself cannot be denied."

One last remark. At historic junctures, leaders must sometimes take crucial, painful decisions, which we refer to as "Ben-Gurion-style" decisions. Ben-Gurion, when offered the partition plan in 1947, had to forsake Jerusalem, but he said, "Let it be so; we need a Jewish commonwealth in Palestine. For that I am willing to pay a price and let us see what the future brings." Arafat may have been seen as a successful leader until the summit, but unfortunately in the summit he showed himself to be a complete failure. He had great achievements while struggling uphill, yet turned out to be a terrible disappointment upon reaching the peak. He was no Ben-Gurion. He could have assumed what is called in Arabic the *burda*, the cloak of the leader, and brought his people to the Promised Land, but he missed the opportunity.

# MOHAMMED S. DAJANI

# The Role of Informal Talks

I VIEW THE CAMP DAVID SUMMIT BASICALLY AS A STATION ON THE ROAD. The title of the conference asks, "What went wrong?" but this refers only to the empty half of the glass. The full half of the glass invites the questions, "What went right?" and "What are the lessons to be learned for future peace negotiations?" I believe this is why we are here today. In my view, we need to view things optimistically in order to look with hope toward the future. Unlike many experts, I believe that the Camp David summit was not a total failure. Indeed, we have actually seen this morning how from this experience many useful lessons can be extracted that would benefit the future search for peace in our region. I apply this approach also to the Oslo Peace process as a whole. I do not think Oslo failed. It was just an earlier station on the long road to peace.

In my view, and contrary to what has been said here, Arafat did not think that there was no solution for the most controversial issue of Jerusalem. Beginning in 1997, I was personally involved, as an academic, in Track II meetings with Israelis, where the issue of Jerusalem was discussed. A few weeks before Camp David, we were meeting with Israelis in Cyprus, in an unofficial forum arranged by IPCRI (Israel–Palestine Center for Research and Information, located in Jerusalem). We were ten people, five from each side. The Israeli colleagues came into the first session of the second day and threw at us the question, "What if we withdraw to the 1967 borders, what are you willing to concede on Jerusalem?"

This was actually the first time throughout our meetings that the Israelis expressed willingness to consider the possibility of withdrawal to the 1967 borders. So we naturally inquired, "What are your demands? What do you want in return?" They responded, "We are thinking in terms of sovereignty over the Wailing Wall, the whole Jewish Quarter, and the large Israeli neighborhoods surrounding Jerusalem, including Ma'ale Adumim and Pisgat Ze'ev, to be exchanged for areas inside the Green Line in the northern regions."

The Palestinians asked to adjourn the meeting to study this proposal and we met amongst ourselves to evaluate its implications. Some of us found it too sudden and suspected a media trap. We wondered, if we were to express interest, would they publicly trumpet it as another Palestinian concession? My own position, as an academic with no political affiliations, was that I personally could voice my support for such a deal. As for those who held official Palestinian Authority posts, if they decided to play it safe, they could voice reservations on this offer.

These proceedings were reported to President Arafat. Hence, in my view, when Arafat flew to Camp David, he believed, based on this and other sources, that a deal could be reached on Jerusalem with which he could live.

I believe that he was really perplexed with what actually happened at Camp David, when Prime Minister Barak pulled two rabbits out of his hat. The first was the issue of sovereignty over *al-Haram al-Sharif*/the Temple Mount. The Palestinians never understood the Israeli mindset concerning the significance of the Temple Mount, since it had never been put on the political agenda in previous negotiations. The Palestinians, in general, were not sufficiently aware that this was a significant, and even crucial, political as well as religious issue for the Israelis, and that it would be one of the major Israeli demands at Camp David.

The second of Barak's "rabbits" was the demand for Israeli sovereignty over the Armenian Quarter. I received a call from a Palestinian official friend who asked me, "Why do you think the Israelis raised the issue of sovereignty over the Armenian quarter? Was this demand ever raised in meetings with them?" I explained that it provided them with a direct access route to the Wailing Wall. Also, it would divide Jerusalem into two halves – one half that included the Moslem and Christian Quarters, and the other half that included the Jewish and Armenian Quarters.

Accordingly, Arafat found himself facing a double dilemma: if he agreed to the first demand, he would have to confront the Islamic world which would accuse him of betrayal; if he agreed to the second demand, he would have to confront those Christians who would accuse him of selling out a Christian stronghold. In both cases he felt it was a decision that fell beyond his authority and realm. To him, both issues were taboos – red lines that he could not cross. In my opinion, these differences over Jerusalem were the main reason why the negotiations failed.

# MENACHEM KLEIN

# Track II Plans

BACK-CHANNEL NEGOTIATIONS CONSIST OF SECRET OFFICIAL NEGOTIATIONS between representatives of contesting parties, such as the secret meetings of Amnon Lipkin-Shahak with Abu Mazen that took take place in early 2000, parallel to the official talks between negotiators Oded Eran and Yasser Abed Rabbo. Track II diplomacy, on the other hand, is not official. Its structure and mode of operation have many variations. It can be run by ex-establishment persons, organizers of people-to-people activities, self-appointed advisors and academic experts. It is important that they have access to decision-makers. Hereafter, I shall deal with the informal diplomacy initiatives conducted by academic experts who indeed had access to decision-makers. I shall try to evaluate their contribution and input to the official negotiating track, mainly on the issue of Jerusalem.

Since 1994, more than 30 Israeli and Palestinian civil groups have discussed the parameters of a permanent status agreement, many of them focusing on Jerusalem.[1] These informal Israeli–Palestinian meetings created a common professional discourse and structure, based on a more-or-less agreed upon data base. Sometimes, the talks stopped at this informative level. At other times, they went beyond that in an attempt to find an operational program that would give a political direction to the points on which the experts had reached a consensus. Some of the groups dealt just with Jerusalem and its metropolitan area, some with the refugee problem, while others included these issues in the wider framework of all the matters pertaining to the permanent status negotiations. Sometimes there were numerous participants in the meetings, while at other times there were only small groups. Regarding the sponsorship of Track II, most of the forums met under Western European auspices – sometimes under the sponsorship of governmental institutions and other times at the invitation of NGOs. Harvard University, as well as several other American institutions, hosted a very important Track II forum, but the official American administration was constrained by the Israeli government's taboo on any discussion on the future of Jerusalem.

The groups that discussed the subject of Jerusalem in these unofficial talks may be divided into two basic categories. The first category includes the groups that did not dare to raise political issues and contented themselves with discussing professionally subjects of a technical nature. Such a group was the joint forum sponsored by the Jerusalem Institute for Israel Studies and the Arab Studies Society. I believe that this type could become an important model in the long-run, in the years following the attainment of a political settlement. Plans designed by experts will flesh out the framework agreements concluded by the statesmen.

This type of work preserves the division of labor between politicians and experts. The danger is that the two will become entirely disengaged. When politicians prepare a framework for a settlement without, or even in contradiction to, the output of professional work, problems will arise. That was the case, in my view, regarding the Israeli map presented in the Taba talks, which drew the borders of Jerusalem, comprising the Ma'ale Adumim and Givat Ze'ev blocs. No one in the Israeli delegation considered the need of the Palestinians in Jerusalem to have a land reservoir for expansion, and for solving their acute housing problems. Moreover, none of the Israeli negotiators paid attention to the problem that Jewish West Jerusalem will face if Israel annexes the open areas around Palestinian East Jerusalem and thus doom it to poverty. Political considerations overrode the requirements indicated by professionals. Negotiating without input from experts will later cause difficulties for the politicians when they face the concrete problems resulting from their handiwork. Conversely, it would be dangerous for professionals to make recommendations without any political input or perspective. There is also the problem that politicians and experts may not understand each other's language – as happened more than once in meetings between members of the two sectors.

The second category of informal channels seeks to deal with this problem. The participants in this model of informal talks believe that dialogue between experts alone is not enough, for without a political framework the professional dialogue cannot go very far. That was the concept that guided these participants. The political dimension was explicitly included in the work of groups belonging to this category. Such channels were opened before Camp David in order to prepare tools for decision-makers and explore ways for political breakthroughs, should negotiations over Jerusalem take place. This category included groups like the one described by Reuven Merhav; and Israeli–Palestinian talks held under the auspices of (a) the Economic Cooperation Foundation and the Arab Studies Society, and (b) the EU and Spain, known as the Madrid Track. Some of the groups in this category managed to reach understandings on political aspects as well, part of which remain secret until now.

It would be difficult to exaggerate the importance of the informal channels and their contributions to the negotiations. They prepared the professional and political infrastructure for agreement and created a common language between the two sides. This is true for both the Israeli and Palestinian participants. Creative ideas formulated in these forums were later brought to the negotiation table and several breakthroughs were achieved. On the issue of Jerusalem they generated new concepts and distinctions, such as suspended, joint and divine sovereignty. Plans developed in these groups included: a common economic regime for Jerusalem and Al-Quds; territorial exchanges and the annexation by Israel of settlement blocs by mutual agreement; cooperation between the Israeli and Palestinian police, and the creation of a joint police force for the zone between East and West Jerusalem; and a Jewish–Muslim–Christian religious council to coordinate the management of the holy places. The Holy Basin concept originated from these groups.

On the issues of the 1948 Palestinian refugees, Track II meetings discussed different types of refugee return and rehabilitation, models of compensation, and formulas for an Israeli declaration recognizing responsibility for the creation of the refugee problem.

However, those meetings had their own shortcomings. Although dealing with the political dimension, they were conducted almost exclusively between professionals. Insufficient effort was made to bring together community leaders representing the two societies that would have to live side-by-side following the conclusion of a peace accord. Government officials and bureaucrats rarely participated. Nevertheless, a few highly placed decision-makers on each side were briefed about the discussions. Among them, on the Israeli side, were: Ehud Olmert, when he was the mayor of Jerusalem; Ami Gluska, from the Ministry of Internal Security; officials of the Ministry of Foreign Affairs; and Prime Minister Ehud Barak himself. In several cases, Members of Knesset took part in Track II meetings, including Colette Avital, Meir Shitrit, Nahum Langenthal, Ofir Pines-Paz and David Tal. Palestinian officials briefed on the discussions included: Abu Mazen, at that time the PLO Executive Committee's second highest official; Feisal Husseini (now deceased), who held the Executive Committee's Jerusalem portfolio; and top Palestinian negotiator Sa'eb Erakat. Yet, most of the time, officials preferred to keep away from the Track II meetings, toward which their attitudes varied. Some of them underestimated the potential of Track II talks for creating understandings, let alone full-fledged agreements. Others used them to float trial balloons without risking any political costs – which is indeed one of the functions of the Track II channel.

There were also two types of Track II initiatives that were more narrowly defined: those that aimed at influencing public opinion and those concerned with religious dialogue. As far as I know, up to the emergence of the Ayalon–Nusseibeh principles and the Geneva Agreement (both in 2003), only one Track II initiative operated with the aim of shaping public opinion on both sides. In January 2000, a joint statement on the principles that were to guide the negotiations on Jerusalem was published by a forum convening under the auspices of the University of Oklahoma and the Rockefeller Foundation. The statement was signed by Israelis, Egyptians, Jordanians, Palestinians and Americans, all of whom had held discussions together over the previous two years. Of the various informal channels, this was the only one whose participants publicized their resolutions, in addition to submitting their papers to the relevant political leaders.

The other type of Track II initiatives focused on the religious dimension. In general, informal professional channels did not devote enough attention to Jerusalem as a religious city. They treated its status as a holy city with respect but were also reluctant to delve too deeply into this aspect of the city. It was easier to discuss the preservation and renovation of historical buildings in the Old City than the links that exist in the historical and religious heart of Jerusalem between political issues and religious sanctity. Only a few meetings dealt with the religious aspects of the city and only a very small number of religious leaders took part in them. When the question was brought to Prime Minister Barak, he refused to let moderate religious leaders – such as MKs Michael Melchior and Avraham Burg – to step in and develop a creative Jewish religious discourse on the subject and engage in an inter-faith dialogue with Palestinian religious leaders. He was apparently motivated also by personal political considerations, and thus refused to allow Melchior or Burg to gain politically from engaging in such activities. Israelis belonging to the "national-religious" camp were regarded by Barak as essentially fundamentalists. In the absence of a moderate religious discourse, the Israeli negotiating team in Camp David followed the mainstream and demanded to have tangible signs of sovereignty on the Temple Mount. They also asked for the designation of an extra-territorial compound within the Mount where Jews could pray. The Israeli team argued that these demands were justified because the remains of the Jewish Temples lay beneath the platform of the Mount. Even when the demand to allocate a site for Jewish prayer was taken off the table during the post-Camp David negotiations, the Israeli argument behind it remained in force. Basing itself on that view, Israel never relinquished its demand to have some expression of sovereignty on the Mount, nor its refusal to grant the Palestinians full and exclusive sovereignty there.

The interaction between Track II experts and official negotiators deserves some elaboration. The taboo on the Jerusalem issue that prevented officials from systematically preparing their brief toward the negotiations over Jerusalem left them no choice but to pay attention to the ideas exchanged, and understandings formulated in the Track II talks. For their part, the Track II professionals were eager to inject their insights, ideas and proposals, whether fully thought-out or half-baked, into the official talks. On both the Israeli and Palestinian sides, however, official–professional dialogue was limited by the decision-makers. Each official selected the particular expert voice he would listen to. Officials placed time limits on the hearing given to external professionals. The outsiders were called in either sporadically, or when the talks faced a deadlock or even serious crisis. The officials also decided which level of the negotiating team the professionals would be allowed to meet, and limited their access to the chief decision-makers. The officials' choices of experts invited to present their views did not depend solely on the experts' capabilities. The Israeli prime minister, in particular, tended to prefer experts who belonged to the mainstream and those that his team felt were loyal to him and to his policies. Former civil servants and experts who had a good rapport with the authorities were preferred. A professional's influence increased to the extent that his ideas were consistent with other components of the deal that the Israeli leader had prepared or already tendered.

In choosing his negotiating strategy and tactics, Barak's approach was naturally shaped also by domestic political and public-relations considerations. He shared those considerations only with a small number of loyal assistants, certainly not with external professionals. The result of all these factors was that the official negotiators rarely adopted complete sets of ideas and understandings formulated in Track II meetings. Such ideas were either completely rejected, or revised, or placed in a different context. Among these were the ideas of working out a special regime for the Holy Basin, refraining from granting sovereignty over the Temple Mount/Wailing Wall compound to any party, and creating a concept of "sovereignty of God" for that site. While these and similar concepts aimed at putting both sides on an equal footing, the Israeli negotiators ignored this consideration. They presented demands regarding sovereignty on the Temple Mount, while not offering the Palestinians the same authority and status regarding the Wailing Wall. Needless to say, these demands were presented in a style that was very different from that employed by Track II interlocutors, whose positive disposition and manner facilitated reaching a common ground with the other side.

Comparing ideas produced in Track II talks with positions taken by Israeli negotiators shows how the influence of Track II on the officials was restricted. The example of the issue of sovereignty in the Holy Basin is instructive. Immediately after the return of the Israeli delegation from Camp David, I was asked, together with Professor Ruth Lapidoth, to write a paper for Ehud Barak on sovereignty. Ten days later, we presented it to him at his home in Kochav Yair. We discussed the various models of sovereignty, including the option of "sovereignty of God." Later on, we learned from leaks to the media how the concept was twisted in its presentation to the Palestinians, and also to the Egyptians who had been called upon by the US to help. In the absence of either Israeli or Palestinian sovereignty, the Israelis asked to keep in their hands several aspects of control. They also rejected President Husni Mubarak's proposal of applying the principles adopted for the Temple Mount to the Wailing Wall as well, a proposal that had some logic since the Wall and the Mount belong to a single compound, holy to both Judaism and Islam. However, Barak rejected Mubarak's suggestion.

A few concluding notes, some of them on a personal level. Experts do not know everything, they do not have answers to all questions, they make mistakes and they are not prophets. The question is whether experts can learn from developments in the course of the negotiations and change direction during their interaction with the decision-makers? Are the experts capable of changing their minds and can they convince the decision-makers to go through the same learning process? As far as I am concerned, I did change my position in the process. Regarding the solution for the city of Jerusalem, I shifted from initially favoring a "functional division" in the eastern part of the city while keeping free movement to both sides, to favoring the partition of the city with controlled border crossings and full Palestinian sovereignty in the east. As is well documented in my current and forthcoming publications, I also became convinced that no final status agreement can be achieved unless: (a) Israel allows the Palestinians to enjoy full sovereignty on the Temple Mount while Israel maintains its sovereignty over the Wailing Wall; or alternatively, (b) it refrains from imposing any sovereignty over places of worship. In other words, from the Israeli perspective, the price of an agreement in Jerusalem is giving up sovereignty over the Temple Mount.

I also made mistakes. At the beginning of the official negotiation I was overly optimistic, or at least my optimism was premature. If I would have to offer an excuse, it will be that I did not know what the real Israeli positions were. After all, I was an external advisor who only partly passed the test put forth by the bureaucrats and senior politicians: the test of loyalty. But later I learned a number of things regarding the style and strategy of the negotiators and the positions of the protagonists and consequently my perspective changed.

My greatest failure occurred twelve days after the outbreak of the *Aqsa Intifada*. I provided Shlomo Ben-Ami with a personal position paper, calling upon him and the Israeli cabinet to acknowledge that the *intifada* had created an "Algerian-like" situation in the Occupied Territories and therefore the government should reconsider its positions *vis-à-vis* the Palestinians. Failure to do so, I wrote, would result in the right-wing ascending to power and in escalating terrorist attacks in Israeli cities. Regretfully, the Israeli choice was a different one than what I had advocated.

## Remarks during the Discussion

Concerning the allegation that the Israelis at Camp David gave up the Temple Mount and handed it over to the Palestinians, I attest that this is not true. At no stage of the negotiations was Ehud Barak willing to hand over the Temple Mount to Palestinian sovereignty. Israel was interested in *improving* the status quo in its favor namely, the idea of allocating a site on the Mount where Jews could pray (which eventually was taken off the agenda). This is the truth, and it must be stated.

The Israeli chief negotiators manifested on matters of religious issues not only insensitivity but also ignorance – they had failed to adequately prepare themselves on this subject for the summit. Of course, the fact that no work had been done to prepare public opinion did not help either, because negotiators cannot proceed beyond the limits set by the religious and nationalist myths prevailing in a society.

Over lunch yesterday, Ehud Barak said something to this effect, "What is public opinion? There are leaders. Leaders decide, and public opinion follows. Had I come back with an agreement, 80% of Israelis would have supported it." To this, I responded, "I think that on the contrary, the parameters of Israel's negotiating positions were in fact formed by Israeli public opinion."

In May 2000, the Jerusalem Institute for Israel Studies published a book outlining alternative permanent status agreements. By accident, the timing was opportune. The Israeli delegation adopted this book, as did the American delegation (Martin Indyk visited the Institute prior to the Camp David summit, listened to a presentation and took a copy with him). The alternatives proposed in this book were a matter of public debate even before the summit began, and the boundaries delineated in the public discussion of these alternatives were quite similar to those of the position presented by Israel at Camp David. The summit began on July 11. On July 17, one week later, Ehud Barak conducted the discussion mentioned earlier by Amnon Lipkin-Shahak and Danny Yatom, which was the most important, pointed Israeli discussion of the issue held at the summit. At that point he came to terms with the idea of handing over the Arab northern neighborhoods of Jerusalem, Beit Hanina and Shu'afat, to full Palestinian sovereignty. Just before making that decision, he asked Yossi Beilin to undertake a tour of these areas – for which I served as guide, together with attorney Danny Seidemann – accompanied by local and foreign television crews. Also present were retired senior security officials, who spoke on record in favor of the idea. The event was designed to convince the Israeli public, as well as some of the members of Barak's own delegation, that giving up those areas would be in Israel's interest. It was not easy for Barak to implement the move. Although the decision to transfer sovereignty of these neighborhoods had already been made, it had not yet fully sunk in. Indeed, as Gilead Sher noted here yesterday, there is a difference between making decisions on paper and learning to live with them.

These were just examples of the inadequate foundation that had been laid prior to the summit. The religious aspects of the talks required meticulous, detailed preparations, and their absence influenced the results. Many things should have been done beforehand, above all the preparation of public opinion. Additionally, I think that the idea of holding Arafat solely responsible for the failure of the summit was ill conceived. To the best of my knowledge, this idea – expressed in Barak's post-Camp David declaration, "we have exposed Arafat's true face" – had been planned in advance for the event that the summit failed. Of all the things that should have been prepared before the beginning of the summit, ironically *this* one was.

# Academic Perspectives

YAACOV BAR-SIMAN-TOV

# An Irresolvable Conflict or Lack of Ripeness?

THE DISINTEGRATION OF THE OSLO PROCESS AND THE OUTBREAK OF VIOLENCE at the end of September 2000, after seven years of talks, engendered frustration not only among the two peoples and their policymakers, but also among scholars studying conflict resolution and peace processes. The Oslo process created the feeling that despite the complex nature of the Israeli–Palestinian dispute and the conflicting interests of the two parties, the conflict could nevertheless be resolved. The interim agreement reached through the Oslo process was to lead to a permanent arrangement between the two sides. The Camp David summit was designed to achieve this final status agreement but it collapsed. For the first time in the history of the Israeli–Arab conflict, a peace process not only failed, but led to exceptionally bloody hostilities that have continued ever since.

From the time of the collapse of the Camp David summit, participants and researchers have been trying to decipher the reasons for the failure of the whole Oslo process. Most of the focus has been on the Camp David summit, which seemed to be one of the most important stages in the Oslo process, if not the most important one. After all, it was at this stage that at least Israel, and perhaps also the US, expected negotiations to lead to a signed peace agreement, thereby ending the conflict once and for all.

As pivotal as the Camp David summit was to the disintegration of the peace process, our review focus should be somewhat broader and encompass the Oslo process from its outset, namely, from the beginning of the unofficial talks that began in Oslo in early 1993. The failure of the summit was the result of cumulative factors that are not necessarily connected with the events of the summit itself. Over the years since Camp David, Israel and the Palestinians have repeatedly accused each other over the failure of the process, and even within Israel and the US no consensus has been reached on the reasons for this failure. It is evident that the subject is not only volatile and controversial, but also far too complex to be explained by any single isolated cause. It was my opinion from the outset that these diverse and complex reasons can only be understood through an interdisciplinary effort. For this purpose I established a multidisciplinary team under the auspices of the Leonard Davis Institute for International Relations and the Swiss Center for Conflict Research, Management and Resolution – both belonging to The Hebrew University.

Our study gave rise to several alternative explanations for the failure of the Oslo process, which I offer here as hypotheses. The working assumption was that these explanations can provide a comprehensive interpretation of the disintegration of the Oslo process only if considered as a whole. The following reasons may explain the failure: (1) the conflict is essentially irresolvable; (2) the absence of ripeness; (3) the mismanagement of the negotiations; (4) failures in the implementation of the Oslo Accords up to the time of the Camp David summit; (5) the illegitimacy of the process in the eyes of both nations and failure by the leaders to secure such legitimacy; (6) strategic, psychological and cultural barriers; (7) inadequate mediation; and (8) the collapse of the Camp David summit.

There are several factors that make it difficult to study today the failure of the process having only a few years of hindsight. The events are still fresh, and we do not have enough firsthand written accounts of the evolution of the various stages of the talks. The resources available to the researchers are mainly interviews that the participants gave to the media, as well as memoirs published by several of the players. Naturally, resources of this kind reflect personal perspectives and therefore tend to be one-sided and subjective. To gather further resources, we decided to interview Israeli negotiators who were involved in the talks in one way or another from the very beginning of the Oslo process. We were hoping that a Palestinian research group would concurrently hold interviews with Palestinian figures and an American group would interview American participants, so that at the end of the study we could examine the various explanations together. However, the violent conflict made it difficult for the Palestinian researchers to operate, and the American group conducted very few interviews.

We were well aware that the testimonies we were collecting constituted personal impressions that offered only partial perspectives. However, these testimonies have proved to be exceptionally valuable, as the interviewees realized the urgent need for our study and gave us insight into additional issues that we had not previously considered. Each interviewee was given the alternative explanations proposed by the research team, and was asked to address these explanations and offer others on his part. The list of interviewees, alphabetically in Hebrew, is as follows: Ami Ayalon, Shaul Arieli, Alan Baker, Ehud Barak, Avi Gil, Yossi Ginossar, Gidi Grinstein, Eitan Haber, Yair Hirschfeld, Yisrael Hasson, Shlomo Yanai, Danny Yatom, Amnon Lipkin-Shahak, Eran Lerman, Yitzhak Molcho, Pini Meidan, Dan Meridor, Oded Eran, Ron Pundik, Dan Rothschild and Gilead Sher. We learned from the interviews that there was no single Israeli version as to the reasons for the disintegration of the Oslo process, and that there were great differences on the relative significance of the alternative explanations.

Instead of analyzing the interviews, I will focus on the first two alternative explanations I mentioned earlier, namely, that the failure of the Oslo process stems mainly from the nature of the conflict, or from trying to end it too soon. In other words: an irresolvable conflict versus the absence of ripeness.

## An Irresolvable Conflict

What are the arguments that support this explanation of the failure? The main argument here is that the Israeli–Palestinian conflict cannot be resolved because it is a protracted conflict. Conflicts of this kind involve interests that are at complete odds with one another and differences in values that cannot be bridged; they usually take the form of zero-sum games. The literature dealing with protracted conflicts is indeed very pessimistic about the possibility of resolving such conflicts, and holds that when there is an expectation that the conflict *can* be resolved, it is only an illusion: the reconciliation process quickly shatters and violence is resumed. If the Israeli–Palestinian conflict indeed fits into this category, then the Oslo process was doomed from the outset. Accordingly, policymakers on both sides were wrong in their decision to try and settle the conflict, since they should have been aware of the fact that it could not be resolved – as had indeed been maintained by both sides before the Oslo process began. This claim is supported by the very fact that no agreement was secured between the parties at Camp David and that since September 2000 serious violence has resumed. Hence, the attempt to resolve this conflict was misguided. Moreover, it turned out to be a dangerous gamble, as the violence that ensued was far worse than what had existed before any attempt was made to settle the conflict. After the great expectations generated by the summit, its failure, which showed that the conflict could not be resolved, generated extreme frustration, particularly among the Palestinians, who once again opted for violence as a more effective tool for accomplishing their goals.

The leading Israeli protagonists of the Oslo process did not subscribe to the belief that the conflict is not solvable. Otherwise, they would not have initiated the process or concluded the interim agreements. Yossi Beilin, Yair Hirschfeld and Ron Pundik believed that the conflict could be resolved, and that a successful process of negotiations could change the state of the conflict. In their minds, the failure of the process was not due to the nature of the conflict but to mismanagement of the negotiations, failure to fully implement the Oslo Accords, cowardice on the part of the leaders and failure of the leaders to secure the public support that would legitimize the process.

Yitzhak Rabin had serious doubts as to whether the conflict could be resolved and a permanent agreement reached with the PLO, because he was aware of the wide differences between the positions of the two parties, especially on the issues of Jerusalem and the Palestinian Right of Return. Rabin nevertheless felt compelled to try and see how far the process could go. The strategy of negotiating a resolution of the conflict in stages, through interim agreements which involved only calculated risks, became the litmus test for the entire peace process. At that stage, intelligence experts such as Ya'akov Amidror and Amos Gilad, who said all along that the conflict with the Palestinians could not be resolved because Arafat and the PLO were incapable of doing so, shared Rabin's doubts. But although their warnings were published, they had no resonance, because Israel's policymakers sided with Rabin, who believed that nevertheless an attempt should be made. Israel's right-wing leaders, including Yitzhak Shamir, Binyamin Netanyahu, Ariel Sharon and Ze'ev Binyamin Begin, flatly rejected any possibility of resolving the conflict, not only because of the unbridgeable differences between the parties but also because they believed that the Palestinians had not yet accepted the legitimacy of the existence of Israel as a Jewish state. They perceived the Oslo process as a dangerous bet that would threaten not only the security, but the very existence of the State of Israel.

Israel's policymakers did not conduct any thorough research on the prospects of resolving the conflict and the price this would entail. One of the reasons why Yitzhak Rabin and Shimon Peres avoided any such study was that they did not want to deal with the issues of permanent status negotiations before the process reached that stage, in order not to reveal Israel's red lines. They were also concerned that a public debate of these issues at that early stage would evoke premature opposition.

Ehud Barak was the first to decide to take action for testing whether the Palestinians were in fact ready to settle their conflict with Israel. His assessment was that if Israel continued to make gradual territorial concessions without resolving the conflict itself, Israel would be left without any leverage for negotiating the permanent status agreement. Barak was prepared to make extensive concessions in order to end the conflict. Thus, the Camp

David summit would become the first test case for the ability of the Oslo process to culminate in the settlement of the Israeli–Palestinian conflict. Despite warnings by Israeli intelligence that Arafat would not be able to end the conflict without full sovereignty over the Temple Mount, the division of Jerusalem and implementation of the Palestinian Right of Return, Barak decided to go ahead.

The failure of the Camp David summit and the negotiations that ensued, including those at Taba, convinced Barak and several of his ministers and assistants, among them Shlomo Ben-Ami, Dan Meridor, Danny Yatom and Gilead Sher, that the Israeli–Palestinian conflict could not be resolved as long as Arafat continued to lead the Palestinian people.

This view was formed against the backdrop of the rejection by Arafat of Barak's far-reaching concessions, including those concerning Jerusalem, which went far beyond anything that Israel had previously been ready to offer. Arafat's refusal to endorse President Clinton's proposed plan or the concessions that Israel was offering at Taba, and the resumption of Palestinian violence, only strengthened their belief. The two basic tests of the Palestinians' genuine readiness to resolve the conflict were the issues of the Temple Mount and the Right of Return. During the Camp David summit and the negotiations that followed, some of the Israeli negotiators realized that the Palestinians were unable to resolve the conflict not only because they could not compromise on Jerusalem, the Temple Mount and the Right of Return, but mainly because of their perception that the unrectifiable injustice that the establishment of the State of Israel had inflicted upon them made it impossible to acknowledge the right of the Jewish State of Israel to exist in this region. At Camp David, some of the Israelis realized that the problem at the core of the conflict was not Israeli expansion in the 1967 Six Day War, but rather the outcome of the war of 1948, and possibly even earlier developments.

The Palestinian refusal to acknowledge the religious and historical links that the Jewish people have with the Temple Mount has become, for some Israeli policymakers, the ultimate proof of the Palestinians' unwillingness to come to terms with Israel's existence in the region. During talks at Bolling Air Force Base in December 2000, Shlomo Ben-Ami realized that the formula of land-for-peace was not even nearly enough to resolve the conflict. His discovery that it was Israel's very existence in the region that the Palestinians considered an obstacle, changed his entire perception of the feasibility of resolving the conflict. In his *Ha'aretz* interview with Ari Shavit, Ben-Ami said:

> The Palestinians were not ready to utter the elementary phrase, 'Because the site is sacred to the Jews.' What upset me most was not just the fact that they refused,

but the way in which they refused, with absolute contempt and an attitude of disregard and condescension. It was at that moment that I realized that they were not Sadat; that they were unwilling to make even emotional, symbolic concessions. *In the deepest sense, they are not prepared to acknowledge any right that we have to this land.* (*Ha'aretz*, September 14, 2001, author's emphasis)

The escalation of the violent conflict with the Palestinians led Barak, and Ariel Sharon after him, to maintain that Arafat was an obstacle to peace and that his departure was the key to settling the conflict. Arafat, they concluded, was not capable of making concessions on the most charged issues, even in return for Palestinian sovereignty, and was unable to recognize the legitimacy of a Jewish state whose very establishment was the source of a national disaster for the Palestinians. This conclusion, eventually adopted by the administration of President George W. Bush, gave rise to the view that while the conflict can be resolved, it required the removal of Arafat and implementation of substantial reforms in the Palestinian Authority.

While the implications of the argument that Arafat was the obstacle may be complex, the argument is relatively simple and convenient, because it focuses on a single individual rather than an abstract collective world-view, namely, it postulated that Arafat behaved this way while others are essentially different; this leaves some hope that without Arafat the conflict can still be resolved. However, proponents of the "irresolvable conflict" school of thought argue that this optimism disregards the fact that other Palestinian leaders were also unwilling or unable to make the concessions that Arafat had refused to make on the issues of the Temple Mount and the Right of Return. Furthermore, it is not at all clear whether they have even accepted Israel's right to exist as a Jewish state. If this is the case, then the conflict cannot be resolved and remains at its core a protracted conflict. Hence, the differences between the parties cannot be resolved and any attempt to do so is bound to fail and might lead to another violent outburst. Only a learning process that would fundamentally change the value systems of both sides would could end this protracted conflict.

This explanation is, of course, exceptionally pessimistic, as it effectively rules out any possibility of resolving the Israeli–Palestinian dispute. Many people are therefore unwilling to accept it and prefer explanations that allow some room for change.

## Absence of Ripeness

Ruling out the assumption that the Israeli–Palestinian conflict categorically cannot be resolved makes room for an alternative explanation for the collapse of the peace process. The main argument here is that the Oslo process disintegrated because the ground was not ready for a resolution of the conflict. The parties failed to resolve the conflict because they were not ripe for an accommodation, and ripeness is a precondition for the resolution of any international conflict. "Ripeness" is a key concept for understanding of the transition from a state of war to that of peace. It tries to determine the suitable timing for the resolution of a conflict, and when the parties are ready to settle their differences through political means. Ripeness is reached only when the parties reevaluate their positions and their chances of realizing their goals. Such reevaluation usually stems from mutual learning processes, driven by continuous failure by the parties to accomplish their goals through violent means. In most cases, ripeness emerges after a war (or a sequence of wars) that did not secure the parties' goals and involved an intolerable level of casualties and costs, leading the parties to realize that they have reached a stalemate. The perpetuation of a situation of this kind is unacceptable to both parties, since another war would not get them anywhere and would be just destructive and costly. Thus, both parties have an incentive to consider resolving the conflict by political means, assuming that this avenue is open to them.

The literature dealing with the role of ripeness in the process of settling ethnic and international conflicts does not differentiate between ripeness for negotiations, ripeness for conflict de-escalation for the purpose of securing interim agreements, and ripeness for conflict resolution. A situation is *ripe for negotiation* when both parties are prepared to sit down and talk instead of pursuing force-based options. It is *ripe for de-escalation* when the parties are not ready to resolve the conflict but only to alleviate it. In this case, mechanisms are created for ceasing violence and maintaining peace through security arrangements. Only when the parties acknowledge that resolution of the conflict is the only way in which they can realize at least some of their goals, and that by necessity such resolution would involve painful concessions, is the time *ripe for conflict resolution.*

The Oslo process reflected ripeness for negotiations and even for an interim agreement, but not for conflict resolution. The parties did not thoroughly study the possibility of completely resolving the conflict, because they felt that the situation was not ripe for that; they did not want to risk an examination that might halt the process. The fact that the most complicated issues – such as Jerusalem, refugees, borders and settlements – were left to the end of the process, proves this point.

The ripeness for negotiations that enabled the Oslo process was the outcome of the *intifada* in the years 1987–91. This revolt brought the two sides to a painful dead end, which warmed both to the concept of negotiations. Yitzhak Rabin, who served as defense minister when the *intifada* first started, was gradually convinced that it could not be suppressed by military means. He was also convinced that Israel could not continue controlling another nation and that a political path was needed for gradually resolving the conflict. Rabin considered the Palestinian autonomy framework that was agreed upon in the 1978 Camp David accords between Israel and Egypt as a model for a first stage that would de-escalate the conflict and pave the road for peacemaking. The Gulf War and the demise of the Soviet Union created a window of opportunity for such a process. It is nevertheless doubtful that Rabin would have initiated the Oslo process on his own. He had three agents to nudge him in this direction: Yossi Beilin, Yair Hirschfeld and Ron Pundik. Without them, in all likelihood, Rabin would have made do with an autonomy of the type that Menachem Begin had accepted in the 1978 Camp David accords. Ripeness for negotiations led Rabin to ripeness for an interim agreement, but not necessarily to ripeness for conflict resolution and a permanent status agreement.

Palestinian ripeness was created by the failure of the *intifada* to bring an end to Israeli control, although it did push the Israelis to reassess their continued rule over the Palestinian population and their position on starting a political process that would end in a permanent status agreement. Grassroots pressure in the West Bank and Gaza Strip to seek an arrangement with Israel, coupled with the isolation of the PLO in general and Arafat in particular after their support of Saddam Hussein during the Gulf War, in addition to the fall of the Soviet Union, pushed the Palestinians to the Oslo talks.

The *intifada* was clearly a primary factor in generating ripeness on both sides, but it only prepared the ground for initiating negotiations and securing an interim agreement. The distrust between the parties, as well as the uncertainty regarding the future of the process, did not encourage the parties to proceed directly to conflict resolution. The failure to secure a permanent status agreement at the Camp David summit, and in subsequent negotiations which peaked at Taba, indicate that the first *intifada* did not create the ripeness necessary for a permanent status agreement. Apparently, the painful stalemate to which it led was not sufficient. The ferocity with which the violent conflict was resumed after Camp David supports this argument.

The assumption held by the parties, especially by Israel, that the interim arrangements and direct negotiations would enhance trust and lead to the ripeness needed for resolving the conflict was proven wrong. Trust was not built; in fact, delays in the implementation of the interim agreements and failure to implement them to the letter shattered the partial trust that had existed at the beginning of the process.

The Camp David summit became the first true test of the question whether the conflict was ripe for resolution. Until that time, no one had genuinely tested the parties' ripeness for making the necessary concessions for a permanent status agreement. For various reasons, all sides preferred to refrain from such examination and ignored the matter altogether. Ehud Barak decided that the Camp David summit would test whether the Palestinians were ripe for a resolution of the conflict. His readiness to make extensive concessions (in Israeli terms) demonstrated Israel's ripeness, as these concessions were not only radical compared to those offered by Barak's predecessors but also compared to Barak's own previously declared red lines, especially on the issue of Jerusalem. Barak's take-it-or-leave-it strategy was designed to force the Palestinians to decide whether they were prepared to make the necessary concessions to resolve the conflict, or not. Barak and Clinton interpreted Arafat's rejection of Israel's proposals as indication that Arafat was not ripe to make the necessary historic concessions. His rejection of President Clinton's Parameters and of the Israeli offers made at Taba, and the initiation of the *Aqsa Intifada*, led to the Israeli call to have Arafat replaced because he was an obstacle to peace. As mentioned above, the revised view of Arafat as an "unripe leader," who could not serve as a partner for peace talks and was actually an obstruction to peace, was eventually endorsed by the Bush administration as well. It seems, however, that the focus on Arafat shifted the attention from the fundamental question of whether the Palestinian people at large were ripe for peace, with or without Arafat.

Arafat, like his public, considered the proposals that Barak had made at Camp David as insufficient and inadequate. In his eyes, they reflected an Israeli–American conspiracy aimed at coercing the Palestinians into an unjust agreement. From the Palestinian perspective, their rejection of Barak's proposals did not necessarily indicate their lack of ripeness for resolving the conflict. To them, the fact that they were prepared to make do with only 22% of the territory between the Jordan River and the Mediterranean Sea reflected complete ripeness. The Palestinians were not prepared to accept any agreement that did not include the establishment of a Palestinian state on that territory, sovereignty over east Jerusalem including the Temple Mount, and the Right of Return for Palestinian refugees to all parts of historic Palestine. They would not consider Israel ripe as long as it was not ready to make these concessions. In their view, Israel's demand to enter into an agreement that would end the conflict and close the door on any further claims could not be complied with unless the Palestinian demands on the issues of Jerusalem and the refugees were also met.

Ripeness studies generally focus on the leaders rather than on the public. The assumption is that leaders are the first to be ready to reach that stage, and then they lead their people in this direction. Apparently, in the Oslo process, the leaders of both sides had failed to prepare their respective communities to make the necessary concessions for resolving the conflict. Indeed, the Israeli and Palestinian societies were probably not ready for the proposals made at Camp David and Taba, and in the interim by President Clinton.

The study of ripeness fails to distinguish between situations that require to compromise concrete interests and those that require to make concessions on fundamental national and historic values, myths and narratives. The latter are by definition not only indivisible but also unopen to compromise. It seems that up to the Camp David summit, neither party gave any thought, either at the beginning of the Oslo process or during it, to the difficulty, and perhaps even the impossibility, of bringing the leaders and their peoples to readiness for compromising some of their values. Moreover, neither side had full knowledge or understanding of the level of readiness of the other party for an accommodation at any given time; nor did they know what kind of concessions their counterparts were prepared to make in order to end the conflict. From the beginning of the process, both parties failed to diagnose their interlocutor's degree of ripeness.

Assuming that the two parties, and especially the Palestinians, were not ripe for making the concessions necessary to resolving the conflict, it appears that starting the Oslo process without first looking into the matter of ripeness was a mistake. The collapse of the process not only attested to the lack of ripeness for resolving the conflict, but also aggravated the conflict, as the Palestinians became convinced that violence would serve them better than talks. This, presumably, makes the emergence of any ripeness in the future contingent upon more violence. Indeed, the *Aqsa Intifada* is ostensibly the new "recipe" that may lead the parties to a hurting stalemate, this time an even more painful than that created by the first *intifada*. Not only the level of violence is higher, but even the limited trust that the two sides had developed in one another and in the peace process has been completely shattered.

Can this horrible violence, combined with external developments such as the September 11, 2001 attacks and the eradication of Saddam Hussein's regime, generate new ripeness? Can the Bush Administration's "Road Map to Peace" help the parties ripen? Are the parties riper today to make the necessary concessions than they were in the past? Although it is hard to answer these questions unequivocally, it seems that the answer at this point is essentially no.

## Conclusions

At first glance, it seems that the two explanations suggested here for the collapse of the Oslo process are quite similar, as it is hard to draw a clear distinction between absence of a solution and absence of ripeness. But there is a difference. An irresolvable conflict, by definition, cannot ever reach ripeness. Only a conflict that is not protracted and is not a zero-sum game can be resolved – but only when it reaches ripeness. If indeed the unique attributes of the Israeli–Palestinian conflict make it an irresolvable conflict, then neither the first *intifada* nor the *Aqsa Intifada* could be considered capable of generating the ripeness needed to resolve the conflict. Wars and violence of various kinds are typical of such conflicts, and by themselves are not sufficient to create the required ripeness. Periods of respites and de-escalation are also typical of conflicts of this kind, because the parties need occasionally to refurbish their resources, but they do not necessarily indicate ripeness. According to the "irresolvable conflict" hypothesis, the Oslo process was, of course, misguided from the outset. Moreover, the conclusion would be that any attempt to try and resolve the conflict again would be dangerous, and that therefore the only option available is to manage the conflict through interim agreements that would at least improve security.

The "no ripeness" explanation holds that the conflict can in fact be resolved. However, to achieve the ripeness necessary for this purpose, the parties must be ready to pay a heavy price. The first *intifada*, according to this hypothesis, was a stage that failed to produce such readiness. The current surge of violence is thus expected to push the parties into the painful dead end that is a requirement for ripeness. As extended and intense as this surge may be, it once again proves that the conflict cannot be resolved by military means. Thus, the parties, through an excruciating learning process, are ripening to the stage where they would be ready to resolve the conflict.

Can the parties learn this by themselves? Do they need a third party to help them through this agonizing process? It seems that any renewed effort to resolve the conflict would require first a meticulous examination of the level of ripeness of the parties for making the necessary concessions. No such study has yet been undertaken. The Road Map does not directly address the issue of ripeness. This omission could prove to be its downfall, since ripeness cannot be forced on the parties – this is a stage that they must reach on their own. This has not happened yet. Although the parties are apparently ripe enough for negotiations, it is doubtful that they are sufficiently ripe for resolving the conflict.

## ASHER SUSSER

# The "End of Conflict" Obstacle

I WOULD LIKE TO PRESENT THREE OBSERVATIONS from the perspective of an academic who has been following the history of the Palestinian national movement.

First: The most important issue raised in the Israeli–Palestinian peace process is that of "end of conflict." The question is, to what extent was Israel able in the past, and is able at present, to make progress toward agreeing with the Palestinians on a formal declaration ending the Palestinian–Israeli conflict?

I believe that the Palestinian issue must be viewed as *sui generis* compared to the rest of the Arab-Israel conflict, which is a conflict between sovereign states. The formation of a Palestinian identity was the outcome of the fight over this land, and the formative event in this process was the trauma of 1948, not the defeat in 1967. Hence, one must distinguish between these two critical phases that are historically relevant to the Palestinian tragedy. In my mind, the failure of the Camp David summit may be seen as a manifestation of this tragedy.

There are two historical narratives, the Israeli and the Palestinian, that are very difficult, if not impossible to bridge. To the Israelis, 1948 is the height of their success story of national revival and their most important victory in the last 2,000 years, a victory in which they proudly defied their past as a miserable and persecuted nation. To the Palestinians, 1948 represents the exact opposite. It is the *Nakba*: their colossal historic catastrophe that cost them their homeland and made many of them refugees. This 1948 narrative defines their attitude to the issue of the "end of the conflict." When Israel asks the Palestinians to declare an end of the conflict and an end to their claims, it is in fact seeking a solution that goes beyond a simple rational balance of interests. In other words, it is saying that the negotiations are about history. It is not the balance of interests that is being discussed in the political process but rather the unbridgeable historical narratives. Obviously, no nation could be expected to negotiate its history away as part of a political give-and-take arrangement while a murderous conflict is still under way. Nations negotiate their history among themselves as they write and rewrite it over the course of generations. This is what historiography is all about. The Israeli people have been engaged in an effort of this kind for more than ten years now, in the discourse of those who are known as the New Historians. But it would be premature to discuss narratives with the Palestinians. This may happen only a long time after peace. Today, an entire lifetime after World War II, Poles and Germans can discuss their national narratives with one another, but this kind of dialogue cannot be an integral part of political negotiations between staunch rivals.

Second: Israel never demanded that the Egyptians, Jordanians or even Syrians declare an "end of conflict." With them, Israel talked about the rational balance of interests – territory, water and security arrangements. But in the case of the Palestinians, Israel's government intuitively felt that it needed to ask more of them than it did of the Arab countries. With them, Israel felt it had to demand an end of conflict declaration, because the conflict with them is truly unique.

Actually, it is precisely because of this uniqueness that Israel should never have made this demand. By requiring the Palestinians to end the conflict, in historic terms, and to declare they had no more claims, all the implications of the historical conflict, from its very beginning, were dragged into the negotiations. Thus, the issue of the Right of Return has become the most important subject on the agenda of the Israelis and Palestinians alike. Inevitably, the intense emotions and exposed nerves that underlie the existential issues encapsulated in the narrative of 1948 – and not in the issues engendered by the 1967 war – have become the focus of public discourse among both Israelis and Palestinians. Ask any Palestinian and he will tell you that the problems that now need fixing all started in 1948. From the Palestinian perspective, there is no way to discuss an "end of conflict" without first going back to where it all began, which is when they lost their homeland in 1948, and not when Israel took the West Bank and the Gaza Strip in June 1967.

With Egypt and Syria, it was possible to limit the discussion to territorial demands, which originated in 1967. The Palestinians, however, have two historical experiences: that of 1967, which is the secondary one, and that of

1948, which is at the heart of their historic narrative. Anyone demanding they end the conflict is, by definition, placing the issues of 1948 on the table – issues that for the State of Israel, as the state of the Jewish people, are virtually impossible to resolve. Instead of focusing on ending the conflict, it would have been wiser to strive toward a practical political arrangement that would allow for peace and coexistence, without any declarations about the way the parties understand their histories. It would have been best to make do with a feasible arrangement that both parties could live with.

Speakers who took part in the Camp David summit said here that the issue of refugees was not the cause of the summit's failure, and was mentioned there in passing only. There is no reason to question their account. But ever since Israel first demanded an end of conflict declaration, the issue of the Right of Return has become the most discordant note in public discourse both in Israel and among the Palestinians, even though it was not negotiated at Camp David in detail. Moreover, within a short time this subject took center stage in public discussions. The failure of Camp David, therefore, resulted to a great degree from the fact that the historical narratives had become integral to the negotiations. This did not have to happen. But if one chooses to discuss history, the issue of refugees will almost automatically lead the agenda, as the two are intertwined.

Third: A comment about the institution of summit meetings. In the political process in the Middle East, the Americans are the ultimate referees. Above them there is only God in heaven. However, it is best to ask the referee to step in only when success is guaranteed. Otherwise, if the ultimate referee is called in and the process fails, despair prevails and a feeling is created that the only option left is the battlefield. Those who argued that holding the summit was the best option even though it was liable to fail were wrong. A summit is the last resort that should be saved throughout the political process to be used only at the very last moment, when it is safe to assume that it is the only piece missing to secure an agreement. As we heard here, the situation at Camp David was quite different: the initial substantive gaps were too wide to be bridged, and failure was therefore inevitable.

# ZEEV MAOZ

# The Strategy of Summit Diplomacy

This chapter focuses on the strategy of summit diplomacy, and particularly on the *wrong* way to go about summit diplomacy. Let me begin by placing the Camp David summit in a broader theoretical and historical perspective. One may start with a hypothesis about the nature of a peace process, which we may call the tragedy of peace, or the paradox of peace. Although this hypothesis has never been tested statistically, I suspect that it is germane to many peace processes. It requires us to examine the agreements that existed before any given war in relation to the outcome of that war. A study of the wars that have taken place over the last 200 years reveals an interesting three-tiered procedure: (1) Most of the wars were preceded by agreements that one or both of the parties breached, thus starting the war. After the war, in retrospect, the parties often realized that the breached agreement was better – sometimes by far – than that secured at the end of the war, even without taking into consideration the loss of life and other damages caused by the war. (2) In most cases, the party that breached the original agreement was also the one that was forced to accept, in the post-war agreement, terms that were much worse than those secured by the party that had not breached the pre-war agreement. (3) The peace paradox applied to both the victor and the loser.

The tragedy of peace is that in many cases, the peaceful alternative is attempted only after all other avenues have been tried, and failed. One such example – and there are many others – is that of the agreement offered to Napoleon in December 1813. Had he accepted this agreement, he would have been able to retain one-third of the continent and would not have been forced into exile when the allied forces took Paris six months later.

But why look to Europe when our own conflict here offers many examples? Abba Eban's famous statement that the Palestinians never miss an opportunity to miss an opportunity (the best example being their rejection of the 1947 partition plan) is true of the Israelis as well. If you examine the peace initiatives taken in the Israeli–Arab conflict, you will find that the Israelis are just as good at missing opportunities as the Palestinians. I will offer three examples relating to one or both sides. The first example of an opportunity missed by Israel was the rejection of the interim agreement proposed by Anwar Sadat in February 1971. Had Israel accepted the offer, the Yom Kippur War would probably have been averted. One of the reasons given for the rejection was Golda Meir's objection to the deployment of Egyptian police east of the Suez Canal. Following the war, in which Israel suffered 3,000 fatalities, Egypt deployed in Sinai, by agreement with Israel, not only its police but also a large military force. The tally of missed opportunities is balanced by the second example. Had the Egyptians recognized the State of Israel within the borders of June 4, 1967, neither the Six Day War nor the Yom Kippur War would have taken place.

The third example of the tragedy of peace brings us to the failure of the Camp David summit – another missed opportunity, this time by both Israel and the Palestinians. As many speakers have already pointed out, there is little doubt that in the future, when the parties return to the negotiation table, they will be returning to the parameters defined by President Clinton and the Taba talks. In other words, they will be starting again from the same point, but only after much more loss of life, pain and suffering for both sides. Tragedies of this kind attest to the shortcomings of leaders and their diplomacy.

Summit diplomacy is one of the many techniques used in resolving disputes between foes. In his book, *Diplomacy for the Next Century*, Abba Eban describes summit diplomacy as one of the attributes of what he terms as today's "new diplomacy" – namely, a type of diplomacy that has emerged due to the advanced means of transportation and communications technology, and also to the democratization of international relations. These developments make statesmen accountable to their electorate even when their countries are not democratic. Abba Eban could have mentioned that there is nothing new about summit diplomacy. It has been prevalent since the 19th century (the Congress of Vienna, the Congress of Berlin, the Treaty of Versailles, and of course the conferences at Yalta and Potsdam at the conclusion of World War II). In fact, this kind of diplomacy was used much less in the latter half of the 20th century.

Israeli–Palestinian negotiations were conducted in various formats:

direct meetings between leaders, meetings between delegates sent by the leaders, meetings between a leader and a representative of his counterpart, etc. The format chosen for the Barak–Arafat attempt to resolve the conflict was that of a summit meeting at Camp David. This format deserves elaboration.

There are three types of summit meetings. The first type is the bilateral meeting, where two leaders meet to resolve their differences after their representatives have already conducted direct negotiations. This is the most common type of summit, one that essentially completes and ratifies understandings that have already been achieved by lower-ranking officials. Some of the examples of summits of this kind would be the Nixon–Brezhnev summit which concluded the SALT I treaty; the Mao–Nixon summit of 1972; the summit meeting between Menachem Begin and Anwar Sadat on March 26, 1979 in Washington where they signed the Egyptian–Israeli peace treaty, and the signing of the Oslo Accords in Washington on September 13, 1993. I refer to this category of summit meetings as "end-of-process summits." The second type of summit is that of multilateral meetings, in which multilateral issues are addressed. The Congress of Vienna and the conferences at Yalta and Potsdam belong to this category.

The third type of summit is a multilateral meeting in which one of the key players is involved only as a mediator. This was the case at the Munich Conference of August 1938, in which Mussolini played the role of the mediator. It is to this category that the two Camp David summits belong.

Why are summit meetings arranged? The "end-of-process summit" is convened to give an opportunity to the principals – prime ministers and presidents – to decide on those issues that can be determined only by them, to tie up loose ends left open by the lower-ranking negotiators, and put the authoritative seal of approval on the agreement.

This was not the case in the first or second Camp David summits. The Camp David summits were designed to resolve *substantial* differences between the parties and initiate a mechanism that would pull the process out of a stalemate. This was to be achieved by convening the principal decision-makers who had the authority to make far-reaching, binding decisions. They were to discuss all the issues on the agenda, in most cases without any media coverage, without any contact with the other leaders at home, and under a very tight timetable. The main advantage of this format is that it gives the leaders an opportunity to tackle all the issues at once, without evading any of the problems. Thus, all the controversial issues are consolidated into a single challenge that may push the leaders to reach a comprehensive agreement. The physical insulation of the leaders creates also mental isolation from all the other matters to which they must attend at home (it has been calculated that principal decision-makers deal, on the average, with twenty different subjects every day), and thus give the subject of the summit their undivided attention. The time pressure makes it impossible for them to procrastinate. If they do, the summit is doomed.

An important advantage, for the participating leaders, in summit meetings that conclude with signed agreements is that they win immediate, large rewards. In other words, the accomplishments are identified exclusively with the leaders. The first Camp David summit, for example, is identified with Menachem Begin, Anwar Sadat and Jimmy Carter, not necessarily in that order. Conversely, the failure of summits may become a stain on the record of the participants. Accordingly, the failure of the second Camp David summit is attributed to the leaders rather than to their staff and advisors. It can therefore be said that just as a successful summit can yield positive results for leaders, a failed summit can seriously endanger their careers

The upsides of summits are also their drawbacks. Since all controversies are rolled into one, the risk of complication is great. Thus, instead of discussing only some of the issues and reaching partial, modular solutions, setting aside the issues that cannot be agreed upon at that stage, everything is treated as one package and the end result is a binary win-all/lose-all.

What are the difficulties in a summit meeting? First of all, leaders are generally under heavy pressure, particularly time pressure, and therefore the quality of their performance suffers. Secondly, the isolation from their support and consulting centers adds to their stress, and they bear the responsibility almost alone. Thirdly, there is the danger of leaks. Confidentiality is a crucial element in summit meetings, because without it the parties would not be able to talk freely and avoid external pressures, but when violated, it turns into a disadvantage. Fourthly, since the parties involved are politicians, who very often have inflated egos, confrontations between them might result in serious difficulties in the talks. As we have seen, at the Camp David summit, the leaders hardly held any direct communication. At the first, the mediator was able to mediate and bridge their differences, at the second he was not.

What then happened at the Camp David summit in July 2000? What factors could have led to its success, and their absence explains its failure? A key factor in the success of any summit is the preparedness of the parties involved. In this case, preparation for the summit was inadequate, not only that of the Israeli and Palestinian parties, but also that of the American team.

Another factor that influences the success or failure of negotiations is the existence in the negotiations of a "single text." In most cases this means that the process of negotiations is based on one text that had been prepared by the mediator. This kind of text was absent from the Camp David summit; it was only added later, in the form of President Clinton's peace parameters. There is no telling whether the introduction of such a text earlier would have altered the outcome of the summit, but its absence surely played a role in the summit's failure.

A third factor that is crucial to the success of a summit meeting is the pivotal role of the mediator in generating a certain level of time pressure and psychological stress. For effective performance, the optimal level of such pressure must be neither too high nor too low: if the pressure is too great, the leaders do not function effectively; if the atmosphere is too relaxed, the incentive to conclude the talks will decrease. The Camp David summit was subject to artificial pressure created by Clinton's scheduled trip to the economic summit in Okinawa. However, the summit's deadline was deferred, because Clinton returned and continued his mediation efforts. The termination date of the summit was therefore unclear, and thus did not play its role.

A fourth factor is the effectiveness of the structure of the agenda. The agenda prepared by the third party at Camp David was apparently unclear; it was tentative or improvised. Negotiators jumped from one topic to the next even before they finished dealing with the first topic. One task of a mediator is to manipulate the agenda in order to link issues. According to Israeli participants, such linkage was hardly created at Camp David. Separate proposals were put on the table about territory, Jerusalem and refugees, but no linkage was created between them.

A fifth factor needed for the success of a summit is the ability of the mediator to empathize with the narratives and myths of the parties and try to harmonize them. One of the problems in this conflict is the existence of disparate premises and truths for each of the bones of contention, which makes it hard to create any mutuality. The mediator should expose contradictory preconceived notions in the positions of the parties. For example, one of the prominent Israeli notions had it that the relocation of the settlers from the West Bank would lead to an internal Israeli civil war and therefore was not negotiable. At the same time the Israelis expected the Palestinians to engage in a civil war for eradicating terror and dismantling the militant organizations

A sixth factor vital to the success of a summit is the political strength of the participating leaders. The mediator must appraise correctly the degree to which the leaders he is working with are firmly established in their positions. This is critical for the success or failure of any talks, and of summit meetings in particular. The American mediator apparently did not give enough weight to the problematical situation of Barak, who had the support of an unstable coalition that included a mere quarter of the 120 members of Knesset. A leader with such little support at home has limited maneuvering scope. Barak and his team should be credited for nevertheless having the courage to transcend the boundaries that even their own coalition members would hardly dare to cross. In any case, the performance of the Israeli chief negotiator was constrained by the fact that he was the leader of a minority cabinet. Similarly, the Americans did not properly evaluate the true level of political strength that Arafat had for concessions, *vis-à-vis* his Palestinian constituency and the Arab world.

Then there is the question of asymmetry of power between the negotiators. If the Palestinians' complaint that they were not ready for the summit and had suggested instead another date is true, it was wrong to twist their arm and force the summit on them at that time. This brought out the basic asymmetry between the stronger and weaker party. Forcing the weaker party into anything, even a technicality, only makes it feel weaker and pushes it into a defiant defensive posture. Having been pressed into a corner, it is harder for the weaker side to make courageous decisions. The Israelis expected Arafat to make "Ben-Gurion-style" decisions but it was difficult to make them from a position of weakness. The mediator should, in fact, do the opposite and instill in the weaker party a feeling that its difficulties and needs are heeded. Therein lay the biggest difference between Carter 1978 and Clinton 2000. Carter realized that Sadat had put his life on the line when he came to Jerusalem. He understood that Sadat was the more vulnerable party and that he was the one to be placated, not only in matters of substance but also in matters of procedure and symbol. Clinton and his team did the opposite: they pushed the Palestinians to the corner. Strategists have long since recognized that the most stubborn adversary is the one who has his back to the wall.

The main lesson to be learned from the Camp David summit, therefore, is that in the future things should be done in an entirely different way. Let me stress that I am not talking about the substantive aspects of the summit but rather about the procedural ones. There are two ways of learning from history: there is the classical concept of learning, according to which he who does not learn history's lesson is doomed to repeat it, and there is the Israeli way of learning, according to which one must study history and learn the lessons of his mistakes, only to repeat them the next time. If we truly want to learn from the failure of the Camp David summit any lesson that we can implement in future summit diplomacy and in negotiations in general, then we must carefully study our own mistakes, not those of the other side. The notion, to which former prime minister Barak subscribes, that the other side was entirely to blame while his moves were unimpeachable and there is therefore no need to revisit them, is unproductive and not useful; it will not help Israel to find a way out of the stalemate.

## Remarks during the Discussion

Did Barak genuinely want an agreement, even if it meant not getting everything he wanted? My basic assumption is that whenever two parties enter negotiations, they calculate that avoiding them will create a worse situation than the existing one and that there is a certain range within which an agreement might perhaps be reached. If this is not the calculation, or if the only purpose of entering negotiations is to make some personal political gains, the negotiations of course are likely to fail. It is my impression that Ehud Barak really wanted to conclude an agreement and knew well that this would require concessions. Otherwise, it is hard to see why he wanted to enter these talks, and take the risk of political suicide. The big question is not whether he really wanted an agreement, but whether he fully understood what kind of concessions he would be required to make.

PETER CARNEVALE

# Psychological Barriers to Negotiations

The "fog of war" concept refers to the difficulty of seeing what is really taking place during the heat of the battle. The concept can also apply to peace negotiations, including the negotiations that took place at the Camp David summit in July 2000. There are many contradictory personal accounts of these negotiations and the follow-up talks in Washington and Taba, and it seems that they just increase the fog. A quote that particularly makes this point comes from an article by Hussein Agha and Robert Malley, "Camp David: The Tragedy of Errors," *New York Review of Books*, August 9, 2001:

> Ask Barak, and he might volunteer that there was no Israeli offer and, besides, Arafat rejected it. Ask Arafat, and the response you might hear is that there was no offer, besides, it was unacceptable; that said, it had better remain on the table.

Another great line comes from the interview of Ehud Barak by Benny Morris which immediately followed the Agha and Malley article ("Camp David and After: An Exchange," *New York Review of Books*, June 13, 2002). This is from a phone call from Bill Clinton to Barak, hours after the publication of Deborah Sontag's "revisionist" article in *The New York Times*, July 21, 2001:

> What the hell is this? Why is she turning the mistakes we [i.e., the US and Israel] made into the essence? The true story of Camp David was that for the first time in the history of the conflict the American president put on the table a proposal, based on UN Security Council resolutions 242 and 338, very close to the Palestinian demands, and Arafat refused even to accept it as a basis for negotiations, walked out of the room, and deliberately turned to terrorism. That's the real story—all the rest is gossip.

Various explanations are offered for the failure. Agha and Malley point to methodological mistakes; Dennis Ross and others point to a personality; and Gidi Grinstein contends that "the foundation of the failure lies in the [un]willingness and the [in]capacity of the respective leaderships to seize a historic opportunity at a high political cost and not in tactical and methodological mistakes" ("Camp David: An Exchange," *New York Review of Books*, September 20, 2001). Other observers say that Taba proved that the teams of negotiators could reach an agreement, but the leaders made the political judgment that it was not the right time for it. Yet others suggest that Arafat was reluctant to say "yes" at that time because both Barak and Clinton were lame ducks and Arafat was afraid that he would be making concessions and getting nothing in return.

About the Taba talks, we have the "Moratinos Non-Paper," but that has not gone unchallenged. One critic, Raymond Cohen, put it this way:

> The importance of Taba has been inflated by Moratinos, and his account bore no relation to what really happened there. He wanted to put the most favorable spin on inchoate events. Taba itself should never have taken place, as the Israeli government no longer had a mandate to negotiate, certainly not under fire. (Personal Communication)

A noteworthy effort to see through the fog may be found in David Matz's report of his interviews with 17 of the 28 participants who were at the Taba negotiations (David Matz, "How Much Do We Know About Real Negotiations? Problems in Constructing Case Studies," *International Negotiation Journal*, Vol. 9, #3, 2004).

However, psychologists know all too well the problematic validity of verbal reports. Add the political context to the reports and matters get worse. Memory is not perfect, people like to exaggerate their own importance, they have scores to settle. Observers, even those who are not naïve (including the European envoys who snoop around the hallway during negotiations . . . ), are still not above political spins.

Given that, the brief analysis offered here is not claiming, "This is what happened, and here is the psychology that explains it." Rather, it tentatively suggests that, "If this is what happened, then it is possible that such-and-such psychological factors were involved." So, rather than debating whether something did or did not happen, the focus here is on the question how psychological processes may operate in difficult negotiations and mediations.

We hear much about "psychological barriers." What do they mean? The term can, of course, mean a variety of different things. It is worth noting that the phrase has appeared in important political statements. It appeared in Sadat's speech to the Knesset in November 1977, and it appeared in the preamble to the October 1994 Treaty between Israel and Jordan. This treaty begins with the statement:

> Bearing in mind the importance of maintaining and strengthening peace based on freedom, equality, justice and respect for fundamental human rights, thereby overcoming psychological barriers and promoting human dignity, etc.

US Defense Secretary Donald Rumsfeld used the same phrase some time ago when he described the change in the US–Russian security arrangements on ballistic missiles. Rumsfeld said:

> There are psychological barriers to creating new security relations with Russia . . . It is a baggage that exists in people's minds – it exists in treaties, it exists in the structure of relationships . . . And it will require, I think, some time to work through these things and see if we can't set the relationship on a different basis.

The term "psychological barriers" is not some sort of psycho-babble about jumping into the depths of someone's mind in order to understand why that person could not make a deal. Instead, it is about the mechanics and processes of negotiation that can get in the way of reaching an agreement, particularly a good one. A good agreement, in this context, means simply some kind of accommodation that all, or perhaps most, of the parties can live with.

The present analysis focuses on three aspects of the mechanics of negotiation and mediation that may be relevant to the failure of the Camp David summit and Taba talks. All these factors can create psychological barriers to agreement through negotiations. The three are: (1) Problems of agenda, (2) Problems of time pressure, and (3) Problems of mediation.

## Problems of Agenda

At a recent conference at New York University, Shlomo Ben-Ami, who led the Israeli effort at Taba, was asked what mistakes were made at Taba. His answer was interesting, especially from the perspective of a psychologist who studies negotiation and social conflict. One part of his answer had to do with the mechanics of negotiation, about the nuts and bolts of the process. He said, "We go in, incrementally, make concessions on the easy issues, then everything collapses when we get to the tough issues."

The question of how to structure the agenda of issues is objective, but it also relates to psychological barriers. Moreover, it is relevant not just to the negotiators, but also to mediators, because a good mediator can often control the order and manner in which issues get discussed. Should the agenda be structured so that the easy issues are dealt with first, and the tough issues later? Or should it be the reverse, with the tough issues scheduled first? In the case of Israeli–Palestinian negotiations – should the discussion deal first with the hard issue of refugees or leave it to the end? This question is related to another dilemma, whether to have separate negotiation teams for each issue, or discuss all issues in the same forum.

Research on issue agendas in negotiations suggests that there are two possible methods, each based on a different concept. One method is based on the concept of momentum. Momentum refers to an increase in cooperation, or an increase in the belief that cooperation will succeed. The idea is this: If we have some early agreements on easy issues, then we have some momentum, and this will increase the chances that our negotiations on the tough issues will result in an agreement. However, most of the evidence supports the second method, which is based on the concept of tradeoffs. It suggests that tough issues should not be saved for later, but should be dealt with at the start. In fact, all the issues should be treated simultaneously. The idea is simple: If we have all the issues on the table in front of us, we might be able to find connections between them and make a better deal. If we can identify tradeoffs and links among issues, the chances of reaching an agreement might be better. This is a proposition that is supported in many studies by experts on negotiation, psychologists and other specialists. It is interesting to note that at the meeting in New York, Ben-Ami mentioned that someone at Taba proposed that some refugees could return to settlements abandoned by Israel. This reflects a promising possible linkage between an agreement on the refugee issue and that on the settlements issue.

Of course, complex negotiations like those in the Middle East can involve a large number of issues, and in this case there is no way to consider all of them simultaneously. It is simply too complicated a task, intellectually and instrumentally. The solution may be found in a framework agreement – like the first 1978 Camp David Accords or the Oslo-based 1993 Declaration of Principles – which deals with the major issues and provides a thumbnail sketch of the final agreement. Then it would be possible to assign the different parts of this framework to committees which will work out the details. I. William Zartman ("Negotiation as a Joint Decision-Making Process," *Journal of Conflict Resolution,* Vol. 21, #4, 1977) refers to this progression of agreements as "formula and detail." In developing the framework agreement, it is important that tradeoffs involving all the major issues are worked out. If there are only a few major issues, they should be discussed simultaneously. However, if there are many cardinal issues, and it becomes impossible to consider them simultaneously, then major issues should be discussed sequentially, while deferring the conclusion of binding agreements until everything has been discussed. This allows skilled participants to propose tradeoffs between issues that were discussed earlier and those now under discussion. These points about agendas are all made by Dean Pruitt (*Negotiation Behavior*, New York: Academic Press, 1981). It should also be noted that sometimes there are preliminaries that must be cleared up before other issues can be discussed. For example, often the parties are unwilling to engage in formal negotiations until an agreement on a cease-fire is reached.

## Problems of Time Pressure

The Camp David summit and the subsequent talks have been characterized as "a hurried, unsuccessful six-month effort . . . to solve a one hundred-year conflict in a matter of months . . . " with "mismatched timetables" (Robert Malley and Hussein Agha, in their above mentioned article). It was reported that both Clinton and Barak announced during the process that all ideas raised during the talks would "depart with the President," that is, would be off the table if there was no agreement by that time.

The value of time pressure is questionable either before or during a summit. But one should keep in mind all the preparations that had taken place, sometimes for a year or two prior to the start of negotiations. It takes time to get all the issues out on the table, think up integrative agreements, test the other side's readiness to make concessions, persuade constituents that the other side will make no further concessions, lower one's own aspirations and those of one's constituents, and wiggle out of unwise commitments. For all these reasons, mediators are advised not to set time limits for the negotiations. The beginning of a summit should not be fixed according to a rigid time-table but delayed until a mutually acceptable agreement is pretty clearly in sight. I doubt if a mutually acceptable agreement was in sight in July 2000.

As for the period of the negotiations, there is a common belief that under time pressure, people tend to make concessions and agreements more quickly. Sometimes this is indeed the case. Often, however, time pressure leads one party to remain unbending, thinking that the other party will make the moves necessary for concluding an agreement. This is especially likely if the strategic game is "chicken," where both parties know that the consequences of non-agreement are the worst possible outcome. When people believe they are in a "chicken" situation, they are tempted to make unilateral, irrevocable commitments to positions and use time pressure as a strategy to force the other to capitulate. In the negotiation literature, this is called "mismatching," and studies show that mismatching is likely to occur especially under the pressure of time. Evidently, time pressure was operating both at Camp David and Taba. Martin Indyk has reported as much in his description of the timing of Barak's proposal just before Clinton had to leave Camp David.

Time pressure can produce a failure to reach agreement, especially if it occurs when trust is low and hostility is high. There is evidence that the Camp David negotiations were hostile in tone and content, and that there was an especially suspicious state of mind on the Palestinian side. Agha and Malley argue, and Dennis Ross did not disagree, that Barak's decisions not to implement some of the interim commitments made by Israel to the Palestinians in the preceding years, and not to turn over three Jerusalem-area neighborhoods to them, contributed to the Palestinians' hostile mood. Adding time pressure to hostility only increases hostility. Sometimes it should be the role of mediators to control the parties' sense of time pressure by influencing the agenda, thus removing these psychological barriers to negotiation.

## Problems of Mediation

It is difficult to get a sense of the style of mediation that was employed at the Camp David summit. Obviously it was problematic: When a mediator gets angry, and yells at one of the parties, using words like, "Give me something better! . . . This is a fraud . . . Let's quit! . . . I should go home . . . Let's let hell break loose and live with the consequences," as Clinton reportedly did, something was not done right. All the more so if the mediator says these things in a forum where people on the other side, and the public at large, could hear about it, and where the recipient is from a culture that places special value on respect and honor.

How can mediators alleviate problems of communication and usage of offensive language? First, the mediator himself must be very accurate in his statements and avoid generating misunderstandings. We have evidence from the "Moratinos Non-Paper" that Clinton made a mistake on one of the toughest issues of the negotiations: the Western Wall. Clinton apparently referred to "the holy parts" of the Wall, which led the Palestinians to claim that only the exposed part of the Wall is considered holy to the Jews, and therefore only this part should be left under Israeli sovereignty. This, of course, ignored the Western Wall tunnels.

There is no doubt that the Palestinians' assertion in the talks that the Jewish Temple had never existed in Jerusalem was shocking and offensive, creating a serious problem in the negotiations. Such problems should be handled by mediation. A mediator needs to control communication processes in direct negotiations so that inflammatory pronouncements do not impact the talks negatively.

We know that at the 1978 Camp David summit, Begin and Sadat met a few times face-to-face, and the communication between them did not work so well. The mediator, Jimmy Carter, understood that he must control the situation. Most of the productive negotiating indeed occurred in separate meetings with the US team, privately and in confidence. Begin and Sadat had only occasional face-to-face contact, some of which took place outside the negotiations. For example, Carter took both leaders to Gettysburg, the US Civil War battlefield (where Begin made quite a positive impression on the Americans there when he recited by memory Abraham Lincoln's Gettysburg Address).

Controlling the communication process allows mediators to manage the negotiation process, and if done well, neither party will feel that the mediator is just running a messenger service for the other side's positions and offers. In fact, there is good evidence that separating the parties and managing the offer-making process is an important element of mediation which helps the parties save face while at the same time progress toward agreement.

How can the mediator deal with internal disagreement within one delegation? There are reports that, at the Camp David summit, the negotiating teams on both sides of the table suffered from internal discord, in particular the Palestinian side. Dennis Ross states, in his criticism of Arafat, that

> he did nothing to control the fratricidal competition in his delegation effectively giving license to those who were attacking other members who were trying to find ways to bridge the differences. (NYRB, September 20, 2001)

According to Gidi Grinstein,

> Rarely was there an integrated Palestinian position. Sometimes more than one Palestinian claimed to have the authority to negotiate. At other times, senior Palestinians would undermine their own official delegation ... It was a messy collective paralysis. (Ibid.)

Groups engaged in negotiations with other groups do not perform well when there is internal disarray within their group. In laboratory research at New York University, groups of individuals were formed and were assigned the task of attempting to reach agreement with other groups in a simulated conflict. The in-group decision process was experimentally controlled: in some cases, a hostile in-group process was artificially initiated and in other cases a cooperative process was created. Then these groups negotiated with other groups. The experiment showed clearly that groups that had high internal conflict were less likely to reach agreement with the other groups.

One implication of this is that mediators of conflicts should pay attention to the within-group processes as much as the between-group processes, and try to encourage cooperation and stability within each side.

There is relevant evidence from field studies conducted among professional labor mediators. Mediation literature shows that dealing with internal-party issues is one thing that labor mediators can do well, and this can have a positive impact on between-group negotiations. There is also evidence that mediators who deal with a situation where there are internal problems within one or both negotiating teams find it harder to build trust between the parties and improve the negotiation.

What can mediators do to reduce biases that come from misperception? Part of the problem in misperceiving a situation is selective memory and selective use of information in order to support one's preferred position. People tend to interpret information in negotiations in a way that serves their own interests. A case in point are the different interpretations of UN General Assembly Resolution 194. Does it actually specify a Right of Return for refugees, as the Palestinians claim, or does it call for a more qualified permission to return for "the refugees wishing to return to their homes and live at peace with their neighbors," as many Israelis argue? One thing a mediator should be able to do is help the parties to correctly use memory and information to support a mutually acceptable agreement, rather than the preferred position of one party or another.

Finally, good deals in negotiations often result from figuring out what the other side really needs, and then coming up with a way to give it to them in exchange for something one needs oneself. Good deals also require creative thinking, as well as the courage to break new ground. This is where a mediator can be helpful. In private meetings, a mediator can try out ideas that may at first sound outlandish but might help break a logjam.

However, it is hard to see how even creative thinking can make it possible to give up assets seen as touching the very core of one's existence. I am reminded of the warning issued to Ehud Barak by Jerusalem's mayor Ehud Olmert who declared to the 100,000 Israelis who paraded at the Old City, "We never forgive those who dare to raise their hands against our most precious treasures." How can people be made to share ownership of sites and buildings that are at the core of their very identity and existence? This is not an easy task, but mediators can help.

## Remarks during the Discussion

Regarding the relative importance of two factors related to asymmetry in negotiations: One of the factors is time pressure, namely which party is under greater or lesser time pressure; the other factor is the walk-away value, that is, which side can walk away with less damage to himself. The two factors may be interconnected, meaning that the effects of walking away are exacerbated under high time pressure. Under less time pressure, the side that can walk away more easily may choose to stick around for a longer period of time since, in this situation, the benefits of walking away are smaller or may even disappear. This suggests that it may have been a strategic mistake for Barak to throw time pressure into the mix.

# Roundtable

YULI TAMIR, YUVAL STEINITZ, DAN
MERIDOR, YOSSI BEILIN

# Past, Present and Future – A
# Political Debate

## ROUND ONE

### David Witzthum, Moderator

In this three-round summing up session we will discuss the past, present and future of Israeli–Palestinian relations in light of the Camp David experience. Although all the panelists represent the Israeli side only, we are sure to have at least four different perspectives. We have here two speakers from the Left and two from the Right. They are all renowned personalities in Israel's political life and at the same time have distinguished academic records. I suggest that in the first round we focus on analyzing "what went wrong" in the Camp David summit.

### Yuli Tamir

I am not sure that the Camp David summit should be judged as a complete failure. The merits of such events and actions should not be measured only by their tangible outcome but also by their contribution to changing public consciousness.

There are moments in which public consciousness changes, for better or worse, as the result of the appearance of exceptional ideas or actions. From this perspective, there were two decisive moments in Israel's history that we can consider. One of them, the Six Day War of June 1967, was considered a great triumph, whereas the other, the Camp David summit of July 2000, was seen as a failure. The Six Day War created a wrong kind of public consciousness, one that idolized power, disregarded the neighboring nations and dictated a misguided order of priorities. This caused extensive political, economic and social damages. In this respect, the Six Day War may have been a military victory, but it was a failure in terms of its effects on public consciousness.

The Camp David summit, on the other hand, was declared a political failure but nevertheless produced positive results in terms of public consciousness. The summit made the public develop new perceptions and new insights concerning the solution of the Israeli–Palestinian conflict. This consciousness will facilitate any future attempt to resolve the conflict. It understands the limits of power, the vital importance of negotiations, the need for compromise and the necessity of recognizing the legitimate political status and needs of the other side.

One of the influential positions that appeared for the first time at Camp David was the willingness to compromise on the issue of Jerusalem. I remember how emotional the discussion of the issue of Jerusalem used to be before that. The experts were saying that even the mentioning alone of a possible compromise on Jerusalem would stir up unprecedented turmoil; people would rally in the streets and the protest would get out of hand. And yet only a few years after the Labor party lost the 1996 elections largely because of a campaign frightening the public that "Peres will divide Jerusalem," Barak proposed at Camp David doing just that and nothing happened. The consensus around the prohibition on any debate over this issue no longer exists. The exact boundaries of the compromise will still require negotiations, but in public consciousness the possibility of the partition of Jerusalem is already a fait accompli.

The Palestinian side also has undergone a process of this kind and the Camp David summit created a new consciousness there too. The concept of two states for two peoples has gained more support. The Green Line is no longer a sacred cow: the Palestinians have agreed in principle to consider, as part of the peace agreement, modifications to this line, including Israeli annexation of certain areas, notably the Jewish neighborhoods around Jerusalem.

The concepts that became acceptable at Camp David will live with us until we finally reach a peace agreement. The effects of the summit were a counterweight to those of the victory in the Six Day War, which led to a disastrous euphoria that lasted three decades. Maybe we needed also the horrendous violence in the years that followed the summit to allow the concept of our vulnerability to sink in, along with the concept of the need for a compromise. Together, these two realizations are part of the comprehensive change in public consciousness.

I would like to point out three causes for the failure of the summit. First of all, the fact that the Arab world was not represented there contributed significantly to the negative outcome. Arafat came to the summit from a position of weakness, and feeling that he had neither the power nor the necessary backing for making substantial decisions. Had he had an Arab shoulder to lean on, his decisions may have been different. It was unwise to isolate Arafat from the other Arab leaders and make him face a united American–Israeli front at the summit. It is very hard to make historic decisions under such circumstances, especially decisions that require making concessions on behalf of large populations and the generations to come, and actually on behalf of the Arab world as well.

Secondly, the perception of the summit as a one-time meeting, without preparing a follow-up, owing to America's and Israel's political timetable, made the failure of the summit become the failure of the entire process. Peace agreements in the Middle East cannot be scheduled around the American timetable. The window of opportunities cannot be shut whenever a particular president steps down. Eventually, all American presidents will find themselves drawn into the Israeli–Palestinian conflict. Changes in the administration may slow down the process, but a leader must not identify personally with a peace process he is steering to the extent that his departure might be seen as ending the process. Sound political processes can survive changes in leadership, but Clinton and Barak refused to acknowledge this. The identity they created between themselves and the process they were leading was misguided and harmful. Unfortunately, this problem is sure to plague us in the future as well.

Thirdly, the biggest damage was not created by the failure of the summit, but by the way it was portrayed after the fact. After the summit, Nabil Sha'ath told me that the Camp David summit was a very productive "first step." Indeed, had we left the summit knowing that it was just the first of more subsequent meetings, the impact of the failure of this summit would have been much smaller. It was wrong to expect that a comprehensive peace agreement would be drafted and signed during a single summit. It was also wrong to assume that if this summit failed the entire process failed with it. We should have summed up the summit as a significant attempt that should be continued.

### Yuval Steinitz

If the Camp David summit can be called a success, I do not know what counts as a failure. In my mind, the summit was definitely a failure. An attempt was made there to make peace and end the conflict. I was very critical of that effort, but I cannot deny that it was sincere and extremely courageous. But this effort, in addition to failing, thrust us into years of a war of attrition and terrorist actions worse even than we had during the bloody years of 1994–97. So if this does not count as a failure, I do not know what standard we use to define a failure. On this, I differ with MK Yuli Tamir.

Let me state who I think is to blame for this failure. In my mind, the blame for the failure of the summit is certainly not with the Israelis or the Americans, and even – and this may surprise you – not with Arafat and the Palestinians, at least not exclusively. I think that the Camp David summit was systematically impeded by the Arab world, the regimes which do not genuinely want the peace process to succeed and find that the process does not promote their essential interests – I speak of regimes, not necessarily nations. Therefore, even if the Palestinians had been ready to compromise at Camp David, I believe that their hands were tied.

I would like to present an interpretation of what happened at Camp David and I feel somewhat uncomfortable doing this in the presence of former Prime Minister Ehud Barak. Some members of academe, including philosophers, believe that the best interpreter of the statements and actions of an individual is that individual himself. I disagree. I can refer you to Ze'ev Bechler's excellent paper on the 17th century scientific revolution, contained in the book, *Science in Context*, which offers a brilliant analysis of this question. I believe that an interpretation from the outside is perfectly legitimate and may be insightful.

When I look back at the Camp David summit, I see an Israeli prime minister, Ehud Barak, who felt that the arrangements of the Oslo interim period were not building trust between the parties as originally intended, but rather eroding it, and that the process that evolved in the years preceding the summit was destructive and fraught with dangers. He therefore decided it was time to terminate this interim process and try to reach a permanent status agreement. In order to convince Arafat to sign a peace agreement and make serious concessions on behalf of the Palestinians, such as recognizing the State of Israel as a Jewish state and almost completely giving up the Right of Return, the prime minister prepared a strategic surprise for the summit that was meant to shake up Arafat and get him to sign a peace agreement, or at least a framework agreement. He prepared it as a strategist and a general who tries to decide the outcome of a battle with a daring and unexpected move at the crucial moment. As we all know, the surprise was his agreement to divide Jerusalem. Not only was Arafat surprised, but also most of the Israeli delegation, for it was the first time that such an offer was made by Israel.

Barak's model for Jerusalem divided the city into Arab and Jewish neighborhoods, with the sites that are holy to Muslims and Christians to be controlled by the Palestinians, and the Western Wall and the excavations near it by the Israelis. Barak evidently expected that the surprised Arafat, who would see this as a real chance to score a substantial achievement on the issue of Jerusalem, would sign the agreement. If Arafat did not, he would be putting himself in a very hard spot, because none of the parties would understand a rejection of such a far-reaching gesture.

The day after Barak sprung his surprise, President Husni Mubarak said on Egyptian TV that Arafat did not have the authority to divide Jerusalem and the Old City. This was an all-Arab and all-Muslim matter, he said, and whoever agrees to the partition would be considered a traitor to Arab and Muslim history. He said he was confident that Arafat would not do such a thing. Another day went by, and other Arab leaders, including leaders of states that still refuse to acknowledge the existence of the State of Israel, echoed Mubarak's statement.

I think that if Arafat had wanted to sign, he could have done so despite opposition from the radical Middle Eastern states – Syria, Iraq and Iran – provided he had the support of the moderate Arab countries, with Egypt taking the lead. Mubarak's statement on TV was exceptional; in most cases, Egypt's interference is much more subtle and is often so sophisticated that it is even hard to detect. But in this case it was all out in the open for everybody to hear. Arafat understood that he could not sign; he backtracked and found no other way but to resume the violence. That is the only explanation I have.

Egypt has consistently opposed peace agreements of other Arabs with Israel. It was unhappy about the peace agreement with Jordan a few years before: Egypt pressured King Hussein not to sign the agreement and Mubarak was conspicuously absent from the signing ceremony, which was attended by Clinton, Rabin and Hussein (although Mubarak did send his foreign minister). Even during the term of the late Yitzhak Rabin, Egypt had pressured other countries, such as Qatar and Morocco, not to normalize their relations with Israel.

Unfortunately, this was consistent with Egyptian behavior in general. While Jordan has been making a serious effort to stop arms smuggling across the border, the smuggling from Egypt's Sinai peninsula to the Territories continues. Egypt has close ties with Hamas; this is evident in its subtle threats to the Palestinian Authority lest it dismantle Hamas, and in its efforts to promote a *hudna* (ceasefire) which would give Hamas a breathing spell.

To conclude, the Palestinians operate under serious constraints, being surrounded by a large Arab world whose interests must be heeded; this Arab constituency is therefore pivotal to the prospect of peace between Israel and the Palestinians. Anyone who believes that peace between Israel and the Palestinians, or at least serious movement in this direction, can be realized without first achieving peace with the Arab world is misguided.

## Yossi Beilin

It seems that the Camp David summit was the political equivalent of the Yom Kippur War. It is seen as the "mother of all disasters," and as such, everything there is now considered to have been misguided, just as everything there would have been considered right if the outcome had been a success. Perhaps if the Camp David summit of 1978 had ended when Begin and his colleagues packed their suitcases to go home, the whole episode would have been perceived as a big mistake. But the success of that summit has turned the whole Israeli–Egyptian process of that time into a model for emulation.

What were the most misguided things about the summit? There is truth to the observation of MK Steinitz that at Camp David a genuine attempt was made to resolve the Israeli–Palestinian conflict with just one stroke of the pen and that Clinton was really seeking Arab support but unfortunately did not receive any. However, my own answer to this question is that the failure of the Camp David summit was caused by a wrong sequence of events.

Before the summit, talks should have been held at a lower level. Granted, such talks had been held in Stockholm, but they were discontinued, for various reasons, and therefore did not reach the stage of a comprehensive discussion of all the issues on the agenda. The prime minister at the time, Ehud Barak, forbade the negotiators in Stockholm to discuss some of the issues that he wanted to leave for the "moment of truth" at the summit (mainly Jerusalem). I think that was a mistake. He should have allowed his ministers or senior officials to reach substantive agreement on as many issues as they could. The negotiators on that level would then have been able to identify the difficult points and divide the issues into those on which agreement had been reached and those which remained outstanding. This was also the appropriate venue to draft a plan of the kind subsequently Clinton proposed (in retrospect, Clinton's plan turned out to be the greatest benefit produced by the summit – to this day it is the only document that both parties have indicated they might accept). The differences between the parties should have been bridged before the leaders met at the summit. The summit itself should have been short, two or three days at the most, focusing on the remaining disputes only.

The core issues in this conflict are the Right of Return and the Temple Mount/Holy Basin. The solution is rather straightforward – Clinton has already drafted it. The summit should have been convened only after the completion of talks like the ones that were later conducted at Taba. Barak may be right when he says that the Taba talks were less committal, but they were good talks conducted on the ministerial level. The results of those talks could have been used to demarcate broad areas of consensus. Then Clinton's proposal could have been addressed, and finally all this could have been taken to the summit. I think that if things had been done in this order, an agreement could have been reached.

What does the presence of a third party in such a summit mean? What would the summit have looked like if it were only a bilateral summit, as many of us wanted it to be, instead of a summit directly conducted by a third party who is also a global leader? Clinton played a key role in those critical two weeks. Barak was writing letters to Clinton and Arafat was writing letters to Clinton. Then Clinton took off to Okinawa, and meanwhile there was trouble in Camp David. This was wrong. The energies of the two parties should have been directed toward each other; instead they were directed at the American mediator. It is possible that at that stage of the negotiations there was no longer any choice but to seek the help of America, which is indeed a great friend of Israel and undoubtedly wanted very much to secure an agreement, but also charged Israel very high "mediation fees."

I am sure that a summit of this kind will take place again in the future, and the contours will not necessarily be any different. But the main lesson is that we must not go to such a two-week summit in which the leaders themselves discuss the fine points of the negotiations and reveal the concessions they are ready to make. This was manifest in the bickering about territory: the percentage of territory which Israel insisted on retaining went down from 13% to 11.3%, to 10.5%, to 9% and then, at Taba, to 6.2%. Such tactics applied by the leader invite additional demands. This rule applies for both sides: the leaders must not hold negotiations themselves.

What role did Egypt play in the summit? Ever since the peace agreement with Egypt was signed, Egypt has played a very positive role. I disagree with the criticism that MK Steinitz has leveled here at Egypt, and not for the first time. However, I do agree with him on one point. After the Camp David summit, one of the Palestinian delegates told me that the Palestinians had received during the negotiations a telephone call from "an Arab leader that everyone here knows," who told them that it was very important that they conclude an agreement, and mentioned that he had spoken about it with Clinton. (By the way, Clinton did not inform any Arab leader of anything that was going on at the summit; all he did was to ask them to support the negotiators and commend them on the progress they were making.) When the Palestinians requested from that Arab leader that he express his support for the conclusion of an agreement not only over the phone but on TV as well, the Arab leader refused. Hence, Egypt certainly could have done more to support the negotiations.

### Dan Meridor

I kept a diary at Camp David, but I did not publish it because I did not see fit to rush and tell the public everything that had been said at the closed meetings of the Israeli delegation, which were very frank because we all trusted each other. I believe that disclosing the information would have been a betrayal of trust and would have impeded such crucial meetings in the future. I have kept the diary and maybe one day I will give it to the Israel State Archives.

I would like to warn against two possible pitfalls that a discussion of this kind may involve. Debates such as these are interesting, fascinating, and reverberate in the media, but can be very dangerous. The first trap is in the assumption of causality: *post hoc ergo propter hoc* – "after the fact, therefore because of the fact." The fact that two events happened consecutively does not necessarily mean that there was a causal relationship between them. Therefore, the various mistakes that were made before and during the Camp David summit are not necessarily relevant to a discussion of "what went wrong," unless it can be established that a specific mistake caused the summit to fail. This is a very difficult analysis to make, but any other analysis would be incorrect. I can point to many mistakes committed by the parties involved, including the Israelis, but to my mind none of them affected the outcome. It is therefore not enough to focus on a given course of action and prove it was misguided, as people here have done. They may be right, but that still does not prove that it was this misguided behavior that caused the failure. For example, it may well be that it was wrong to hold the summit when the sides still had a great deal to do at the pre-negotiations stage, as Yossi Beilin argued. It may be worth noting that this was exactly what Menachem Begin and Anwar Sadat, and a third leader Jimmy Carter, did, and yet their actions led to peace. Had they failed, people would have said, as MK Beilin argues today, what a fool Begin was to go to a summit before the proper time, and then we would be sitting here analyzing the terrible mistakes he had made. Well, that is the wrong way to go about it.

The real question should be that of causation: what is it that really caused the summit to fail? Let me present my opinion, although I am not at all certain that I am correct, because it is extremely difficult to offer an unequivocal answer to this question. The summit involved numerous factors and variables. It involved many players, each of whom had his own perspective. I was there during those fourteen days and nights, at that beautiful place, with friends who are here today too, and of course I formed my own impressions. But they are just that, impressions, and I am not sure beyond a shadow of a doubt that my conclusions are correct. There are many uncertainties. So much for the first pitfall.

The second pitfall concerns the distinction between academic debates and deliberations that a political cabinet holds prior to operative decisions. In academe, you can present a chosen course of action, describe it, analyze it, and even point out its risks – all on a theoretical level. The life of the decision-maker is not that simple. He cannot make do with theoretical analyses. He is forced to choose between options that are all dangerous. When he considers a risky option, he must always ask himself what the alternative is. Decisions like the Road Map to Peace, the Camp David summit, or the Oslo Accords should be judged in light of what the alternative was, and no criticism is valid unless the critic can point out a better alternative. A decision-maker must say to himself, I am preferring this option over the others because the balance of threats and opportunities of this option seems more favorable than all other alternatives.

These are my methodological comments. If they help us be a little less sure of ourselves, and maybe even more humble about the certainty of our conclusions, then that is good enough. Having said that, let me expound my own views on Camp David.

In the world of law, it is said that in order for parties to reach an agreement they must have *consensus ad idem*; in other words, both parties must mean the same thing. In my mind, at Camp David the two sides did not want the same thing. I agree with MK Tamir that the problem was not in the details. In fact, unofficially, there was agreement on many of the details, and concessions were made by both parties, albeit at that stage only in a noncommittal way. Differences remained on very few issues only, but those were the issues which could determine the success or failure of the summit.

The first unresolved issue was that of the Right of Return. Perhaps I should ask Yossi Beilin why, during the Oslo negotiations, he did not demand that the Palestinians give up this demand. I assume he did not insist, because he knew they would not relinquish this claim. This, I think, was a serious mistake. I think that this is the heart of the matter. They did not relinquish this demand. Unfortunately, the Oslo Accords had not stipulated that we must reach an agreed decision on the matter of the refugees prior to talks on final status issues.

Let me talk about the alternatives. What were the alternatives on the eve of the Camp David summit? Ehud Barak, who is here today, surely remembers a conversation we had on the Saturday before leaving for the summit. He asked me to come to his home, the prime minister's residence, which is a three-minute walk from my home. I came over in the afternoon, just as he finished playing what I believe was one of Beethoven's sonatas. He said to me, "I feel as though this were 1973, just before the Yom Kippur War. Everyone is content, not realizing what is about to happen. We are now sailing calmly, people are sitting on the deck, the water is blue, the sky is bright, and everyone is having a good time. But I can see the iceberg." This "iceberg," which at that time still had no name, was the *intifada* which started at the end of September 2000. This conversation took place at the beginning of July 2000. Even then, Ehud Barak predicted that unless we initiated some kind of serious diplomatic move, everything would explode in our faces. "We must make a last-ditch effort to steer clear of the iceberg," Barak told me.

In this conflict, as in many others, time plays a crucial role. A party may agree to compromise if it feels that as time goes by and no agreement is reached, the situation will become worse. However, if a party feels that time is on its side, that party will have no incentive to compromise and conclude an agreement. For many years, time was on Israel's side, and we have grown very strong. But over the past few years, demographics – not security – are working against us. Had I been in Arafat's shoes, I would not have fired a single shot, but just kept refusing to sign any agreement. Once the demographic balance in the area between the Jordan River and the Mediterranean Sea changes in the Palestinians' favor, I would also change my demand. I would no longer demand a Palestinian state, but a unified state without any border in the middle, and the application of the principle of one-man one-vote. Not a single shot, but no bilateral agreement either. This may explain Arafat's opposition to signing an agreement. Maybe he believed that time was on his side. But this is also why it was in Israel's best interest to reach an agreement *now*, even at great risk. The logic is simple: the absence of a border between them and us undermines the Zionist enterprise, not its security but its demography.

These were the reasons why the Israeli delegation to Camp David so badly wanted to reach an agreement that would resolve the problem of 1967. To this end, Ehud Barak agreed to offer far-reaching concessions. I opposed some of them, but that is beside the point now. At the same time, it seems to me that Arafat was not even interested in the problem of 1967, because to him 1948 was the main issue. In one of his well-known articles, *New York Times* columnist Thomas Friedman told the Palestinians, "If it's '67 – we are with you; if it's '48 – forget about it."

My feeling that, from Arafat's perspective, the problem was 1948 not 1967, is based on talks with many people, including the Palestinians at Camp David. It was there that I realized what the Right of Return meant to the Palestinians. I was working on this issue with Elyakim Rubinstein and Oded Eran from our side, and Sa'eb Erekat and Yasser Abed Rabbo and others on theirs, and saw how emotional they were about this issue. In one of our nighttime conversations, one of them, talking to me about my parents and others of their generation who immigrated to the country, said, "Do you realize what you Israelis have done here? Hundreds of thousands of you came to this land without asking our permission." I could feel the clashing of two narratives. Zionism, which to me is a movement of profound justice, is to them the epitome of injustice.

It was not out of good will that we decided to tackle the issue of the Right of Return; the Oslo Accords provided that at the final status stage we were to resolve the issue of refugees. Indeed, we went to Camp David with the intention of solving the problem and putting an end to the conflict. However, it was rather obvious that Arafat did not want to end the conflict there.

My feelings about the role of the Arab world are different than those we heard here earlier. The Palestinians are the only Arabs who stand to gain from a peace agreement. They need the wisdom and the courage that it takes to make this move. It would be a mistake on their part to wait until the other Arab countries, including Egypt, give them their blessing. I do not know whether it is in Egypt's best interest to see the Israeli–Palestinian conflict end or not, but even if it is, I am not sure whether Egypt is ready to take the risk of supporting an agreement that would end the conflict. It is clear that had Sadat waited for the rest of the Arab world – from Qaddafi to Saddam Hussein – we would not have had the peace treaty until this very day. The same is true of King Hussein. An Arab country prepared to enter a peace agreement with Israel always takes a risk. Sadat was assassinated because of his pro-Western policies, which included peacemaking. It happened in Israel too: Yitzhak Rabin paid with his life for advancing the peace process. Opting for peace, then, presents a big risk, certainly in the Arab world. But it is only natural that the party that has the most to gain should be ready to take such a risk. This peace process offers the Palestinians a state, an offer never made to them in their history, and they should consider taking the risks for achieving this goal.

Egypt has nothing substantive to gain from the process. The question whether Egypt wants stability in the region or not is an open question. I do not think we should hang our hopes on the Egyptians taking risks to help resolve the conflict. The Americans asked Mubarak to persuade Arafat, and he did not comply. His viabiliy was more important to him than helping Arafat, whom, incidentally, he did not like. I therefore believe that the backing of the Arab world is not the main issue. I wish the Arab world would help, but we cannot expect salvation from them. The decision must be made by the Palestinians, and by them alone.

Although I did not agree with some of the moves that Ehud Barak made, I would like to explain the dilemma he was facing. As I mentioned, he felt that time was working against him and that serious violence was about to erupt. Some intelligence experts believed that from the Palestinian perspective the conflict could not be resolved without violence, and I think they may have been right. Ehud Barak felt that the whole situation was getting out of hand and that as time passes Jews might no longer be a majority in this land. He therefore concluded that an agreement was imperative. Under these circumstances, he had two options: (a) He could show all his cards, to the limit of the concessions that he was prepared to make, in order to truly have done everything possible to reach peace. This would guarantee that if the attempt failed and war broke out, everyone, especially his own people, would be convinced that justice is on Israel's side. And (b), he could choose to tread a more cautious road. Knowing that if an agreement is not reached, any concession would weaken Israel's position later on, he could make more prudent offers, without showing all his cards. The advantage would be that, if no agreement is reached, his positions would not be compromised, but on the other hand he would not be able to convince the public that he had really left no stone unturned in his attempt to reach a peace at that juncture. This was Barak's dilemma.

Ehud Barak chose the first alternative, which – as I said – came at a price. When we resume negotiations in the future, we may have to start from the concessions Israel was prepared to make, as revealed at Camp David. Although they were submitted unofficially, these proposed concessions were extensive. By the way, the Palestinians also made some concessions, but ours seem to me to be more far-reaching, and unnecessarily so. It should, however, be admitted that there was no third alternative: Barak had to be either cautious, or go all the way.

Finally, as MK Tamir already said, the basis for an agreement in the future was laid down at Camp David. There was a feeling there that an agreement had almost been finalized. There was a group of Palestinian delegates at Camp David that genuinely wanted to sign an agreement and felt frustrated by Arafat's position. I remember one of them criticizing Arafat and his decisions, saying, "It is 1947 all over again, another missed opportunity." However, there were also Palestinians who wanted to thwart the process – apparently because they personally had been overlooked; they later admitted so themselves.

## ROUND TWO

### David Witzthum
In the second round, I am inviting you to focus on the lessons to be learned from the Camp David summit.

### Yuli Tamir
I think we have learned two lessons in the wake of the Camp David summit. Dan Meridor already mentioned one, and I would like to underscore it. While Camp David enhanced the level of Palestinian support for a two-state solution, the Palestinians keep holding another option, the option

of a bi-national state. For some of them, this option is becoming increasingly attractive. The fact that they have this option while we do not consider it possible puts us in an inferior position, because a party that knows it has alternative options in times of crisis has an advantage over an opponent that has not. Was it the existence of this alternative that dissuaded Arafat from cooperating at Camp David? It is hard to say. I do not know whether at this point we can fully reconstruct what happened at the summit. But I am confident that the fact that the Palestinians consider this alternative did have an impact on their behavior at the summit. I first heard this option mentioned long before the summit, and it concerns me that I am hearing it increasingly these days. This option endangers the two-state solution. As long as the Palestinians do not feel that partition is the most desirable and perhaps most readily available option to them, there will be no progress. If the Palestinians conclude that they have a "third option," in addition to continuous fighting and a negotiated peace, and choose to sit back and demand equal civil rights, in other words, if they opt for what might be dubbed the South African "one man-one vote" option – no peace agreement will be reached. The time factor is therefore critical.

A serious Israeli mistake, which we have not mentioned yet, predates the Camp David summit: despite a cabinet resolution to this effect, we did not pull out of the Palestinian neighborhoods around Jerusalem before the summit. Moreover, we carried on with our settlement activities. In other words, on the eve of the summit (just as today) we continued to make the Palestinians feel that the occupation is irreversible. This belief competes among the Palestinians with the understanding of the logic and desirability of partition and may lead them toward the "third option."

We must understand this when we think about the future. Maybe Sharon has finally realized the seriousness of the threat that Israel might become a bi-national state, and that partition is the only option that is compatible with Zionism.

The danger is that the continued occupation will erode the partition concept among the Palestinians, to the point where an agreement will not be reached even when our side will have reached political ripeness. This prospect should worry us very much. It is therefore clearly in our interest to convince the Palestinians that we are prepared to end the occupation and that our presence in the Territories is reversible.

Another thing that has happened since Camp David is that as a result of the *intifada* – as difficult as it is to admit – we have realized that we are vulnerable. I think that the Israeli public, which before the Camp David summit was very sure of itself, has lost some of this confidence. The good years we had before the summit made us feel that we are immune, but now this feeling has disappeared. One of the great philosophers of the 17th century, Thomas Hobbes, said that arrangements founded on equality require "equal vulnerability"– namely, both parties must realize that they are vulnerable. Granted, one of the sides can be stronger, but as we learned, the weaker side can injure the stronger one, and no one is completely immune. The *intifada*, and especially the suicide bombings, have created this feeling on the Israeli side and made Israelis understand the limits of power.

A debate took place here as to whether the Arab world wants or does not want an agreement with the Palestinians to materialize. I believe it definitely does. I would like to remind MK Steinitz and Dan Meridor that one of the basic interests of Egypt – as well as other countries in the region – is to weaken fundamentalism. Although fundamentalism has its roots in many issues apart from the Israeli–Palestinian conflict, it thrives on this conflict. Thus the conflict is an undesired burden on the Arab regimes.

I believe that Egypt is interested in calming the region, especially after the events of September 11. The Arab world knows that the Israeli–Palestinian conflict plays into the hands of Usama Bin Laden. Its leadership has no choice but to try and contain the conflict. Arab leaders are therefore seeking stability and a way out of the Israeli–Palestinian conflict, and if they can win a few fringe benefits on the way, all the better. It therefore seems to me that in future negotiations, we will see the Arab world playing a much more significant role. Maybe this will give the Palestinians, and especially Abu Mazen, for all of his weakness, the shoulder he needs to lean on.

### Yuval Steinitz

Our role in this conference is to elucidate differences. For the sake of this debate, I will devote my comments to the following short remarks: the first will deal with methodology, the second with strategy and interests, and the third with the future. In broad terms, I agree with the approach proposed by Dan Meridor, disagree with the analysis and comments offered by Yuli Tamir, and even more so with those proposed by Yossi Beilin – even though they are prevalent in academic circles in Israel as well as in the media.

Regarding methodology, two great 20th century philosophers wrote excellent books which offer opposing theses for the analysis of the nature of science and the nature of revolutions. Karl Popper authored *The Logic of Scientific Discovery*, which suggests that the refutation of a theory and the switch from one theory to another can be logically analyzed. According to Popper, there is a recognizable underlying logic in the process which allows disregarding all the secondary elements. Thomas S. Kuhn's main thesis in *The Structure of Scientific Revolutions* is that science advances not by logical transition from a theory that was rationally refuted by experiments to another, but by what he calls "science in context." In his view, all things depend on context, which can consist of personal factors, different political perspectives, and cultural and religious influences. All these elements blend together and determine the transition from one scientific theory or paradigm to another.

I feel that the analysis proposed by Yossi Beilin is a classic Kuhnian analysis. In his analysis of a historical event, or the failure thereof, he places emphasis on procedure, or environmental factors, on the way that the event was structured, the atmosphere that prevailed and whether inter-personal chemistry existed or not. I remember that Barak – who was harshly rebuked for his poor inter-personal skills and his inability to develop good chemistry with Arafat – invited Arafat to his home at Kochav Ya'ir. They enjoyed together a typical Middle Eastern snack and their amiable meeting lasted until 2 A.M. Everyone was impressed and thought that this was very significant, as though this was really at the core of the issue. It was not.

Analyses which are based on factors of this kind are useless because, first, they offer no historical insight and second, their validity can never be confirmed or refuted, given the multitude of details and the uncertain relationship between them. In other words, not all the elements in a given context are necessarily interconnected and it is incorrect to assume that all such elements contribute to the outcome. For example, we all saw on television how Ehud Barak physically nudged Arafat to enter the cabin first. Had the summit succeeded, surely it would have been explained that this nudge, reflecting a warm and friendly relationship, contributed to the success. Now that it failed, it is said that Barak was rude, failed to develop any personal relationship with Arafat and that this was an important factor in the failure of the summit. In fact, keeping one's distance from his interlocutor may sometimes be helpful.

I think there is a tendency in the world in general, and in the Middle East in particular, to attribute too much weight to matters of procedure. In the case of Israel's unsuccessful relations with Syria's Asad, there were also many interpretations stressing relationships, timing, excessive suspiciousness and other psychological factors. Granted, a specific meeting might fail because it was insufficiently prepared, because there was poor chemistry between the principals or because one of the protagonists was bad-tempered or moody, but the consistent failure over the years of such a momentous process cannot possibly be blamed on factors of this kind. After seven years since Rabin first proposed withdrawal from the Golan Heights, Asad was still unable to conclude an agreement with Israel, not because of his psychological makeup, but because of his interests. As Rabin had so eloquently put it, "Asad cannot take any less than Sadat did." Analysts who attribute too much to atmosphere, procedure, the mediator's skills, relationships between delegates, etc.

are, in a way, disrespectful of the leaders. They do not regard them as serious statesmen who define strategic goals and pursue concrete interests, but as people who are guided by such marginal questions as the existence or absence of an amiable relationship. Obviously, this is not the relevant foundation on which the success or failure of a political process is built.

So let us focus on the interests at play. Dan Meridor talked about understanding interests over time. I agree. This is what really matters. But the interests that should be considered over time, in this case, are not only Palestinian but also all-Arab, and this is where I differ with Dan Meridor. Arafat was not Sadat, and the Palestinians are not the Egyptians. Thanks to its power, size and status, Egypt was able to withstand years of opposition from the Arab governments that objected to peace with Israel. The Palestinians, however, are a small people. The ability of the Palestinians to stand fast in the face of Arab opposition cannot be compared with that of Egypt, certainly not without the backing of Egypt.

The roots of the disintegration of the Oslo process were embedded in the very essence of the process itself. This process threatened the Arab regimes in the region. Their sense of threat was enhanced by the vision of a "New Middle East" proclaimed by Shimon Peres, and by the Israeli messages at the regional economic conferences that were held in Casablanca and other Arab cities. The Israeli vision that was intended to benefit Syrian, Egyptian and Iraqi citizens was perceived as a colonialist threat to the Arab world. It was seen as involving "dangerous" democratization, liberalization, pluralism and open media. The leaders of Egypt, Syria, Iraq, and Saudi Arabia did not see what they could gain from this process, and certainly did not wish to support it.

As for the future, my three colleagues have said that if any agreement is eventually signed, its parameters will be more or less those that were laid down at Camp David. It was rightly noted that these parameters, which were meant to serve as a finish line, turned instead into the starting line for additional Israeli concessions. These parameters are too far-reaching and dangerous, especially since there is nothing final about them. I subscribe to the school that believes – because of the demographics, among other reasons – that we should eventually separate from the Palestinians. I am prepared to make substantial concessions in order to promote any prospect of a new peace process that would be fundamental and turn a new page. But it should be a peace that frees us from some of the damages caused by the previous process (Oslo) and from the Palestinian terror and incitement that have accompanied it since 1993. I believe that the accommodation that would give us peace and security cannot be worked out with Arafat's Palestinian Authority and all its associated mechanisms. Elections in the Territories may produce a new leadership to work with, a leadership that will have learned the historical lesson that the Israelis will not be the only losers if the process fails.

I agree with Yuli Tamir that we have a lot to lose if we do not accomplish a reasonable separation that would provide the basic conditions Israel needs for its survival, such as demilitarization and security zones. I would like to hope that even the current process may be able to secure an agreement that will be good for both sides and will be universally supported, but after the failure of the Camp David summit I am more skeptical about this than I ever was.

### Yossi Beilin

I envy those who think we can manage without the leadership of the Palestinian Authority. Sitting with us are a few members of this Authority. They took part in the discussions here. They made certain points to which some of us agreed while others did not, but they also criticized frankly *everyone* that was involved in the Camp David process – the Israelis, the Americans and themselves. It is wrong and very dangerous to dispense with them up so easily, because the alternative may be the Hamas leadership. The current Palestinian leadership is the most we can expect in the present circumstances. They are secular pragmatists. The alternative is religious fanatics who will not agree to anything that involves the existence of Israel. We cannot "invent" any other leadership. We cannot generate another Mustafa Dudin, whom Sharon once "appointed" to lead the Palestinians in collaboration with Israel, nor establish another version of the Village Leagues which was created to serve this purpose. It is in the best interest of all of us to make sure that the pragmatists in the Palestinian leadership are strong enough to conclude an agreement with us.

We must not forget that the Right of Return was addressed already in Oslo. We had agreed there on the procedure to be followed in negotiations and about the agenda. It became obvious that asking the Palestinians to give up the demand that refugees be allowed to return to areas in Israel proper became linked to a Palestinian demand that we withdraw to the borders of 1967. That is where negotiations on the permanent status agreement can begin – from this linkage. Although in Oslo we did not reach a permanent status agreement, only an interim agreement, I started even then pushing for negotiating a permanent status agreement because I believed that it could be reached. Indeed, two years later Abu Mazen and I drafted a document that looks a lot like a permanent status agreement and is quite similar to the partial understandings subsequently reached at Camp David and to Clinton's Parameters. I think it would have been wiser to reach a permanent status agreement then, including the resolution of the problem of the Right of Return, rather than wait another five years.

The Palestinians know that no Israeli government will ever allow Palestinian refugees into sovereign Israeli territory under the principle of the Right of Return. All Israeli governments, Right and Left alike, have allowed Palestinian refugees into Israel under the humanitarian umbrella of family reunification, but no government will ever agree to incorporate a Right of Return in any permanent status agreement – this is totally unacceptable. Therefore, the Palestinians will keep the Right of Return as their last card, waiting for the right time to play it. The assumption that the Palestinians will always insist on the unrestricted Right of Return is a mistake.

"Determinists" believe that no agreement could have been reached at Camp David in the first place because Israel's sole purpose was to expose the "true face" of the Palestinians, and the Palestinians' sole purpose was to merely go through the motions and avoid reaching an agreement. This was not the case. There were people on both sides who truly wanted to reach an agreement, and the failure should not be attributed to everybody at the negotiation table. If the negotiations were run differently, the summit may have succeeded, and I think this can still be done in the future. There is a version of the deterministic approach that is very easy on the Israeli side. It claims that the Palestinian side never wanted to reach an agreement – this exempts the Israelis from any responsibility for the failure of the talks. The Israelis came there in good faith, it says, and for fourteen days they conducted *bona fide* negotiations, but the opponent never really wanted to negotiate. Again, I must say that this was not the case.

"Determinists" say that the reason why the Palestinians never wanted an agreement to begin with is that they want to wait until the Palestinians become a majority in this land. I am not saying that these themes cannot be heard among them. A pointed debate goes on within the Palestinian leadership, in the Authority and in Fatah. The Israeli public is not monolithic and neither is the Palestinian. But alongside those who advocate sitting back and waiting until Palestinians become a majority, there are others who understand that even if they become a majority, it will not entail that their dream of a Palestinian state in the whole area between the Jordan River and the Mediterranean Sea would come true. The bloodshed between Jews and Palestinians can go on for decades before one side might win. But these people want to live. They are not prepared to wait. I therefore believe that the "determinists" are wrong and that they are simply choosing a way to exempt Israelis from any responsibility for the failure of the negotiations on the one hand, and place all of the blame and guilt on the Palestinians, on the other.

Let us examine the matter from a different perspective: What was the big Palestinian threat that prompted the Israeli government to take action? Why were the Israelis in such a rush to start negotiating? Why did Barak say at the time, "Everything must be concluded by September"? What was that threat that Barak mentioned in almost every cabinet meeting? The answer is clear: the threat was the unilateral declaration of independence. Initially, the Palestinians were saying they would declare independence in May 1999. This startled the world and made it run for solutions. The Germans convened all the European representatives in Berlin in March 1999. It was decided there to call on the Palestinians not to take this unilateral step, and to promise them that if within one year a Palestinian state was not established through an agreement, Europe would consider recognizing a state that would be declared unilaterally. Clinton also implored Arafat not to make the move, as did many others. This is what created a sense of urgency and pushed Barak to Camp David.

### Dan Meridor

Contrary to what was said here, at Camp David there *was* a proposal for an interim agreement. During the final two days of the summit, Barak received Clinton's proposal for an interim agreement. Arafat rejected it, as some of the people here today can confirm. Since, ostensibly, agreement had been reached on most issues – including Jerusalem except for the Temple Mount – Clinton did not dub his plan, which reflected those points of consensus, an interim agreement. His proposal was to announce everything that had been agreed upon, and leave the issue of Jerusalem for further negotiations. Three options were proposed: (a) to leave open the question of the Temple Mount only; (b) to leave open the question of the Holy Basin; or (c) to leave open the question of the city as a whole, and continue negotiations for two more years or so. Is this not an interim agreement? You can call it by different names, such as "non-final" agreement but essentially it was interim.

The Israeli delegation discussed the plan. Most of us thought we should oppose it, but Barak thought we should let the Americans know we were willing to go ahead with it. Arafat turned it down. I know that these facts pull the rug out from under the story that has been told over the last few years, but it is the truth: Arafat did not agree to an interim agreement. Why? Because the open-ended issue left was Jerusalem while he wanted to leave the Right of Return as the open issue left for the final stage. He did not say so but I believe that this was the reason why he rejected the agreement.

The borders were almost agreed upon. No agreed boundaries were drawn, but the area figures were pretty clear both to us and the Americans, and the feeling was that the Palestinians were close to agreeing as well. American delegates who attended a meeting between Clinton and Arafat told me later that the Americans were talking about Israel keeping 8%–10%

of the West Bank. The Americans were thinking also of a token land swap of nine to one – 9% for us and 1% for the Palestinians. Clinton offered to allocate $10 billion for the refugees, but the matter of the refugees was still amorphous. His proposal included, of course, the end of occupation and the establishment of a Palestinian state. The issue of Jerusalem was almost resolved – against my will – leaving unresolved the question of sovereignty over Temple Mount. Arafat response was a flat "no." That is the truth: an offer was put on the table, and the Palestinians turned it down.

I would like to add that we might not have fully appreciated the seriousness of Arafat's ideological commitment. Some of us believed that he could not have really meant what he said. This reflects a condescending attitude. We do take seriously people on our side who have adamant ideological commitments. I know Israelis who would rather die than accept a non-Israeli sovereignty in Gaza. They genuinely believe that a Palestinian state may not be allowed to exist on any part of the Land of Israel. They will never endorse any document recognizing such a state, even if the price is endless war.

After the summit, Arafat repeatedly said that he had raised the issue of refugees there. I think we are taking the easy way out when we say that Arafat did not really mean it when he raised the flag of the Right of Return, that he was just talking about it but would have taken it off the table when the time was right, that he was bluffing – and after all, he had a lot of experience with such tactics. I may be wrong, but I saw in him, and not just in him, true dedication to this objective, much more than to many other subjects. This is not to say that he did not want an agreement. I think he wanted it very much, but I think the agreement he wanted was not one that involved giving up the continuation of the struggle. I cannot prove it, but it seems to me that he did not want to be the one who gave up the perpetuation of the struggle. Arafat knew that large parts of the Arab world understand that the Right of Return is a lost cause. Israel exists, it is strong, and it will survive. He saw himself as the last of the Mohicans, and felt that once he stopped carrying the torch, the Palestinian story would be over. Historically, proclaiming such a concession would mean a recognition of the finality of the fact that the Jewish state exists in parts of Palestine. To him this was the crux of the problem, not the details of borders. Giving up that claim is a concession for generations to come; it is not a matter for interim agreements. In his perspective, this is what "no more claims" and "end of conflict" mean, and this is why he felt he had to reject it. I never heard him say so explicitly, but this is the interpretation that can clearly explain his political behavior. I know of no other theory that provides a better explanation.

In this context, I would like to tell you a story that may indicate that Abu Mazen is different. I met with Abu Mazen at my home at his request, in 1997 or 1998. We had a long talk, just the two of us. I told him I was happy to meet with him, because he was the first Arab leader to talk about territorial concessions, in line with the agreement he had drafted with Yossi Beilin. After all, no Arab leader, including Sadat and Hussein, had ever agreed to give up a single inch of land. He immediately corrected me and said he did not have any agreement with Beilin; that was just an exchange of views. I said to him:

> Do you understand that refugees will never be allowed to immigrate to Israel? If I know that you do, I will try to convince my friends in Israel to reach a permanent status agreement and even to make concessions for this purpose. But if you say you insist on the Right of Return, I will conclude that there will be no final-status agreement, and will suggest an interim agreement instead.

I did not explain my motivation but I will now: I think that the demographic threat I mentioned before makes the continuation of the present situation the most dangerous alternative.

Abu Mazen did not give me a direct answer. Instead, he told me that when he came to Israel after the Oslo Accords were signed, he took his children to Safed, to the house where he was born, and told them, "This is our family home; this is where I was born; we do not return here." This, of course, was not an official waiver of the demand to allow refugees to return, but it gave me the feeling that what he was trying to say was that he understood that the demand of return was unrealistic.

I think that this man is a pragmatist, even though he may not say things explicitly. Pragmatism is a quality Arafat did not possess. Does Abu Mazen have the power to lead his people to a real peace agreement? I do not have a clear-cut answer to that.

Regarding my conclusions from the summit. I think that theoretically Yossi Beilin might be right, and the Palestinians may have raised the issue of the Right of Return just as a tactical maneuver for the sake of negotiations, while in their heart they knew very well that there will never be a Right of Return to Israel; that just as Jews can come to Israel, Palestinians who want to return would be allowed to go to the state of Palestine, but there never will be cross-border return. So, theoretically, Beilin's interpretation may be right and the Palestinians' rigid position was just a tactical maneuver, but personally – as I mentioned before – I think that this is not very likely. In any case, I think it is wrong to found Israel's policy on such an optimistic assumption. However, if eventually it turns out that they are ready to completely give up the claim to return to Israel, I will not shut the door on them. If that happens, we will have to make mutual concessions: with a heavy heart, we will have to give up the right of Jews to return to Jericho and Nablus, which are part of our historic homeland, and they will give up their claim to return to Jerusalem, Haifa, Jaffa and Beersheva. If we reach that point, all the better, but it would be wrong to build Israel's policy now on an assumption of this kind, because the facts indicate that it is shaky at best.

This brings me to questions beyond the failure of the summit, to those of an agreement with the Palestinians in general. Since 1967, all the Israeli cabinets that agreed to make territorial concessions made them contingent on reaching a comprehensive final-status agreement. The first to diverge from this principle was neither Yossi Beilin, nor Shimon Peres, nor the late Yitzhak Rabin, but Ariel Sharon. Sharon was the first Israeli prime minister to propose the establishment of a Palestinian state independently from a demand to sign a final status agreement. He proposed establishing a Palestinian state while both parties retain their claims, and those would be deferred to a later stage. This was a revolution. Sharon first proposed the acceptance of a Palestinian state to the Likud party in a speech at a neighborhood near Haifa and then at Latrun, and repeated this plan during the prime ministerial election campaign. Later, he offered to agree to a Palestinian state within the framework of a partial agreement. Sharon understood how dangerous it was to let things continue as they are, and estimated that in the present circumstances there was no way to secure a permanent status agreement. Sharon therefore may have preferred the option of two states with a continuing border dispute between them, much like the situation between Israel and Syria where a border dispute over the Golan Heights exists. Politically and strategically, the occupation would end there and then. That was a radical change in his thinking. My conclusion was that if it were feasible, I would support the move.

Although this strategy would involve much heartache and would force us to give away parts of our historic homeland, the benefit it represents outweighs by far the cost. It would give us more oxygen to deal with the conflict, since it would free us of the demographic menace, which jeopardizes the success story of Zionism. I hope that eventually we shall have peace, but if neither a permanent status agreement nor an interim agreement can be reached, because Abu Mazen's efforts are thwarted by Hamas or others, or for any other reason, we must try to establish a border, albeit temporary, between us and them. If this can be done through peaceful coordination, all the better; if not, we will have to put up a border unilaterally. If they fight us, we will fight back – but from within our own borders. If we can have neither a peace agreement nor an interim agreement, we will have to take unilateral action and put up a border ourselves. In these circumstances, the conflict will continue, but this time it will be a conflict between two states, with Israel freed from the demographic threat. These are the issues that should concern us, more than the question of whether the Camp David summit failed because of one reason or another.

## ROUND THREE

### David Witzthum

Dan Meridor has led the discussion to the subject of Israel's post-Camp David concerns and future policies. Do you agree with Meridor that Sharon's choice is truly a revolution?

### Yuli Tamir

When Sharon refers to our presence in the Territories as "occupation," this is a positive change in his discourse. I remember that sometime after he said that, I told friends of mine from the Likud, "I have a lot of 'Stop the Occupation' bumper stickers in my trunk. I can give you a few if you like . . . " This is certainly a real change, and once it was pronounced, the situation changed.

Sharon's statement made it clear that the public in Israel is moving toward left-wing views. Sharon today is saying what even Golda Meir did not dare to say thirty years ago. The concept of Greater Israel is no longer mentioned, and the assumption on which current discussions are based is that we are an occupying force and that this occupation must come to an end. The only debate now is how this should be done – how to end the occupation, how to demarcate the borders, how to relocate the settlers. These are the questions that are now on the agenda. Looking back at the political careers of some of the people at this table, we can recall that the debate started out quite differently, but now demographic concerns, and several other factors, have narrowed the gap between Dan Meridor and myself.

Nevertheless, there is a big "but" here. I think Sharon's conception of a temporary Palestinian state does not resolve the demographic issue, and therefore his solution is an illusion. Sharon has presented no maps, but he talks about percentage points, and I am familiar with the terrain. His map that eventually gives the Palestinians 50% or 52% of the territory will not resolve the demographic problem. Therefore, there is no other way than to conduct the process fully in line with the parameters laid down at Camp David, or according to any other similar parameters; otherwise we accomplish nothing.

Much has been said here about the far-reaching nature of the Camp David initiative, but only a drastic solution can settle the dispute, and such a solution must address all the fundamental issues – including withdrawal to the borders of 1967, the partition of Jerusalem and a solution to the problem of the Right of Return. There is no way to avoid confronting these issues. I will say something that may not be popular, but is nevertheless true.

It makes no sense that on the one hand we oppose the Right of Return – and I too oppose it – while on the other we make moves that will lead to the inclusion of hundreds of thousands of Palestinians into Israel. It is illogical to refuse to let a single additional Palestinian immigrate to Israel and at the same time demand the annexation of East Jerusalem with its 212,000 Palestinian residents.

The fear of the demon of the Right of Return and of the Palestinian immigration that it might entail, while there is a readiness to absorb hundreds of thousands of Palestinians in annexed territories, reflects an emotional approach rather than rational thinking. This is why Sharon's map cannot resolve the problem. Sharon has indeed made a leap forward, and the fact that he began talking about dismantling settlements and started using the term "occupation" in his discourse led Israel into a new era. The old right-wing terminology is buried under the rubble of reality.

When Sharon spoke in front of Likud members about these issues, he made no reference to Divine Promises. The word "forever," so popular in right-wing vocabulary, was only mentioned once, and with a different connotation: the Prime Minister asked a rhetorical question, "Does anyone want us to stay forever in Nablus, Hebron and Jenin?" Apparently, the concept of "forever" is no longer the asset of settlers but of those who want to relocate them.

Many people have said, some out of concern, some out of wishful thinking, that these were "just words." But words have a power of their own. Words affect realities, form consciousness, and define the scope of public thinking. When a "liberated territory" becomes an "occupied territory," the future of that piece of land is affected. When "eternity" is associated with the partition of the country rather than with the annexation of territory, the attitude to settlements changes.

Of course, the distance between words – with all their great import – and actions is great. Only God has the power to create a world with words; for human beings, creation, or destruction, takes longer. The distance between Sharon's statements and the ensuing acts on the ground may be great, but the words have been uttered, and they cannot be taken back. Words are not just hot air, as they are often said to be. Words are the solid ground on which reality is formed.

Another person who recently understood this is Uri Elitzur, the former bureau chief of Prime Minister Binyamin Netanyahu and editor of *Nekuda*, the monthly journal of the Council of Jewish Communities of Judea, Samaria and Gaza. He wrote, with deep frustration, that the Road Map is a triumph of left-wing consciousness. In the long run, Elitzur said, "the battle is over consciousness, and it will be won with words. While we are creating facts on the ground, the left-wing is creating facts in our consciousness. We build and plant real houses and trees, and they demolish and uproot them with words." Eiltzur's description of the present-day battlefield is accurate. This is a battle over words, and Sharon is the most recent member of the vocabulary revisionists. Elitzur has good cause for concern. After years in which the Right managed to dictate the lingo, erasing the term "occupied territories" and replacing it with "Judea and Samaria," the word "occupation" is back. Sharon's comments close an era that began after the Six Day War. That was an era of baseless euphoria that created in the Israeli fiber deep social, economic and ethical wounds that will take many years to heal. Only very few of us noticed the wounds when they first appeared, others noticed them when they started hemorrhaging, but now most of the public is aware of them. A correct diagnosis is a good start toward full recovery.

### Yuval Steinitz

Regarding the prospects of salvaging this peace process, a process that even Yossi Beilin agrees is defective and faltering, the truth is that the Camp David summit was just the last stage of a ten-year misguided process. And if that summit was a failure, so was the whole process.

Yossi Beilin asked whom we expect to see leading the Palestinians if Arafat's Palestinian Authority is discarded and the militant organizations are dismantled. Let me tell you that a few months before the war in Afghanistan started, when it was already clear that the Americans would be allying with the Northern Alliance of the Mujahidin against the Taliban, I asked some senior officials at the Pentagon and the State Department, "What will the US do after they have taken Afghanistan? Who will rule that country?" Their answer was the Mujahidin, after disarming the Taliban. When I reminded them that the Mujahidin are just a chip off the same block as the Taliban, and in terms of their hatred for the West, there is very little difference between them, they responded that it was true that the people in both organizations are similar, but once the Mujahidin are in power, they will have learned the historical lesson about the fate of a regime that supports murderous terror. It is the same with the Palestinians. The question is not just who will be leading the Palestinians and whether they will be more pleasant than the current leadership. Elections will be held under international observation, and the Palestinian voters and the leadership they elect will have learned their historical lesson about carrying out murderous terror against Israel.

As for Sharon's concept of implementing a partition into two states, with or without an agreement, or perhaps with an interim agreement, Dan Meridor, in his criticism, has already explained the pitfall involved in this plan. Under a plan of this kind, even if it involves temporary borders, Israel would be conceding, not just in words but in deeds, a great deal and getting very little in return. The border dispute would persist. Even worse, the conflict would not be confined to a border dispute; it would remain an existential conflict, with the Palestinians continuing to demand the return of refugees to the Galilee, the Negev and the coastal plain. In this existential conflict, the rest of the Arab world will always loom large in the background.

Unilateral withdrawal is problematic, and we should always remember the bitter experience of withdrawal from South Lebanon. There are now thousands of rockets in the hands of Hizballah in South Lebanon. Some of them are the equivalent of a Scud missile with a warhead of more than half a ton. They easily can hit Haifa. This is a serious threat to Israel's security. A temporary Palestinian state without a demilitarization agreement and without an end of conflict agreement may perhaps afford us some temporary, relative quiet, but we may subsequently witness a process of stockpiling of weapons, including artillery and missiles, either manufactured locally or smuggled into the West Bank and the Gaza Strip. They would threaten not just Haifa and the north but also Tel Aviv and the entire coastal plain, including most of Israel's airbases. This can generate not only local border disputes, but could become an existential conflict. I can therefore only partially agree with Dan Meridor's analysis.

When the future of the Territories is discussed, there are two considerations, one demographic, the other strategic; the Left highlights the former, and the Right the latter. Both considerations are valid, but unfortunately lead to conflicting conclusions. The demographic argument is an existential one, and it ostensibly leaves us no choice but to part with the Territories. The Right argues that any foreign military force in the Territories would present a strategic threat to Israel's existence, and therefore, ostensibly, we are left with no choice but to stay in the West Bank (and I am setting aside ideological arguments concerning the historic Land of Israel and how they influence the situation, although these arguments are also important). What we need is an arrangement that will enable us to separate from most of the territory, and from its residents who represent a demographic threat, and at the same time prevent a terrorist and military threat from building up in the evacuated territories. In and of itself, this threat may not be existential, but in the context of regional escalation it could well become so.

### Yossi Beilin

Actually, MK Steinitz and I agree on many things. We both oppose the separation fence; we both are not keen on the concept of a "temporary Palestinian state" because it requires major concessions with little in return; and we both regard, by a process of elimination, a permanent status agreement as the ideal solution. What is it that we still differ on? The nature of the "partner." All the plans that we agree on do not necessitate a partner except for the permanent status agreement. Steinitz proposes discarding the Palestinian Authority and the militant organizations, and holding elections. But what will happen in these elections? Have we not tried this before, in various configurations, since 1978? We tried in the past to get alternative leaders elected but they refused, and directed us to those who really represented the Palestinians – the PLO leaders in Tunis. The true representatives, they said, were Abu Mazen, Yasser Abed Rabbo and others – those who are in the Palestinian Authority today. Without them, the West Bankers told us, no agreement could ever be signed.

In the debate over a permanent status agreement, we may disagree on the possible goals, but as Professor Tamir said earlier, the discussions we shall have in the future will be very different from those we would have had ten years ago. The scope of the debate has considerably narrowed. The debate will focus only on the details of the agreement, because we have already agreed that most of the territory will be handed over to the Palestinians. The main issue remaining is that of the partner. If MK Steinitz wants to conduct a consistent analysis of the situation, he must reach the conclusion that hoping for another unnamed partner instead of those we have today is futile.

The Road Map is an arrangement tailored to fit Sharon's measurements. Sharon is interested in implementing the first and second parts of the Road Map. The first part talks about reducing violence and pacification, and those outcomes he definitely wants. The second part calls for the establishment of a temporary state, which Dan Meridor, like me, has reservations about. In my estimation, this solution is still better than none, but it is not my preferred solution because – as it has been mentioned before – under this plan we are made to pay a price without getting our money's worth. Nor does it resolve the long-term problems. All it will accomplish is putting the Palestinians into a compound that occupies some 50% of the territory and thus gain, for Israel, some time. A state of this kind would not genuinely solve the demographic problem either. It does not offer the Palestinians territorial contiguity and therefore does not enable them to develop normal national life. Israel would pay the price for this problematic arrangement.

Sharon has been promoting his own plan for more than twenty years, at least since 1982: his map of Palestinian sovereignty consists roughly of Oslo II's zones A and B. If you add some territory to these zones, create a temporary Palestinian state and resolve the demographic problem, that will bring Sharon to the end of the second part of the Road Map. From then on continuous negotiations about the border between two sovereign states will take place; and Sharon could drag these talks on and on. Even if the agreement stipulates that a permanent status agreement must be reached in 2005, Sharon can always say, as did Rabin at the time, that there is nothing sacred about dates. At that point, he presumes that the relations with the Palestinians will switch from a protracted historic national conflict to an ordinary border dispute, similar to at least seventy-two other disputes that exist around the world. The international community will get off Israel's back and Bush will not send emissaries to pressure Israel. The world will tell us to solve our border disputes on our own. As far as Sharon is concerned, that will have resolved the problem.

Therefore, if we want to be practical, we must arrive at a formula of an interim arrangement that Sharon can live with and the Palestinians will not view as a deception. After that it will be Israel's responsibility to prepare a permanent status agreement which both parties can accept, and I think it will follow, more or less, the lines of Clinton's Parameters, because there is hardly any other alternative. Optimally it should be concluded in 2005; alternatively, conditions must be created that will enable the Palestinians to wait a little longer until a permanent status agreement is reached.

### Dan Meridor

Look at what happened to Israel's public opinion. Fifteen or twenty years ago, in the elections of 1984 and 1988, there was a party called Hadash (a communist, predominantly-Arab party), whose slogan was "two peoples, two states." At that time almost everyone was against them. It is said nowadays that Israeli society has veered right, but in fact the entire electorate, apart from a negligible minority, supports the idea of "two peoples, two states." Whether it veered right or left, it is clear that the Israeli public has undergone a serious transformation. It has accepted the two-state solution and the debate now is over the parameters, over the demarcation of the border. This is entirely different than what the majority believed twenty to thirty years ago.

The Likud underwent this transformation mostly after the Oslo Accords were signed, when Netanyahu, the party's candidate for the premiership, announced before the elections of 1996 that he accepted the Oslo Accords. I believe that was the right thing to do, and at that time I indeed pushed him to go in this direction. Initially, Likud had opposed the Oslo Accords, but once they were concluded and implementation began, Netanyahu announced that the party was accepting these accords as a given fact and as a binding agreement. This meant parting with the right-wing ideology that half of Israel had historically believed in, the ideology of Herut and Likud, coming to terms with realities and moving toward the center.

The same center-bound movement is also evident in parts of Israel's Left, which after the Camp David summit had to confront the same realities, only from the other end. Their platform was no longer compatible with reality. Nowadays, 80% of Israelis are in the center of the political spectrum. They support striking the terrorists with everything possible – even employing measures to which I would be opposed – and at the same time they are prepared to make far-reaching territorial concessions. The depth of this revolution cannot be overstated.

Can a similar trend be detected among the Palestinians? Are they also willing to make concessions that, from their perspective, are far-reaching? I do not know. What really matters is the change in the positions of Palestinian decision-makers, not those of the Palestinian masses. I do not wish to sound undemocratic, but with the situation as it is, the opinion of the people is not as important as that of the leadership. Sadat made sure that almost 100 percent of the Egyptians voted in favor of his peace agreement with Israel. He made the decision, and his people found it necessary to follow. It is a question of leadership. Do the Palestinians have a leadership that can introduce the same kind of transformation that took place in Israel? This is the key question in this discussion.

I would like to comment on a few things that were said here. I want very much to see the realization of a permanent status agreement, because that is the best arrangement we can possibly have. I want this agreement even though it would necessarily involve substantial risks and concessions. But wanting it is not enough, it also has to be feasible, and I am not sure that this is the case. I am afraid that today a permanent status agreement would be very hard to reach. I am not closing the door on this option. To me an interim agreement is just second best, a fallback. I am ready to accept an interim arrangement because of all the reasons I explained earlier. But if that too is not feasible, I am prepared to make a unilateral move. I know the price we would have to pay for a unilateral move would be higher than the price we have been paying for the withdrawal from Lebanon, which was nevertheless the right thing to do. There, too, the question was that of alternatives. The alternative to withdrawal was a situation in which soldiers would continue getting killed and Israel's morale would continue to be eroded, as would its deterrence and military capabilities – a process that had been going on in the years before the pullout. Once again, facing the Palestinians, we now have to weigh the alternatives. A unilateral move unfortunately translates into an extremely high price, but it also would provide great benefits and turn out to be better than the other options.

I would like to comment on what Yuval Steinitz said. Incidentally, he is a good example of the revolution in Israeli thinking. At the time, he left Peace Now to join Likud, and now people are asking him why he had to do that considering the fact that Likud adopted the same positions that he promulgated when he was in Peace Now . . .

Regrettably, there are some people in the Likud who think that we can go on controlling the entire territory permanently, without granting the

Arab population citizenship and voting rights in Israel. To me, this is not a legitimate alternative. We will not be an apartheid state. What are the implications of their position? Does it mean that Zionism cannot exist except in a racist form? That Zionism cannot survive unless it controls the Arabs without giving them voting rights? Does it mean that the UN resolution equating Zionism with racism was right? God help us if this is the conclusion we must reach.

We therefore have no choice but to make a decision. If we decide not to decide, it would mean that we have chosen the apartheid option. It is a very hard decision to make, but it is imperative. Either you support keeping hold of all the land and giving equal rights to all the inhabitants, which would mean the end of Zionism, or you support giving up parts of this land, as painful as this may be, in order to preserve the Zionist enterprise, which is built on a Jewish majority. There simply is no third option.

# The Clinton Parameters

*Points Made by President Clinton at a Meeting with Israeli and
Palestinian Officials, December 23, 2000*

## Territory

○ Based on what the President heard, he believes that a fair solution
would be in the mid-90s – i.e., 94 to 96 percent of West Bank territory to the Palestinian State.
○ The land annexed by Israel should be compensated by a land swap
of 1 to 3 percent, in addition to other territorial arrangements (e.g.,
Permanent Safe Passage). The parties also should consider the swap
of leased land to meet their respective needs. There are creative
ways of doing this that could address Israeli or Palestinian issues or
concerns.
○ The President thought that the parties should develop a map consistent with the criteria: 80 percent of settlers in blocks of
settlements, contiguity, minimum annexation of territory to
Israel, minimum number of Palestinians to be affected by the
annexation.

## Security

○ The President believes that the key lays in an international presence
that would only be withdrawn by mutual consent. This presence
would also monitor the implementation of the agreement by both
sides.

○ It is the President's best judgment that the Israeli withdrawal should be phased over 36 months, while the international force is gradually introduced into the area.

○ At the end of this period a small Israeli presence would remain in specified military locations in the Jordan Valley under the authority of the international force for another 36 months. This period could be reduced in the event of favorable regional developments that would diminish the threat to Israel.

○ Early Warning Stations: Israel should maintain three facilities in the West Bank with a Palestinian liaison presence. The stations should be subject to review after 10 years, with any change in status to be mutually agreed.

○ Emergency Deployment areas: The President understood that the parties still have to develop maps of relevant areas and routes.

○ Emergency means the imminent and demonstrable threat to Israel's national security of a military nature that requires the activation of a national state of emergency. The international force would need to be notified of any such determination.

○ Airspace: the State of Palestine would have sovereignty over the airspace but the two states should work out special arrangements for Israeli training and operational needs.

○ The President understood that the Israeli position is that Palestine should be defined as "demilitarized" while the Palestinian side proposed a "State of Limited Arms." As a compromise the President suggests "non-militarized state." This would be consistent with the fact that in addition to a strong Palestinian security force, Palestine will have an international force for border security and deterrence purposes.

## Jerusalem and Refugees: General

The President's sense is that remaining gaps would have more to do with formulation than with practical reality.

### Jerusalem

○ What is Arab should be Palestinian and what is Jewish should be Israeli. This would apply to the Old City as well.

○ The President urges the Parties to work on maps that would ensure maximum contiguity for both sides.

○ *Haram (al-Sharif)* – Temple Mount: The gap is not related to practical administration but to the symbolic issues of sovereignty and finding a way to accord respect to the religious beliefs of both sides.

○ The President knows that the parties discussed different formulations. He wants to suggest two additional ones to formalize the Palestinian de-facto control over the *Haram*, while respecting the convictions of the Jewish people. With regard to either one, there should be international monitoring to provide for mutual confidence:

1. Palestinian sovereignty over the *Haram*, and Israeli sovereignty over the Western Wall and (a) the space sacred to Jews, of which it is a part; or (b) the Holy of Holies, of which it is a part.

2. Palestinian sovereignty over the *Haram* and Israeli sovereignty over the Western Wall plus shared functional sovereignty over the issue of excavation under the *Haram* or behind the wall. That way mutual consent would be required before any excavation took place.

## Refugees

○ The President believes that the differences are over formulating the solutions rather than with what would happen on the practical level.

○ Israel is prepared to acknowledge the moral and material suffering caused to the Palestinian people as a result of the 1948 war and the need to assist in the international community's effort in addressing the problem.

○ An international commission will implement all aspects that flow from the agreement: compensation, resettlement, rehabilitation, etc. The U.S. is prepared to lead an international effort to help the refugees.

○ The fundamental gap is over how to handle the Right of Return (ROR). The President knows the history of the issue and how hard it is for the Palestinian leadership to appear to be abandoning this principle. At the same time, the Israeli side could not accept any reference to the ROR that would imply a right to immigrate to Israel in defiance of Israel's sovereign policy on admission or that would threaten the Jewish character of the state.

○ Any solution must address both needs and be consistent with the two-state approach that both sides have accepted as a way to end the Israeli–Palestinian conflict: The State of Palestine as the homeland for the Palestinian people and the State of Israel as the homeland for the Jewish people.

○ In a two-state solution, the State of Palestine will be the focal point for Palestinians who choose to return to the area, without ruling out that Israel would accept some of these refugees.

○ The President believes that the Parties need to adopt a formulation on the ROR that will make clear that there is no specific ROR to Israel itself, but that does not negate the aspirations of the Palestinian people to return to the area.

In light of that, the President suggests the following two alternatives:

**1.** Both sides recognize the right of Palestinian refugees to return to historic Palestine;

**2.** Both sides recognize the right of Palestinian refugees to return to their homeland

○ The agreement would define the implementation of this general right in a way that is consistent with the two-state solution. It will list the five possible final homes for the refugees: the State of Palestine, areas of Israel being transferred to Palestine in the land swap, rehabilitation in the host countries, resettlement in third countries and admission to Israel.

○ In listing these options the agreement would make clear that return to the West Bank and Gaza or the areas acquired through the land swap would be a right for all Palestinian refugees while rehabilitation in host countries, resettlement in third countries or absorption into Israel would depend upon the policies of these countries.

○ Israel could indicate in the agreement that it intended to establish a policy so that some of the refugees would be absorbed into Israel consistent with Israel's sovereign decision.

○ The President believes that priority should be given to the refugees in Lebanon.

○ The parties would agree that these steps constitute the implementation of UNGAR 194.

## End of Conflict and Finality of Claims

○ The President proposes that the agreement clearly marks the end of the conflict and its implementation put an end to all claims. This could be manifested through a UN Security Council Resolution that notes that UNSCRs 242 and 338 have been implemented and through the final release of Palestinian prisoners.

○ The President believes that this is the outline of a fair and lasting agreement. It gives the Palestinian people the ability to determine their future in their own land, a sovereign and viable state recognized by the international community, Al-Quds as its capital, sovereignty over the *Haram* and new lives for the refugees.

○  It gives the people of Israel a genuine end of conflict, real security, the preservation of sacred religious ties, the incorporation of 80 percent of the settlers into Israel and the largest Jerusalem in history recognized by all as its capital.

### Final comments

This is the best that the President can do. Brief the leaders and let the President know if they are prepared to come to discussion based on these ideas. If not, the President has taken it as far as he can. These are the ideas of the President. If they are not accepted, they are not just off the table; they go with the President as he leaves office.

# Contributors

**Samih al-Abed** (Ph.D.). Deputy Minister of Planning, Palestinian National Authority; member of the Palestinian negotiating team from 1993; member of the Palestinian delegation at the Camp David Summit and Taba talks.

**Shaul Arieli** (Col., Res.). Former Military Commander of the Gaza Strip; former director of the Israeli government's "Peace Administration" in the Barak government that prepared the background material for the negotiators; member of the Israeli delegation at the Camp David Summit.

**Ehud Barak** (Lt-Gen., Res.). Former Prime Minister of Israel; former Chief of the General Staff, Israel Defense Forces; former Defense Minister, Interior Minister and Foreign Minister; head of the Israeli delegation at the Camp David Summit.

**Yaacov Bar-Siman-Tov.** Professor of International Relations, incumbent of the Chair in Peace and Regional Cooperation Studies and Head of the Leonard Davis Institute for International Relations, The Hebrew University of Jerusalem; Head of the Jerusalem Institute for Israel Studies.

**Yossi Beilin** (Ph.D.). Chairman of the Yahad Party; former Minister of Justice, Minister of Economics and Social Development, Deputy Minister of Foreign Affairs, Deputy Minister of Finance; former Member of Knesset; one of the prime architects of the Oslo Framework Agreement; former head of the Israeli delegation to the Multilateral peace process working groups; member of the Israeli delegation at the Taba talks.

**Peter Carnevale.** Professor of Social Psychology, New York University.

**Mohammed S. Dajani** (Ph.D.). Director and Founder of the American Studies Institute, Al-Quds University, of the Palestinian National Institute for Public Administration, of the Jerusalem Studies and Research Institute and of the ISBN Palestine Agency.

**Munther S. Dajani.** Professor of Political Science and Director of the Issam Sartawi Center for the Advancement of Peace and Democracy, Al-Quds University.

**Johannes Gerster** (J.D.). Head of the Konrad Adenauer Foundation's Israel office; former Member of the Bundestag; former member of the Rhineland-Palatinian Federal State Parliament.

**Yossi Ginossar.** Former senior official in Israel's General Security Service (*Shin Bet*); member of the Israeli delegation at the Camp David Summit.

**Martin Indyk** (Ph.D.). Former US Assistant Secretary of State for Near Eastern and South Asian Affairs; former US Ambassador to Israel; member of the Clinton Administration's "peace team" for Arab–Israeli negotiations; member of the US delegation at the Camp David Summit; Director of the Saban Center for Middle East Policy, Brookings Institution.

**Menachem Klein** (Ph.D.). Senior Lecturer, Department of Political Studies, Bar-Ilan University; Research Fellow, Jerusalem Institute for Israel Studies; former Counselor on Jerusalem Affairs and Israel–PLO final status talks to the Minister of Foreign Affairs; member of a professional advisory team on Palestinian affairs, office of Prime Minister Barak.

**Amnon Lipkin-Shahak** (Lt.-Gen., Res.). Former Chief of the General Staff, Israel Defense Forces; former Minister of Tourism, Minister of Transport and member of the Security Cabinet; senior member of the Israeli negotiating team in the Barak Administration; member of the Israeli delegation at the Camp David Summit and Taba talks.

**Bruce Maddy-Weitzman** (Ph.D.). Senior Research Fellow at The Moshe Dayan Center for Middle Eastern and African Studies, Tel Aviv University.

**Robert Malley** (Ph.D.). Special Assistant to President Clinton for Arab–Israeli Affairs and member of Clinton Administration's "peace team" for Arab–Israeli negotiations; former Executive Assistant to the US National Security Advisor; member of the US delegation at the Camp David Summit; Middle East and North Africa Program Director, International Crisis Group.

**Zeev Maoz.** Professor of Political Science, former head of the Jaffee Center for Strategic Studies and former head of Hartog School of Government and Policy, Tel Aviv University.

**Reuven Merhav.** Former officer in the Israeli security and intelligence community; former Director-General in the Ministry of Foreign Affairs; former Director-General of the Ministry of Immigrant Absorption; member of the Israeli delegation at the Camp David Summit; Research Fellow at the Jerusalem Institute for Israel Studies.

**Dan Meridor** (J.D.). Former Minister of Justice, and Minister of Finance; former Cabinet Secretary; former chairman of the Knesset Foreign Affairs and Defense Committee; member of the Israeli delegation at the Camp David Summit.

**Aaron David Miller** (Ph.D.). Advisor to six US Secretaries of State; former Deputy Special Middle East Coordinator for Arab–Israeli negotiations; served as a Senior Member of the State Department's Policy Planning Staff, in the Bureau of Intelligence and Research and in the Office of the Historian; member of the US delegation at the Camp David Summit; President of Seeds of Peace.

**Sari Nusseibeh.** Professor of Islamic Philosophy, founder of the Issam Sartawi Center for the Advancement of Peace and Democracy, and President of Al-Quds University; former PLO Representative in Jerusalem; member of the Palestinian Steering Committee to the 1991 Madrid conference; co-author of the *People's Voice* initiative to build grassroots support for a two-state solution.

**Ron Pundik** (Ph.D.). Participant in Track II activities with Palestinians; Director-General of the Peres Center for Peace; among the initiators of the Oslo Framework Agreement.

**Itamar Rabinovich.** Professor of Middle Eastern History, incumbent of the Yonah and Dina Ettinger Chair in contemporary history of the Middle East, and President of Tel Aviv University; former Israeli Ambassador to the United States; former head of the Israeli delegation in negotiations with Syria during the Rabin Administration.

**Gilead Sher** (Col., Res.). Attorney-at-law; former Bureau Chief and Policy Coordinator for Prime Minister Barak; senior negotiator with the Palestinians; member of the Israeli delegation at the Camp David Summit and Taba talks.

**Shimon Shamir.** Professor Emeritus of Middle Eastern History, and Head of The University Institute for Diplomacy and Regional Cooperation, Tel Aviv University; former Israeli Ambassador to Egypt; first Israeli Ambassador to Jordan.

**Yuval Steinitz** (Ph.D.). Chairman of the Knesset Foreign Affairs and Defense Committee; Senior Lecturer in the Department of Philosophy, Haifa University.

**Asher Susser.** Professor of Middle Eastern History and Director of The Moshe Dayan Center for Middle Eastern and African Studies, Tel Aviv University.

**Yuli Tamir.** Professor of Political Philosophy, Tel Aviv University; former Minister of Immigrant Absorption; Member of Knesset.

**Danny Yatom** (Maj.-Gen., Res.). Former Head of the Mossad; former Chief of Staff and Security Advisor to Prime Minister Barak; former Military Secretary to Yitzhak Rabin and Shimon Peres; former participant in peace negotiations with Syria, Jordan and the Palestinians; Member of Knesset; member of the Israeli delegation at the Camp David Summit.

# Index

# Index

# Personal Notes

*Personal Notes*

*Personal Notes*

*Personal Notes*

*Personal Notes*

*Personal Notes*